Selected Sermons

SELECTED WRITINGS
OF C.F.W. WALTHER

Selected Sermons

Henry J. Eggold, Translator

Aug. R. Suelflow, Series Editor

Publishing House
St. Louis

Copyright © 1981
Concordia Publishing House
3558 South Jefferson
Saint Louis, Missouri 63118

Manufactured in the United States of America

1 2 3 4 5 6 7 8 9 10 WP 90 89 88 87 86 85 84 83 82 81

Library of Congress Cataloging in Publication Data

Walther, C. F. W. (Carl Ferdinand Wilhelm), 1811-1887.
    Selected sermons.

    (Selected writings of C. F. W. Walther)
    1. Lutheran Church—Sermons. 2. Sermons, English—Translations from German.
3. Sermons, German—Translations into English. I. Title. II. Series: Walther, C. F. W.
(Carl Ferdinand Wilhelm), 1811-1887. Selections. English. 1981.
BX8066.W3S47213   252'.041322   81-3097
ISBN 0-570-08276-5   AACR2

Contents

Introduction   8

Translator's Preface   10

Sermons for the Church Year

First Sunday in Advent, 1842
Matthew 21:1-9
The Gracious Entrance of Christ the Heavenly King into the
Temple of the Human Heart   13

Christmas Day
Luke 2:1-14
Rejoice! The Savior Is Born; Heaven Is Open for You   22

First Sunday After Epiphany
Luke 2:41-54
The Holy Family, an Instructive Example for Christian Parents
and Children   30

First Sunday in Lent
Matthew 4:1-11
Christ's Battle with the Prince of Darkness and His Glorious
Victory   40

Palm Sunday Confirmation Address
John 6:66-69
Your Answer to Christ's Question: "Do You Also Wish to
Go Away?"   51

Maundy Thursday
1 Corinthians 11:23-32
How Important and Necessary It Is That We Also Henceforth
Hold Fast to the Pure Doctrine of the Lord's Supper . . . with
Constant Faithfulness   59

Good Friday, 1846
Luke 23:27-40
There Is Nothing Which So Strongly and Compellingly Urges
Us to Turn to God with All Our Hearts as the Death of the Son
of God for Our Sins on the Cross   69

Easter Sunday, 1852
1 Corinthians 15:55-57
True Freedom, the Glorious Fruit of the Resurrection of Our
Lord Jesus Christ   76

Ascension
Mark 16:14-20
The Ascension of Christ, a Sure Foundation of a Joyous Faith   87

Trinity Sunday, 1844
John 3:1-15
Baptism, the Powerful Means of Regeneration   99

Tenth Sunday After Trinity
Luke 19:41-48
God Does Not Desire the Death of Any Sinner, Even Though So
Many Perish Eternally   108

Eleventh Sunday After Trinity
Luke 18:9-14
The Justification of a Poor Sinner
Before God According to the Gospel   115

Twelfth Sunday After Trinity
Mark 7:31-37
The Daily Renewal of a Justified Christian   123

Thirteenth Sunday After Trinity 1846
Luke 10:23-37
Love for the Neighbor—a Fruit of Faith   131

Sermons for Special Occasions

Sermon for the Opening of a Synodical Convention
Psalm 119:23-25
How Comforted We Can Be in the Face of All the
Reproaches We Experience as Long as We Stand
on God's Word Without Wavering   140

Address at the Dedication of Concordia Publishing House
Feb. 28, 1870   149

Day of Repentance, 1870
Galatians 5:7
We Are No Longer What We Were   155

Installation Sermon; Third Sunday of Advent, 1878
 1 Corinthians 4:1-5
  When Is the Day of the Installation of a Pastor a Day of Festive
  Joy for a Congregation?   164

Sermon on Predestination, Christmas 1881
 Ephesians 1:3-6
  Concerning Predestination   173

Wedding Address for Magdalene, Walther's Daughter
 Numbers 6:24-26
  My Threefold Fatherly Blessing upon You   183

Funeral Address for Mrs. Caroline Barthel   188

Notes   191

Bibliography   192

Introduction

It is an ambitious project to permit C. F. W. Walther (1811—87) to address English readers. Efforts to do so have occurred in the past from time to time. But this English edition constitutes one of the most significant contributions made to the study of the theology of Lutheranism in America within past years. The stereotype of Walther heretofore imposed upon him by those who were unable to read his German writings will now be significantly altered! It is to be regretted that a rich treasury of many other works from Walther's pen still await a future project.

Dr. Henry E. Jacobs (1844—1932), late president of Lutheran Theological Seminary in Philadelphia, Pa., said of Walther:

> He is as orthodox as John Gerhard, but as fervent as a pietist, as correct in form as a university or court preacher, and yet as popular as Luther himself. If the Lutheran Church will bring its doctrines again to the people, it must be as faithful and as definite in its doctrine and as interesting and thoroughly adapted to the times in form, as is the case in Walther. He is a model preacher in the Lutheran Church ("Dr. Walther as a Preacher, *Lutheran Church Review,* III [October 1889], 319).

In each of the volumes a special effort was made to select the most significant and relevant materials and to have Walther speak contemporary English. We have further endeavored, wherever possible, to quote from the American Edition of *Luther's Works* and to utilize the Revised Standard Version of the Bible for Scriptural references. Quotations from the Lutheran Confessions were keyed to the Tappert edition of the *Book of Concord.* It was helpful to be able to consult some resources which Walther had in his own library.

Walther was an exceedingly involved church leader. A founding father of The Lutheran Church—Missouri Synod, he served as its first president 1847—50 and 1864—78. He was Concordia Seminary's (St. Louis) foremost instructor from 1849 until his death in 1887, and served as its president 1850—87.

His concern for Lutheran unity is demonstrative. He conceived the "Free Conferences" in the aftermath of the confessional crisis in 1855. Later, in 1872, he was elected the first president of a new pan-Lutheran federation, the Evangelical Lutheran Synodical Conference.

The project to translate Walther into English received support from The Lutheran Church—Missouri Synod in 1962, when a special committee was formed. When funds were not available, the project was transferred to Concordia Publishing House. It has now become a pioneer in publishing both Luther's and Walther's select works in English.

Walther's classic *Law and Gospel,* generally considered one of the most important books produced within American Lutheranism, deserves a volume of its own. In it we see him as theological professor, with his students gathered around him.

Another volume acquaints us with Walther the preacher. He made a great impact on his hearers, and much of his sermonic and homiletical material was published in German during his lifetime and in the years following his death. In spite of this, several thousand sermon manuscripts still remain untouched.

In a further volume we see Walther the convention essayist. None of these essays, presented to Western District conventions between 1873 and 1886, with their ever-recurring theme "To God All Glory!" have seen the English light of day until now.

Of particular importance were Walther's writings on the church, and one of our volumes brings a condensation of these. *Church and Ministry* (1852), *The Proper Form* (1863), and *The True Visible Church* (1866) give the theological foundation for the Missouri Synod's strong emphasis on the congregation and on lay involvement.

We include a volume of Walther's correspondence. It lets us see him in his intense and complex relationships with many different people. Concordia Historical Institute, with funds provided by the Aid Association for Lutherans, has in recent years transcribed several hundred original *Fraktur* letters. Only a few have been published in English heretofore, and we too can bring only a selection.

Finally we take a look at Walther the editor—one of his most important functions. Through *Lehre und Wehre* (from which we bring articles never before presented in English) and *Der Lutheraner* Walther exerted a strong influence toward orthodox Lutheranism.

The translators of this edition hope that readers and users will develop a new appreciation for this 19th-century hero of faith, but above all, that Walther, as the preceptor of Luther in America, will direct the readers to the very cross of our Lord Jesus Christ, his and our only hope.

Aug. R. Suelflow, *Series Editor*

Translator's Preface

Walther, the preacher, represents a synthesis of Orthodoxy and Pietism. He entered the scene at a time when the two forces of Orthodoxy and Pietism joined forces in opposing Rationalism. Moreover, Walther himself imbibed something of the spirit of each in his formative years.

That he was influenced by Orthodoxy, Walther would be the first to admit, and with a great deal of pride, too. Moreover, his sermons bear the marks of the influence of Orthodoxy. Walther builds his theology on the three *solas: sola Scriptura, sola gratia,* and *sola fide.*

Each of these is an affirmation of Orthodoxy and, at the same time, a repudiation of Pietism. Walther proclaimed Scripture alone as opposed to feeling; grace alone against the notion that one must himself establish a degree of contrition; faith alone against any thought of the merit of one's conduct before, in, or after conversion.

But Pietism left its mark on Walther too, for good and for ill. He learned from the Pietists to accent experience, but he purified that accent. In Pietism experience was viewed in terms of autosuggestion. Walther's experience is that of a sinner under the influence of Law and Gospel. Again, Walther never lost Pietism's concern for making religion something personal, a matter of heart and life. His sermons, though strongly didactic, are nevertheless personal, intended to awaken and strengthen faith and love in the heart. So intensely does he feel that Christianity is a matter of the personal relationship between a Christian and Christ that he at times employs mystical imagery to describe this blissful relationship. Moreover, he consistently emphasizes that the end of justification is the new life. Avoiding Pietism's weakness of mixing sanctification and justification, Walther always emphasizes that a genuine faith is active in love. Where there is no love, there is no faith; where no faith, no grace; where no grace, no salvation. A cold, intellectual affirmation can never pass for saving faith.

A critical appraisal of Walther's sermons will not cause one to close his eyes to the influence of Pietism which introduced faults into Walther's preaching, namely his tinge of legalism and his occasional advice to the terrified sinner to pray for grace without directing him to the Gospel.

Summing up the twofold influence of Orthodoxy and Pietism in

Walther's preaching, it is probably safe to say that Orthodoxy provided the content for Walther's sermons and Pietism gave them their practical bent. The one gave the sermons substance and a solid basis; the other provided their direction.

As to form, Walther's sermons are more goal-centered than text-centered. The text suggests the theme for Walther, but from that moment on the theme is the master of the sermon. His sermon divisions are taken from the theme, but not necessarily from the text. As a result, Walther has sermons which are quite textual and others which use the text only as a point of departure.

As a stylist, Walther does credit to the great age of German literature. His sermons bear the marks of painstaking care in their exactness and beauty of style. But Walther's main asset is his ability to maintain unity of subject, goal, and mood. Here he demonstrates his consummate artistry.

But the chief legacy which Walther has left us is his view of the sermon as a confrontation of man by God in His justice and mercy. His sermons leave one with the unmistakable impression that one has been in the holy of holies. There he has seen God, the God of Sinai and the God of Golgotha, the God of awful justice and the God of infinite mercy.

The sermons of this volume are intended to give a panoramic view of Walther's preaching. Some, like the sermon on predestination, are strongly didactic. Others emphasize God's grace in justification and conversion, as well as the Christian's responsibility to live the new life. Sermons like the funeral sermon, the wedding address, and the Palm Sunday confirmation sermon evidence the warmth of Walther's love for people.

My thanks to my wife Madalene for typing the manuscript.

Henry J. Eggold

SERMONS
FOR THE CHURCH YEAR

First Sunday in Advent, 1842
Matthew 21:1-9

The Gracious Entrance of Christ the Heavenly King into the Temple of the Human Heart
(Festklaenge, pp. 1—11)

O Jesus, in Your name we today again enter upon a new church year and with heart and mouth praise Your mercy which during the past year You have shown our souls. But where shall we seek and ask for new help and grace for the new year except from You? Ah, Lord, what would it help us to live longer if Your grace were not with us? Without Your grace our life would be a death, the earth a hell. Therefore we pray You as once Your servant Moses did: "Lead us not where Your face will not go before us." Let Your glory go before us. Send us also in the new year Your Word and Sacrament pure and clean and let it at all times be a power in us; through these means preserve in us always a repentant heart which ever realizes and feels its sin and unworthiness with remorse and pain, so that we may steadfastly comfort ourselves in Your grace. Whatever in the past year has remained in a state of sin, through Your Word transform into a state of grace in the new year. O Lord, come, come into our hearts and make Your dwelling place in our souls, also those of our children; be and remain the One who pities us in time and eternity. We hope in You, let us not be put to shame. O Lord, hear; O Lord, help and let things turn out well. Amen. Amen.

Beloved brothers and sisters in Christ Jesus!

A short time ago we still hoped that on this first day of the new church year we would be in our own house of the Lord to bring to God the first offering of our praise and thanks. Our hope was not realized; also today we have had to assemble here as guests and foreigners.

As sad as this may make us on the one hand, let us surely not in contemptuous ingratitude forget what great blessings of God we enjoy, that in spite of the delay, we have not had to interrupt our worship together. Oh, what faithfulness of our heavenly Leader it is that this shelter which belongs to others has remained friendly and open to us for so long, until the doors of our own church open to us. Oh, what would we perhaps now be if a hospitable reception from benefactors who are strangers had not made it possible for us Sunday after Sunday to unite in hearing the Word of God, in our use of the holy sacraments together, and in our common prayers? How many of us would perhaps have gone over to the world or embraced one of the enthusiastic sects! Was not the public worship held here the chief bond which held us together and bound us to the public confession of our faith? Yes, the memory of the benefits we have enjoyed here must be indelibly written and remain in our thankful hearts.

Yet, my beloved, we know from God's Word that nothing, not even the least thing, happens by chance. We would, therefore, certainly not judge in a Christian way if we ascribed the delay in our church dedication to blind fate, and wanted to look only at human causes. No, the God who according to His eternal wisdom guides the whole enterprise to its goal by directing each detail, God, without whose will no sparrow falls from a roof and no hair from one's head—He it is who with this delay surely has His holy and wise purposes for the salvation of our souls.

If I wanted to share with you my Christian reflections about the delay, they are these: We were not permitted today, as we hoped, to enter our own house of God so that we first might have a living, godly reminder that we are in no way worthy of this great blessing. We were not permitted to enter it today so that we could first examine ourselves and ask: Have we diligently, earnestly, humbly and believingly called upon God for the successful completion of this building project which is so important for us? Yes, just believe it, no person is more to blame for the delay than the one who has been negligent in prayer. Furthermore, we were not permitted to gather there today, as we hoped, so that we first might realize all the better what a great blessing this is, so that this good may become still more dear to us. It is also furthermore true that an unexpected delay has occurred so that we may realize well that our church building is not our work, so that the truth may once more be laid upon our heart which we considered at our cornerstone laying: "Unless the Lord builds the house, those who build it labor in vain."

Yet, finally, my beloved, another reason above all hovers before my

14

soul, one which I find in the meaning of this day. Today we are celebrating the entry of Christ into Jerusalem; say, why could we not therefore with our songs to the entering King of heaven cry Hosanna in our newly built church? I think Christ wants to say to us that He wants to enter, not that stone house but rather the little church in our hearts; as St. Paul writes to the Corinthians: "For God's temple is holy, and that temple you are."

Oh, let us therefore, as an eternally salutary preparation for the dedication of our visible house of God, today first conduct the dedication of our hearts. May Jesus Christ to this end give us the light and power of His grace.

Text: Matthew 21:1-9

On the basis of the Gospel lesson for today, just read, consider with me:

The Gracious Entrance of Christ the Heavenly King into the Temple of the Human Heart

We shall consider:
1. *how this entrance was brought about;*
2. *who may hold himself in readiness for this entrance;*
3. *what Christ in His entrance brings with Him;* and finally
4. *how a person must festively adorn and celebrate this entrance.*

O Jesus, we are assembled here today for the last time, so we pray You now for Your last blessing. Ah, if there is one who perhaps until now has not been blessed here, lay hold of him with Your grace even in this last hour. We know that conversion is not our work but Yours—so turn us, and we shall be turned; help us, and we are helped. Even today take a great catch with the net of Your Gospel, that we all, all may be Your blessed captives. Ah, Lord, deny us not this last prayer here, for the sake of Your faithfulness. Amen.

I

My hearers, no one can someday enter the heavenly Jerusalem into whose heart Christ has not already here made His gracious entry. He Himself says: "If a man does not abide in Me, he is cast forth as a branch and withers; and the branches are gathered, thrown into the fire and burned." And St. Paul says: "Anyone who does not have the spirit of Christ does not belong to Him." And in another place the same apostle therefore confesses: "It is no longer I who live, but Christ who lives in me." Christ's entry into Jerusalem is a visible picture of this necessary entrance of the heavenly King into the temple of the human heart; and our text sets forth, first of all, how that is worked and brought about.

What did the city of Jerusalem do to prompt Christ to enter it? Nothing; without the desire or the calling of its inhabitants, He came; and when some came to meet Him, he had already begun His entrance. Christ made the first arrangement when He sent His disciples to bring an ass and a colt so that riding upon them He might make His entry into the city of David.

O man, do you ask: "What shall I do that this noble guest may come also to me? What gates of honor shall I build that through them He may make His entry? How shall I make ready the house of my heart that the King of heaven may have the desire to enter it? Where is material for a bed to which I can invite the heavenly Wanderer so He can take His rest?" If you ask that, then know that if a person had to make the beginning for the entrance of Christ into his heart, it would never happen; if a person had to lay the first stone for the little church for Christ in his heart, it would forever remain unbuilt. Man has nothing with which he can prepare a suitable refuge for Christ. Before Christ comes into our heart, all our thinking is only sinful; our willing only sinful; our speaking, our doing, our beginnings are only sinful.

How? Do you say "I can indeed pray that Christ come into my heart"?—No, O man, before Christ has already come to you, you cannot pray, for we are all by nature dead in sin. But if you begin genuinely, with heartfelt desire, to ask: "O come, my Savior!" then He has already come. The inner longing of your heart after Him is a sign that you have tasted of His grace; for that very reason you hunger and thirst after Him. If in your room you begin to cry: "Hosanna to the Son of David!" that is, "Lord, help the Son of David; let Him win also my heart for His kingdom," then Christ has already entered the door of your heart.

Yes, my beloved, not we but Christ Himself initiated His entrance; not we, Christ made the beginning; we do not seek Christ; He seeks us; we do not find Christ, He finds us. O man, you do not come to Him, but it says: *"Behold, your King is coming to you."* Everything we ourselves want to contribute to Christ's entry is in vain. Before anyone was created and before we could ask Him, He of His own free will resolved already in eternity to dwell among us in order to save us sinners. When the fallen Adam had forsaken God and did not want to return, but fled from God, God's Son again made the beginning and followed him and called: "Adam, where are you?" Of His own free will Christ came also to miserable Bethlehem. Freely and uncommanded He finally came also to Jerusalem in the days of His last redemptive suffering. So He also comes, freely and uncommanded, to the doors of our hearts. Ah, if Christ first came when we sought Him, He would not come to us in all eternity.

But you ask: "By what means does He come to us today without any activity on our part?" By no other means than He used once to enter the city of David; namely, He sends His apostles, that is, His holy Word and sacrament. The Word of God is always calling: *"Behold, your King is coming!"* and the holy sacraments are the visible, effective signs of His most holy presence. Whenever a person is baptized, the King of heaven enters his heart. As often as God's Word is preached, Christ makes ready to enter the souls of the hearers; the church in which the Gospel resounds is changed into a Jerusalem; every word which you there let enter your heart is a step farther which Christ takes to your hearts; as often as through the Law you are convicted of your sins and are led to despair of yourselves, the bolts fall from the closed doors of your soul; and as often as, by the preaching of grace, you are moved, softly enticed, and stimulated, Christ steps across the threshold of your being. As often as you receive the Lord's Supper, Christ enters the shelter of your heart. Therefore, whoever has the Word of God and the holy sacraments does not fail to have Christ come to him, for He comes with every word.

The failure is only that the majority do not receive Him. Christ desires nothing of us except that we just hear His Word, take it to heart, through it be persuaded of our sin and of His grace, and that we do not push Him aside. Then He will in grace unite us with Himself. Oh, what can be more fearful than this, that a person either does not hear God's Word, or if he does hear it, does not receive it with a willing heart, does not let it work in his soul, but resists the Holy Spirit! Such a person does nothing else to prevent Christ from entering his poor, sinful heart.

I fear that this has happened with many of us in the past church year: The seed of the Word fell either on the footpath of an indifferent heart; or on the stony ground of a hard, unbroken soul; or, probably most frequently, among the thorns of the riches or cares or lusts of this life. O you unfortunate people, I proclaim to you the Word of Jesus Christ according to the grace which has been given me; how will you excuse yourselves before God when you die without having Jesus in your heart? Ah, I plead with you for the sake of the blood shed for you on the cross, open not only your ears to the Word of God, but open also your hearts, that Jesus Christ may come to you and eternally, eternally make His dwelling place with you.

But dare all of us also in the new church year hold ourselves in readiness for His entrance? Let me, in the second place, answer this question.

17

II

The entrance of Christ into Jerusalem was, as we heard, a picture of His entrance into the human heart. Of the former we are told: *"This took place to fulfill what was spoken by the prophet, saying 'Tell the daughter of Zion, Behold, your King is coming to you, humble, and mounted on an ass, and on a colt, the foal of an ass.'"* The prophet Zechariah says: *"Tell the daughter of Zion."* "The daughter of Zion" refers, to be sure, in the first place to the Israelite church. Zion was a mountain, on which was built not only David's castle but, at its side, also the temple. Because the Israelites honored this place as their spiritual home and embraced it with a love like that for a mother, they were all called the daughter of Zion. Christendom now in the New Testament is also called that; its Zion is the church, which it embraces with a daughter's love as its spiritual mother.

If we consider more closely the place cited in the prophet, we find that under the phrase "daughter of Zion" more is to be understood than Christendom. For Zechariah says immediately following: "And He shall command peace to the nations; His dominion shall be from sea to sea, and from the River to the ends of the earth."

From this we see that the daughter of Zion includes all people of all times, zones, and lands, for whom the King of heaven came into this world. Evangelical preachers are to call to all of these: *"Behold, your King is coming."* Without a doubt it was for this very reason that Christ chose the Eastertide for His entry, when an astounding throng of Jews and heathen were gathered in Jerusalem. We hear also in the Gospel of John that heathen Greeks took notice and laid before an apostle the request: "Sir, we wish to see Jesus." For no other reason Christ now did not enter in an unnoticed, quiet manner but with a great sensation, so that no one would be left who had not heard about Him, so that young and old, poor and rich, the high and the lowly would notice Him and ask: "Who is He?" so that they could hear the answer: *"Behold, your King is coming to you."*

See from this, my beloved, the divine instruction we evangelical preachers have. Whoever asks us today or throughout the whole year: "Who should hold himself in readiness for the entrance of the King of heaven? to whom does He come?" we should always answer: *"Behold, your King is coming to you."* Yes, to you, O man, who ask. Yes, if today I could approach each one of you, I would, unasked, say to each one of you: "See, my brother, see, my sister, today your King comes also to you; He wants to enter also your heart. Oh, open it! Do not say: "I am not worthy to have Him come under my roof." Indeed, you are not worthy, but it is your King's will to come into the lowly, dark, unclean hut of your heart. Oh, only believe it; then He gladly is and remains the Guest of your soul.

But you who harbor in your heart the wealth, the vanities, the honors, the lusts of the world, ah, sin, ah, Satan, you who until now have granted no place to your King, do not say also today: "I have no room for Jesus." How? Would you rather let the ruler of darkness live in you than the King of heaven? Oh, throw them out, those shameful guests, and say: "Come in, O blessed of the Lord, why do You stand outside?" [Here Walther inserts a hymn verse.]

Yet, my friends, is it something so precious to have this Guest in your hearts? Yes, yes; hear therefore, in the third place, what Christ in His entrance brings with Him.

III

In our text we read: *"He comes to you, humble."* From this the daughter of Zion is to observe: Although Christ is the great King of heaven, yet there is nothing frightening, nothing fearful, nothing threatening about Him when He is on the way to our hearts; He does not come in the splendor and majesty of His righteousness and holiness. When He entered Jerusalem, He did not come riding on a snorting cavalry horse, not with armed soldiers, not with powerful artillery, as a frightening world conqueror, but meek, full of love, humble, riding upon an ass, accompanied by His dear disciples, escorted by the simple people and surrounded by a group of children; in such a loving way He also draws near to the gate of our poor, sinful heart.

And what does He bring? First of all, He says: *"Go into the village opposite you, and immediately you will find an ass tied, and a colt with her; untie them and bring them to Me."* Here we see how Christ finds us all when He comes, namely, bound with the bands of sin, death, and God's disfavor. Christ's advent in our souls releases us from all these; He brings us forgiveness of all our guilt and freedom from God's wrath and all His punishments. When Christ enters, everything damning leaves, and lovingly, like the morning sun, God's fatherly countenance rises over us.

Yet, the gift of Christ is twofold: First He gives us freedom from evil, and then He gives us Himself. The person in whom Jesus dwells can then say: "What belongs to Jesus belongs also to me; His righteousness is mine, His holiness is mine, His life is mine, His suffering and death are mine, His sonship is mine, His glory, His salvation, His heaven are mine. Hallelujah!"

Therefore St. Paul says: "Therefore, since we are justified by faith, we have peace with God through our Lord Jesus Christ. Through Him we have obtained access to this grace in which we stand, and we rejoice in our hope of sharing the glory of God.—Who shall bring any charge against God's

19

elect? It is God who justifies; who is to condemn? Is it Christ Jesus, who died, yes, who was raised from the dead, who is at the right hand of God, who indeed intercedes for us?"

Oh, how blessed, therefore, is the person who does not forget his baptism but who considers it valuable and dear above all else and who in faith daily comforts himself therewith! For in baptism Christ held His triumphal procession over sin, death, devil, and hell in our hearts. Oh, how blessed is the person who gladly hears God's Word and who permits himself to be corrected, enlightened, awakened, and comforted by it! For if a person keeps the Word in his heart, he also has Christ in his heart, and with Him grace, righteousness, life, and salvation. And whoever in life lets Christ dwell with him will not in death be forsaken by Him. If the believer lies on his last sickbed, he can also conquer the fear of death; for his faith calls to him, also into his breaking heart: "*'Behold, your King is coming to you!'* Rejoice; now He is receiving you into His heavenly kingdom."

But, my beloved, shall a Christian only take, and give nothing?—In the fourth place, let me say a few things about how a person should festively adorn and celebrate Christ's entrance.

IV

The heart of a Christian should be a continuously open road where Christ lives and walks; therefore his whole life should be a continuous endeavor festively to adorn the way of his Savior with thanksgiving and voluntary love.

It is true, we cannot do anything in order that Christ come to us, He comes voluntarily through His Word and sacrament and makes us dead people alive, us prisoners free, us sinners righteous. But after He has come to us, we should openly show to the world through a new life that we have a holy, important, heavenly guest in our hearts.

Our Gospel shows us what we should do. The disciples and the people took off their garments and spread them on the way. So a believing Christian should take off the old, spotted garment of the flesh; he should no longer walk according to the old lusts, according to the old wishes, according to the old evil thoughts of his sinful heart, but should say from the heart [*The Lutheran Hymnal,* 347:5]:

> Sinful life, thy bonds I sever,
> Leave thee now forever.

But the crowd also cut down branches and strewed them in the way. So a believing Christian should spread out everywhere the fruits of the tree of his faith. Through his good works and new life, through his love to God and all men, through his humility, through his meekness, through his heavenly mindedness, through his denial of everything worldly, through his patience under the cross, through his firm hope in trouble—through all this a Christian should show that Christ dwells in him.

Finally, the people and with them even the children cried: *"Hosanna to the Son of David; blessed is He who comes in the name of the Lord! Hosanna in the highest!"* My beloved, this is not only a chant of praise but also a wish for good fortune. "Hosanna!" means, "O Lord, help!" So the people cried out to God that He would help His Anointed, that His kingdom would continue to spread. So also a Christian should show that Christ has taken up residence in him not only in this, that his mouth is always full of praise and thanks for the grace he has received, but also in this, that he longs and pleads and entreats that Christ's kingdom may win more and more blessed citizens, that more and more may come to know the heavenly King of grace, accept Him, and through Him be saved.

Now, my beloved, you all want to be considered as people in whom not the spirit of the world but Christ dwells; but who can think it of those in whose life one cannot see that they festively adorn and celebrate Christ's entrance? Is Christ's triumphal entry there where one still wears the old garments of a worldly life and has not cast them at the feet of Christ? Can Christ have made His way there where one sees no palm branches of good works and a new life in love and humility? where one adorns not Christ's way but one's own? where one offers oneself not to Christ but to the world? Can the Savior already have come there where one hears no Hosanna cry of believing thankoffering and intercession? Ah, you who until now have still blocked Christ's entrance and until now have despised His grace, accept Him today, yet today!

But you who would want no other guest in your hearts but Christ, do not trouble yourselves whether He has come also to you; your unworthiness and your misery do not hold Him back from you but draw Him to you. Yes, He is with you. Just look at Him with the eyes of faith and joyfully praise His goodness. Here Christ still hides Himself in a poor, lowly form. But be comforted; hold to His holy Word. Then one day when He appears in His glory you will enter with Him through the open doors of heaven. Amen.

Christmas Day
Luke 2:1-14

Rejoice! The Savior Is Born; Heaven Is Open for You
(Lutherische Brosamen, pp. 9—18)

Lord Jesus, You Son of the living God, who once came into this world and became a child in order to open Your heaven to us, who once let sinners have a place in the inn while You lay in the manger in a dark stall in order to prepare for us an entrance into the eternal dwelling place of Your heavenly Father, we pray You, in these days let us in a living way recognize the blessed mystery of Your wonderful birth, find comfort in it in undoubting faith, and by this means become citizens of Your heavenly kingdom now and forever. Oh, in these days do not lead us only to the gates of heaven, which you have opened by Your holy birth, but also lead us in, in order that one day we may be with You eternally and glorify and praise You, our Savior, throughout eternity. Amen.

In our newborn Savior, heartily beloved hearers!

The will of our eternal, good God is that we humans should get to heaven, that we should be saved and should live eternally. After we were created, we should now not only never revert to nothingness, but in seeing God eternally and in everlasting fellowship with Him and all the blessed angels we should enjoy God's love for all eternity, be eternally happy, eternally joyful, eternally have reason to praise God's goodness toward us and rejoice in it. For that purpose alone God created us, for that purpose He gave us an immortal soul, and for that purpose He sank deep in our hearts an unquenchable longing for freedom from all evil and for perfect knowledge and salvation. For that purpose also God once placed the newly created humans in a paradise on earth. This was to serve as the vestibule of an everlasting heaven; and the short life in it was to be the prelude to an everlasting life in the kingdom of divine glory.

But ah! we humans fell, and as we were therefore banished from the earthly paradise into this world full of pain, fear, and tears, this was only a silhouette of what at the same time took place above before the face of God. For also the heaven of glory was closed to us after our fall. As once a cherub with a flaming sword guarded the entrance to the earthly paradise and to the tree of life, so now God's holiness and righteousness guarded the entrance to the eternal city with the threatening sword of His holy law, which irrevocably excludes all transgressors.

Ah, beloved, if now we had no Savior who opened again for us the closed door of heaven, it would be better for us had we never been born and never seen the light of this world, better that God had never conceived and carried out the plan to create us, better that we remained eternally locked into our oblivion. David thought so too. When there was danger that his family, who alone had the promise of the Savior, would be exterminated, David, holding God's promise up to Him, sighed in Psalm 89: "For what vanity Thou hast created all the sons of men!"

Yes, without a Savior all human beings would have been created in vain. For who can break the diamond-hard bolt of God's righteousness and holiness with which the door of heaven is closed to all unclean sinners? Or who can say to them: Open, you golden gates, you doors of righteousness! and thereby open them? As surely as God cannot cease to be just and holy, so surely can He open the gates of His holy city of God only to those who are holy and righteous. Our conscience says this to all of us. Even the most unbelieving person does not deny that; for why does he seek to dissuade himself from belief in an eternal life and to change the fleeting life here into a heaven on earth?—Because he despairs of a heaven after death.

Yet, beloved, as useless as is all human endeavor to open the doors of heaven, we do not have to despair that they will open to us. For concerning the eternal city of God it is written in God's holy revelation: "Its gates shall never be shut." And if you ask, Who has opened the doors of righteousness to us? I call to you: Come, come, my brothers and sisters, let me today lead you to the open door of heaven itself. Let us go to Bethlehem; there you will not only see Him who has opened heaven for us, but you yourselves will look into the open heaven, so that all doubt is removed.

But, my beloved, before we go to this most holy and most blessed place on earth, let us first lift up our hearts to God in silent prayer after we have sung a hymn.

Text: Luke 2:1-14

Permit me then on the basis of this story of all stories to bring you the joyful Christmas message:

Rejoice! The Savior Is Born;
Heaven Is Open for You

Therefore listen to these two thoughts:

1. *that through the birth of the Savior heaven has really and truly been opened;* and

2. *that we therefore have nothing to do except joyfully enter heaven.*

I

There can be no doubt, my beloved, that through Christ's birth heaven stands open for all people. For what do we hear and see today! Hardly has Christ been born in the stable in Bethlehem when outside on the fields of Bethlehem the angel of the Lord appears, radiant in the glory of the Lord, and calls to the shepherds terrified by the heavenly brightness: *"Be not afraid; for behold I bring you good news of a great joy which will come to all the people; for to you is born this day in the city of David a Savior, who is Christ the Lord."* And more! The heavens open, the whole multitude of the heavenly hosts comes down and in heavenly responsive choirs sings to the amazed shepherds: *"Glory to God in the highest, and on earth peace among men with whom He is pleased!"*

Behold, in Bethlehem and its environs we see everything which belongs only to heaven: The Lord of heaven Himself is there as a friendly child lying in a manger; the brilliance of the Lord shines upon the shepherds and illumines the night with heavenly light; the heavenly hosts are assembled and mingle with men who are speechless with enchantment; and the music of heaven fills the air. It is as if not only the door of heaven had opened but also heaven itself had come to earth and had already taken up and enclosed the earth in its circumference.

No, my hearers, do not say: "Indeed heaven once opened over those shepherds of Bethlehem, yes, came down over them, but what does that help us? Are we not still on earth and does not God's righteousness and holiness still hold heaven tightly closed to us sinners?" Oh, don't talk like that! The beloved shepherds were sinners as we are; otherwise they would not have been so afraid, as our text says, at the sight of the glory of the Lord. Therefore if at that time heaven had still been closed to sinners, it would have been closed also to our fellow-sinners, the beloved shepherds. But since today long ago, in the hour of our Savior's birth, heaven was opened without them asking, yes, even came down to them, it must now be open and must have come down also to all *sinners*.

But if you still want to have doubts about it, I ask you: Tell me, who is that newborn child who lies in the manger? He is, as the angel of the Lord

24

himself announced so loudly, *"Christ the Lord,"* Jehovah; He is the Son of the living God Himself, who became a child of man, like us. In Bethlehem on this day God in human form once did not only *visit* a few people. We could surely find no comfort in that. No, there God's Son Himself *became a human being* like us; a descendant of our fallen father, Adam, like us; a member of our whole human family, like us; a blood relative of all fallen humans, like us; a brother of all sinners! Therefore what once happened in Bethlehem does not concern only the Bethlehemites, but all whose nature the Son of God took on, therefore all that calls itself human, all that calls itself sinner; therefore also the angel of the Lord calls aloud: *"I bring you good news of a great joy which will come to all the people";* hear it well, *"to all the people."*

At the bottom of this lies an unspeakably great, unfathomable divine mystery. God's holiness and righteousness had to close heaven to us sinners, and God knew well that neither we ourselves nor any creature in heaven and on earth could open it again. But a long time ago, yes, already in eternity, He made the most blessed decision to do Himself what we could not do, and indeed in a way that, to His eternal praise and glory, would reveal to all creatures how divinely great, how wonderful, how unfathomable, how immeasurable His love is. Namely, God made the decision to send into the world His only begotten Son Himself, to let Him carry them through all the deepest humiliation to the death on the cross in order to make satisfaction for them, and so to atone for all our sins completely and eternally. And what we today see with our eyes in Bethlehem is the final carrying out of that eternal decision of God the heavenly Father.

As soon as God's Son became a man, already then the unbearable burden of sin was taken from all people and laid on Christ; already then the holy child of God lying in a dark stall on a hard manger atoned for the sins of all sinners as God's sacrificial Lamb; and in God's eyes, which look into the future and therefore saw the Son of love already dead on the cross, the payment for the sins of all sinners was now already as good as made, the satisfaction for God's injured holiness and righteousness as good as accomplished, the eternal redemption carried out, and God already reconciled with us all. Then God also immediately opened all the gates of heaven to sinners, reconciled to Him and redeemed. And as a sign that this happened, God sent to the reconciled earth the highest servant at His throne, accompanied by the whole throng of the heavenly hosts; here let the wonder of His love that had come to pass (so that everyone would accept it) be proclaimed to the least of the people, the poor shepherds; and at the conclusion let the air be filled by the singers of heaven with the festive song about the accomplished redemption of the world.

25

Now there is no sinner for whom heaven is not open. Now there is no place, no corner of the earth, no city, no hamlet, no single cottage, no mountain, no valley, no field, no forest, no glen, no depth of the sea, where the gates of heaven do not stand open to every sinner. Although you, as all sinners, have been *born in sin,* this does not close heaven to you any longer. The birth of the most holy Son of God has hallowed your birth as a sinner. If you have lived in *the lust of the eyes* [1 John 2:16], that is, in the love of the tangible, and have said idolatrously to the nugget of gold in your heart: "My comfort!"—also this does not close heaven to you anymore; because for that the One born in Bethlehem denied Himself everything tangible and temporal, became the poorest among the poor, and in that way eternally atoned for your lust of the eyes. Or if you have wasted your life until now in *the lust of the flesh,* sought your peace, your rest, your heaven in unclean lust or in the vanity of this world—also this no longer closes heaven to you; for the sweet child Jesus renounced all the joys of the world, willingly became the most miserable of all the miserable, and in that way eternally atoned also for your lust of the flesh. Or if you have given yourself to *the pride of life,* sought your own honor, and in that way robbed God of His honor and made yourself God in your heart—also this does not close heaven to you anymore; for the Christ Child, although the King of all kings and Lord of all lords, in incomprehensible humility became a subject of an idolatrous, heathen Caesar, submitted to his tax, became the obedient Son of a sinner, a servant of all servants, obedient unto death, yes, to the death of the cross, and so through His deepest humility eternally atoned for your damnable pride. Or, finally, if you were *the sinner of all sinners,* the most deeply fallen of all the fallen—also this no longer closes heaven to you; for the Most Holy became your Brother and therefore stands as near to you as to the most pious on earth. In Bethlehem He took also your sins upon Himself, carried them up to Golgotha, took them with Him down into the grave, and buried them there eternally—heaven is open for you.

Oh, therefore, let us be joyful and happy today; today let us shout for joy; let our mouths be full of laughter and our tongues filled with praise, for—oh, blessed Christmas message!—*heaven* is open for us, that is, God's everlasting grace without wrath, Christ's everlasting gracious righteousness without sin and guilt, everlasting life without darkness, everlasting joy without sorrow, everlasting riches without want, everlasting health without sickness, everlasting youth without the weakness of age, everlasting vision of God without weariness, everlasting enjoyment without satiety, everlasting life without death, everlasting fellowship with God, with His holy angels, and with all saints without separation; in short, an everlasting city of God, an everlasting fatherland, and an everlasting home in complete blessedness of body and soul, without end and without ceasing. All this now stands open for us. [*The Lutheran Hymnal,* 105:8:]

> He opens us again the door
> Of Paradise today;
> The angel guards the gate no more.
> To God our thanks we pay.

II

Now the question arises: What should we do so that today the door of heaven has not been opened to us in vain?—Let me now, in the second place, answer this question.

Beloved, there are many who admit that through Christ's coming into this world of sinners heaven has been opened; but how do they understand this?—Some mean by this that Christ has only shown us the way to heaven and only *taught* us what we must do in order through our own works to deserve an entrance to heaven. Others understand it this way: Christ through His birth, His suffering, and His reconciling death won grace for us so that through our conversion and rebirth, through our praying, wrestling, and fighting, we might reach the point where God is reconciled to us and heaven is opened to us.

But all these do not as yet know the true power and fruit of the birth of Christ. For they all manifestly mean that heaven is really still closed to the sinner and that he must now do something in order that it be opened to him. But that is not the way it is. No door of heaven is any longer closed to us sinners; everywhere all are wide open for everyone. Now after Christ's birth there is written so to speak with the blood and tears of Christ, in large letters over the 12 pearly gates of the heavenly Jerusalem, as we read in the 21st chapter of St. John's Revelation: "Its gates shall never be shut." Therefore when Christ started to preach publicly, He began with the words: "The kingdom of God has come near." And when the first disciples came to Him, He called to them: "Truly, truly, I say to you, you will see heaven opened, and the angels of God ascending and descending upon the Son of man." And Christ not only makes it clear that with His coming into the world He opened heaven for everyone, yes, that with His coming heaven came to earth, but He says also that the kingdom of heaven which came with Him is like a wedding feast to which all whom the servants would find would be invited with the words: "Come, for all is now ready."

Tell me yourselves, my hearers: What is it we have to do so that heaven, opened again through Christ's birth, may not stand open for us in vain?—We have to do nothing except joyfully enter in through the wide-open gates.

What would you say if over the open gate of a most wonderful garden

27

these words were written in large golden letters: Here everyone can enter free; or if the words were written: Come, come in, everyone, and enjoy yourself in this beautiful garden!—What would you say if someone would then first ask what he must do to be permitted to enter? You would say: Have you not read what is written here? Go in as you are; here everyone is welcome.

But perhaps you will ask: Where are the open *gates* of heaven through which we should enter? That is easy to answer: Where Baptism is administered, where the preaching of the Gospel sounds forth, where the sinner is absolved, where the holy meal of reconciliation is celebrated— there, there heaven is open; those, those are the wide-open doors of heaven for everyone.

But perhaps you will ask further: How does one enter through these doors?—In a word, the sinner does that when he *believes.* Whoever is baptized and believes that thereby God has received him as His child; whoever hears the preaching of the Gospel: *"To you is born this day . . . a Savior,"* and believes that the child Jesus born in Bethlehem is also his Savior, born also for him; whoever is absolved and believes that thereby God Himself speaks to him the forgiveness of all his sins; whoever goes to the Lord's Supper and believes that through it he becomes partaker of all the fruits of the suffering and death of his Savior—that person, yes, that person goes through any of these four gates of heaven on earth into heaven.

Finally, perhaps you will say: Even after receiving Baptism in faith, hearing the Gospel in faith, receiving absolution in faith, partaking of the Supper in faith, am I not and do I not still remain *on earth?* I reply: Indeed you remain on earth; but in spite of that you are already in heaven, for you have at your side a gracious God, because your unworthiness can no longer separate you and your God; you have within you a blessed joy because you know that you have become God's beloved child; and you have around you the holy angels and with you blessed brothers and sisters, for through Christ's birth heaven and earth are united in peace. What more do you want? Is that not already heaven on earth?

It is indeed true: As long as a believing person is still on earth, so long it is not yet evident what we shall be, but still such a person is already in the midst of heaven and has eternal life as a seed in his soul, as the Lord expressly says in John 6:40: "For this is the will of My Father, that everyone who sees the Son and believes in Him should have eternal life; and I will raise him up at the last day." The believer lacks nothing more except that at last the curtain of his sinful flesh be put off; then with ecstasy he will see that for a long time heaven already vaulted over him.

True, the light of heaven in the believer here on earth is still like a glowing ember; but it is already lit, and in death it will suddenly be changed into a full sun of heavenly light. True, the joy of heaven in the believer here on earth is still only like a drop; but it already refreshes and sweetens the heart, and in death it will be changed into a full stream, into a whole sea of heavenly joy. True, the eternal sanctification in the believer here on earth is only very incomplete, is hindered by the sinful flesh, and is often hardly recognizable; but it is already begun, and in death it will quickly and suddenly be completed as soon as the believer here arrives there and sees God; and the one who falls asleep in Jesus will awake with songs of rejoicing, completely renewed in the image of God.

O my dear hearers, in conclusion I therefore call to you once more: *Rejoice! The Savior is born; heaven is open for you.* Now let none of you remain irresolute and hesitant as you stand before the open gates of heaven. Do you perhaps want to remain outside for the sake of the joy which the world and its sin and vanity gives you? Oh, consider this: This joy is nothing but apparent joy, and its end is everlasting mourning! Or do you perhaps not want to enter because of your many and great sins? Oh, think about this: The gates of heaven have been opened so wide precisely for the sake of sinners, for great sinners! Or do you think you must first do something in order to be worthy of it? Oh, consider: *As long as you remain outside, you remain unworthy; you will become worthy by going in!* Oh, therefore, believe the joyful Christmas message which I have brought you today. Then you also today will go through it as through an open gate of heaven, into heaven opened wide for you today. And when one day your bodily eye is closed in death, then the eye of your soul will behold all the glory of heaven. You will "rejoice with unutterable . . . joy" [1 Peter 1:8], and "no one will take your joy from you" [John 16:22].

So then, say with me: [Here Walther inserts a hymn verse]. Amen.

First Sunday After Epiphany
Luke 2:41-54

The Holy Family, an Instructive Example for Christian Parents and Children
(Amerikanisch-Lutherische Evangelien Postille, pp. 59—65)

Grace, mercy, and peace from God the Father and the Lord Jesus Christ, the Son of the Father, in truth and love be with you all. Amen.

Beloved brothers and sisters in Christ Jesus!

Only a few who immigrated to this country did this from the right motive, letting God lead them. Most left their homeland to find here freedom of the flesh, earthly riches, or at least a comfortable life. Only a few did it in order here, better than in their old fatherland, to be able to lead a quiet and peaceable life in all godliness and honesty. And even those who only for the sake of heavenly riches exchanged the land of their birth for this distant western country have in part fallen into a gross error. For some thought they had to do it so that through them the true church would be preserved. That is a great error, as I said.

The true church is so constituted that it can exist in every land and under every form of government. Indeed, it is true that here and there in our old German fatherland the authorities, the temporal as well as the so-called spiritual authorities, did not permit the pure doctrine of the true church to be preached, but instead forced upon the congregations false teachers and false books for school and church, while *here* Christians are granted a completely free exercise of their faith in every respect. However, the experience of all ages has established the fact that just when the church lay under the greatest outward oppression it was strengthened the most inwardly, and that persecution is the very thing that trained the best Christians; but as soon as the church was free and unoppressed, it sank little by little into indifference, security, indolence, and spiritual satiety.

It is particularly noteworthy and a source of shame that many thought they had to emigrate, not for any earthly consideration but particularly for the souls' salvation of their children, and yet it cannot be denied that right here our beloved youth stand in particularly great spiritual danger.

Under the shield of religious liberty and freedom of conscience here in all streets and in all public places such horrible blasphemies are uttered against God, His Word, and everything holy, and are even spread in eagerly read daily papers, as probably happens in no other land in the world. Under the cloak of freedom in a republic all sins and shame are so brazenly carried out in broad daylight, and the authorities and their laws and all discipline and order are so insolently scoffed at, as hardly happens in other lands and in our old fatherland. Add to this the fact that here so many ways are open to children to earn money and to be independent of their parents that it can almost be looked upon as a miracle if a child here still retains a childlike frame of mind and remains obedient. The danger of being led astray reaches its peak in the fact that here as nowhere else the land is filled with a countless host of heterodox sects, who are often surrounded by such a deceiving and holy appearance that even those who are really concerned about their soul's salvation can easily be decieved and led on byways dangerous to their soul.

Whoever among us is a father or a mother and has the heartfelt wish that his children not only come through the world but above all that they be saved—must he not think of the future with trembling when he considers the condition of our new fatherland according to the Word of God? Who must not cry out with anxiety and concern: Ah, what will happen to my poor children after my death? Will they not be drawn into the fearful storm of ruin and lose their dearly bought souls?

Beloved, as well founded as such a concern is, we would sin if we despaired on account of it. In fact, we would fall into the same error which once prompted many to come here from the old, beloved fatherland, namely the error that one could not be saved everywhere on earth. May such thoughts be far from us! No, since we now are here by God's permission, we should think for our comfort: God, whose grace reaches so far, as far as heaven, is also here; Jesus Christ, to whom the heathen have been given for an inheritance and the ends of the world for His possession, has His kingdom of grace also here; God's Spirit, from whom one cannot escape even with the wings of the morning, moves and works also here. Also here this word applies: "Everyone who calls upon the name of the Lord will be saved." Also here heaven is open; also here is the tree of the church, whose branches spread out to all parts of the earth; also here God stretches out His hands to sinners. Therefore also here we and our children can be protected from being led astray and can be saved.

In this hour, on the basis of our Gospel lesson for today, permit me to speak to you about what parents and children must do in order that this may happen.

Text: Luke 2:41-52

Now that within the past so-called 12 nights we have considered Christ as an infant on the lap and in the arms of His mother, our Gospel lesson for this Sunday, just read, presents Him to us in His holy *youth* at the side of His earthly parents. Therefore consider with me:

The Holy Family, an Instructive Example for Christian Parents and Children

In this connection we ask:
1. *What does it teach parents?* and
2. *What does it teach children?*

O Jesus, may You Yourself bless the preaching of Your Word so that it mightily penetrates the hearts of parents and children so that we henceforth faithfully direct all our children to You, and our children willingly permit themselves to be led to You, so that also then when we parents sleep in our graves, our children still all together may serve You here and bless us as their pious fathers and mothers; until You finally will have brought us all together in the triumphant congregation of Your perfected saints. There we will sing Your praise always and eternally. Amen.

I

What is told us in our Gospel lesson for today is the only report which the holy evangelists have preserved to us about the holy family during the youth of our Savior. The presentation of this one occurrence, singled out from all the others, nevertheless suffices to give us a vivid picture of the nature of Christ's entire life as a youth until He entered upon His public ministry.

The first thing we learn from the report of our Gospel lesson is the way Mary and Joseph carried out their task as the earthly parents of Christ. We learn here that, after they had the holy Child circumcized according to the law of the Lord, they trained Him with the greatest care; and therefore they asked Him, already from His 12th year on, to accompany them when, according to the law of the Lord, they journeyed to Jerusalem. Here, where the only temple of God's people was, they served the Lord publicly and celebrated the Easter festival with the whole congregation of Israel.

How instructive this is for us parents, to whom God has entrusted children as pledges of His love! If Mary and Joseph painstakingly had to rear the holy Child, in whom the Lord of Glory had disguised Himself; if even they dared not think this Child would grow by Himself without their assistance and that God would without them watch over Him and keep

32

Him, how much more should we realize our calling to be instruments of God in the rearing of our helpless little ones! If the parents of the most holy God-man recognized it as their obligation to bring Him to the house of the Lord, how much more should we realize our responsibility to bring our children, who are sinners in need of grace, to the Lord early in life!

It is true, beloved, that it is not in our power to convert our children, to cleanse and change their sinful hearts, and to preserve them in God's grace; but we can indeed neglect them and be guilty if their souls are lost. Therefore, if they let themselves be saved, we should indeed be God's helpers. They have not been given to us for playing and joking, much less that they be only our servants; rather, they have been entrusted to us by God that we should direct them to their heavenly Father already then when they as yet know nothing about Him. One day God will demand at our hands the souls and the blood of our children and say to us: Where are they, My children whom I have given you?

It is of the utmost importance, and our first duty as Christian parents, to bring our children immediately after birth to Jesus through Holy Baptism; for He said: "Let the children come to Me, and do not hinder them; for to such belongs the kingdom of God." But with that we as parents have in no way discharged our debt to them. No, after our children have been baptized they carry Jesus Himself in their hearts; then, like Mary and Joseph, we have with our child a Jesus-child in our house and in our arms. For that reason our heartfelt concern for their protection should be doubled. Then the salvation of our dear child should be the subject of our daily care and our sighs and prayers; daily and hourly we should place him in Jesus' arms and, so to say, let the love of Jesus and the fear of God flow into him with his mother's milk. As soon as the child can possibly grasp it, we should tell him that he is baptized and what great grace has thereby been given him, and teach him to say with joy: I am baptized! My Jesus is mine! My sins are forgiven!

We should by no means wait with that until our children go to school. No, before we can send our children to school, we should daily be their teachers and guides to God. Those are truly unfaithful parents who permit their child to grow up as it is and set their minds at ease with the fact that in his sixth year he will go to school; for the more tender the child is, the more important is what is sown in his delicate heart in these years. If we neglect the souls of our smallest children, we are laying the foundation for a possible later ruin that cannot be rooted out. If we do not plant God's Word in their heart, only too soon after baptism it will be like an uncultivated field, in which the weeds of sin, yea, thorns, thistles, and hedges of vice, disrespect, and shamelessness will shoot up abundantly.

33

Oh, shame on those parents who bring a wild child to school; for, as I said, already in these first years the faithful training given by parents does unbelievably much, whereas neglect during this time brings irreparable harm.

But what shall we say of parents who have the opportunity to send their children to a Christian school for a small fee—yes, and if they are truly poor, free of tuition—but do not take advantage of this opportunity to do something for the souls of their children, but who look upon their children as their slaves who must earn money for them and for that reason keep them out of school? Oh, how blind are such parents! How is it that they do not realize at all why God has entrusted them with immortal, dearly redeemed souls? What a heavy, fearful accountability they load upon their conscience with such neglect! One day such conscienceless parents will wish they had never had children, when they must appear with them before God!

Yet, beloved, even this is not enough, that we simply send our growing children to school, perhaps only to be free of them and to be relieved of all personal concern for their instruction and upbringing. No, by simply sending them to school our responsibility is in no way finished. What can the few hours in school profit if we are not concerned to watch over our children so that the good seed sown in their hearts is not again smothered by bad example, keeping bad company, and many other kinds of seduction? And how can what the teacher plants in their souls grow and bear fruit when at home the parents do not through questions, admonitions, warnings, and loving remonstrances water and cultivate what has been planted?

Yet, my beloved, even if parents did everything they could for their children during the time they were in school, their parental responsibility by no means comes to an end when this time is over. But what happens most of the time, especially in our new fatherland? Parents almost begrudge their children the last weeks of their preparation for that important day of their life on which they confess their faith before many witnesses, publicly renew their baptismal vow, and swear everlasting faithfulness to the triune God; and if they permit this to happen, they immediately unmercifully push their children out into the world and do not inquire whether their souls are in danger or not, if only they can find a place where their children can earn more money than elsewhere!

Oh, curse-laden greed, when for the sake of base gain parents place their children into situations where they know that because of the greatness of temptation they can hardly escape ruin! Oh, conscienceless parents who place their poor child, unsure and inexperienced in faith and knowledge, either among the heterodox, who with subtle fallacies and false piety crowd in upon the blinded child in order to win him for a false faith and enthusiasm; or among people who care as much about one religion as about another, and therefore about none, and who call a zeal for the one pure, true religion a narrow fanaticism; or among profligate scoffers, where the unfortunate children from morning to night hear nothing but ridicule, slander, and filthy jokes! Oh, conscienceless parents who knowingly and willingly let their poor, innocent child work in such places where a crowd of seducers surround him and set almost inescapable traps for his innocence! Oh, conscienceless parents who unnecessarily place their children in the midst of murderers of souls and who for weeks and months, yes years, do not investigate whether the child still has the Lord Jesus in his heart and confesses Him before the world!

Those, too, are conscienceless who, when they must permit their child to go into a dangerous place, yet do not bring his need to God in fervent prayer, and who do not with tears beseech and encourage their child to remain faithful to his Savior! Oh conscienceless parents who hire out their child in such a way that in his service to man he cannot even publicly serve the Lord on the Lord's day, strengthen his weak faith through the hearing of God's Word, rouse his sluggish heart again, confirm his feeble knees, and strengthen his already staggering foot and again set it on the already forsaken narrow way!

"Yes," someone says, "we have had concern enough to get our children through school; now they must fend for themselves as best they can; we, too, had to go out into the world in our tender years." Ah, those who can think so indifferently about the danger to the souls of their children show thereby that when they themselves went out into the world they were overcome by the corruption of the world. They have no concern for their own soul; therefore they have even less concern for the soul's need of their children. Instead of lighting the way for their children through their God-pleasing example, through their zeal and seriousness in their Christianity, they seduce them to a similar ungodly way of life through their bad example, through their lukewarm, sluggish Christianity.

Ah, you unfortunate people who act like that, if you considered what you are doing, and if you would hear the woe that God calls down upon such conscienceless parents, you would be horrified. God says in His Word: "Seek first His kingdom and His righteousness, and all these things shall be yours as well"; but you do the opposite and seek first the kingdom of this world. God says further in His Word: "For what shall it profit a man, if he shall gain the whole world and lose his own soul? Or what shall a man give in exchange for his soul?" [KJV]. But you consider the souls of your children a thousand times less than the whole world; yes, what shall I say? You sell your children, body and soul, to the servants of the devil so that they can gain a few rusty dollars. Christ says: "Whoever causes one of these little ones who believe in Me to sin, it would be better for him to have a great millstone fastened round his neck and to be drowned in the depth of the sea." But you cause your children to sin, whom God has bound to your heart before others; therefore woe to you always and eternally!

Oh Lord God, how in all eternity will you people answer for the neglect of your children?—Look at Mary and Joseph: Although they were very poor, every year they made the expensive journey of 18 German miles on foot to Jerusalem, to the temple of the Lord, with their little Boy whom no one could either seduce or teach. And when out of weakness they lost the precious little Child only according to the body, how anxious they were, how they lamented, cried, and sighed and sought for Him without rest day and night, until they found the Child entrusted to them! Therefore believe this: Misery and woe will come upon your heads if because of shameful greed you plunge the dearly redeemed souls of your children into the least danger. Yes, as Christian parents you will have to suffer a more severe punishment than those heathen parents who threw their children into the red-hot belly of the iron god Moloch.

O father, consider this: *God* placed your child into your arms. Consider this, O mother: *God* placed your infant in your lap. From your hands and from your lap God will demand your child again. Woe to you if you then must remain silent to the question: Where are My children? Consider Eli, upon whom God's fearful judgment fell particularly because he did not rear his sons in the nurture and admonition of the Lord; yes, did not even look with disfavor on their knavery. Don't say: Yes, my child will not listen to me anymore! Perhaps you let him grow up in early youth without the rod of correction; now you are already reaping the fruit of your foolish love. Oh, therefore, hurry to recover as much as possible what you have previously neglected. If you did not neglect the necessary discipline of your children in their earliest years, you should not think that your children have now outgrown your discipline. But you should continue to use your parental authority which God has given you, and even now make your children subject to you. Do not cloak and excuse their sins, but earnestly punish them; do not neglect to admonish and warn them; and let your tears as father and mother speak so that, if God wills, the hard hearts of your children may still be softened. But, above all, you should cry to God day and night that He may move the hearts of your lost sons and daughters that they be converted. Yes, if nothing will help, then you should show that you love Christ more than your children; take from them your parental blessing and no longer recognize them as your children, if they insist on continually despising your parental warnings.

But you, dear parents, who day and night carry your children on your heart and still see no fruit, do not despair on that account! God sees your silent tears; God hears your sighs; God notices the fervent longing of your hearts. Just wait for His help; your care and labor are not lost. Either God will still draw your godless children to Himself, as once He did in the case of Augustine, who was living deep in the service of sin. His faithful, godly mother, Monica, daily prayed and wept for him for more than 20 years. Therefore Ambrose said to her: "It is not possible that a child of these tears should be lost." Or, you God-fearing parents, if your children are absolutely not to be saved, your concern and prayers for them will not be lost, but the blessing of your parental faithfulness will return upon you a thousandfold.

II

But let this suffice about what our Gospel lesson for today says to parents; on the basis of our Gospel lesson let us now consider, in the second place, the lovely boy Jesus as an instructive example for you, dear children.

Dear children, the example of Jesus teaches particularly two things: first, how already in your youth you are to serve God and, second, how you are to be subject to your parents.

You see, the Son of God could have come into the world as a grown man. But He did not want to. He wanted to be also a child and a youth in order to redeem us through His holy childhood and youth from the sins of our childhood and youth and to give all children and young men and women an example and pattern of a genuinely pious youth in order that they might follow in His steps.

Consider, beloved children, the holy boy Jesus was at the same time God's Son in one person. He was therefore not obligated according to the law to appear in the temple in Jerusalem and to celebrate the Easter festival; and yet He, still young and delicate, accompanied His parents and undertook with joy the long, laborious, and difficult journey, on which His poor parents surely could not always give Him the necessary nourishment. Consider this: In the holy boy Jesus lay hidden all the treasures of wisdom and knowledge; therefore the teachers had to marvel at His high, marvelous understanding when He asked questions and when He answered. And yet this Child, full of God's wisdom, as soon as He came to Jerusalem went into the temple and sat among the teachers. He was not attracted by the beautiful city with its splendid royal castle or by the shining palaces of the rich; He passed by all that without marveling at it, and hurried to the temple in order to hear discourses about God's Word and to talk about it Himself. Are you like this holy Child? Is God's Word now already the joy of your heart?

Yes, some may perhaps say, Jesus was God's Son; that is why already as a child He was so pious. Can one expect that also of us? I reply to them: Yes, dear children, many other children have followed the Lord Jesus and have been like Him. The holy apostle Paul says of Timothy that from a child he knew the Holy Scriptures; yes, of the little God-fearing Samuel is said practically what is said of the Lord Jesus: "Now the boy Samuel continued to grow in stature and in favor with the Lord and with men." And of the eight-year-old Josiah we read: "He did what was right in the eyes of the Lord . . . and he did not turn aside to the right hand or to the left."

Beloved children, you see from this that one can be pious already in his youth; yes, that is the time when it is easiest to be pious, for then one does not have so many hindrances: no great cares, no lofty wishes, not so much work; also then one is not so easily hated and persecuted on account of his piety, for a pious child has a good standing not only with God but also with men. Everyone likes that and loves such a child. On the other hand, an ungodly child is most unfortunate; for he is an abomination to God, and the holy angels do not love him, and people want nothing to do with him. It is true, in your own strength you children cannot be pious, as little as other people can. For only Jesus was from birth holy, blameless, and separate from sinners; but all other mortals have an evil heart when they are born into the world. But see, in Holy Baptism God gave the Holy Spirit into your heart and cleanses it through faith. If you still believe in your dear Savior, namely if you believe that He redeemed you and has already washed you of all your sins, He also gives you power to live according to His holy example.

Oh, therefore, follow after Him. Like the holy boy Jesus, also you should go into the house of the Lord with heartfelt desire and diligence. Let the precious Word of God be also your best-loved activity—to speak of it, to ask questions about it, and to let others ask you questions. Let that be your highest desire. Therefore, as often as evil rascals tempt you not to go where you are taught God's Word, don't follow them but say with the boy Jesus: *"Did you not know that I must be in My Father's house?"*

Yet of this most holy Child we are told not only that He had such great joy in the Word of God, but also especially that when His parents found Him in the temple and wanted to return home, *"He went down with them and came to Nazareth and was obedient to them."*

Oh, that I could write these words: *"And He was obedient to them"* with indelible script on the hearts of all of you who still have parents or foster parents. Consider what an adorable humility it was that He to whom all creatures are subject and before whom all angels and humans must bow the knee was subject to His parents! Consider what a wonderful, incomprehensible condenscension it was that He who made the firmament and who was the Maker of the universe let His foster father employ Him when he wanted to build a hut for some poor person!

But realize from this also what godless children those must be who do not imitate this great example and do not want to be subject to their parents! What will Christ one day say to you who despise your parents, who let their warnings go in one ear and out the other, who grieve them daily, and not once pay attention to the tears and sighings which you with your disobedience have provoked? The Savior will one day say to you: You wicked children, I thought you would be moved to listen to your parents when you would hear that I, your God, Lord, and Savior, was subject to My poor parents. But, behold! Even My example could not melt your disobedient, obstinate heart and move you to childlike obedience. Oh, because of that, woe to you now and always! Yes, "Depart from Me, you cursed, into the eternal fire prepared for the devil and his angels."

Ah, how those who on earth were godless, disobedient children will then wish they once again could be children! Then they will think: Oh, how gladly we would obey our parents! But then it is too late. Therefore *now,* in heartfelt repentance and firm faith, ask God, for the sake of the holy obedience of the child Jesus, to forgive your previous disobedience; then God will be gracious to you and will help you to become better while there still is time. Do not listen to the voice of those who would deceive you by saying that obedience to parents is a heavy yoke. That is the voice of Satan. Listen rather to the faithful voice of your father and your mother! Their voice is God's voice; their blessing is God's blessing; their curse is God's curse.

Ah yes, beloved children, consider what Sirach says: "My child, forget not how bitter you have been to your mother; for whoever forsakes his father will be disgraced, and he who brings sorrow to his mother is an accursed child before the Lord. The father's blessing builds children's houses, but the mother's curse tears them down again." Consider what Solomon says: "The eye that mocks a father and scorns to obey a mother will be picked out by the ravens of the valley and eaten by the vultures." Finally, consider also what God Himself says in His holy Law: "Honor your father and mother (this is the first commandment with a promise), that it may be well with you and that you may live long on the earth." God help that this precious promise can be fulfilled in us all here in time and there eternally. Amen.

First Sunday in Lent
Matthew 4:1-11

Christ's Battle with the Prince of Darkness and His Glorious Victory

(*Amerikanisch-Lutherische Evangelien Postille*, pp. 108—15)

May grace and peace be multiplied to you in the knowledge of God and of Jesus our Lord [2 Peter 1:2]. Amen.

Dear brothers and sisters in Christ Jesus!

Among the Christian doctrines which today are disputed within Christendom, the teaching that there is a devil who ceaselessly, maliciously tempts men is perhaps attacked most frequently and vehemently. Yes, it has come to this that many assert that they believe in the entire Scriptures, but they cannot possibly believe that there is a devil, at least that he can still work among men.

It is just about impossible to debate on this point with one who rejects God's Word. The doctrine of Satan concerns the invisible world of spirits which cannot be opened up to us by our reason, but by the Word of divine revelation. To the person who rejects the entire divine revelation the teaching about the mysterious power of darkness must naturally be foolishness. What would it help atheists, followers of natural religion, or moralists if they believed in an invisible enemy of the soul, tempter and seducer of men, but did not believe in the grace and redemption of their Savior? In the explanation of the sentence of Peter: "Always be prepared to make a defense," Luther says:

> If you hear people who are so completely blinded and hardened that they deny that [Scripture] is God's Word or are in doubt about it, just keep silence, do not say a word to them, and let them go their way. Just say: "I will give you enough proof from Scripture. If you want to believe it, this is good; if not, I will give you nothing else." Then you may say: "Ah, in this way God's Word must needs be brought into disgrace!" Leave this to God [*Luther's Works,* American Edition, 30, 107].

So far Luther.

Today the poison of unbelief and doubt have so taken over in

Christendom and infected so many that even those who do not simply want to reject Scripture doubt the existence of Satan or at least his present influence among men. But, beloved, as surely as there is a God who has revealed Himself in Holy Scripture, so certain is it that there is a devil. In Holy Scripture Satan is not only named here and there, so that a person could think that this referred to evil thoughts and lusts, but the Bible describes in detail the whole history of his origin, his being, his qualities, his works, his influence upon the whole human race, his kingdom, his abode, and his present and future fate. We find the doctrine of Satan in all the books of the Old and New Testaments, in Genesis as well as in the Revelation of St. John. In Holy Scripture Satan is not mentioned only incidentally, but the doctrine of Satan is so interwoven with the whole teaching of divine revelation that the whole structure of Christian doctrine collapses as soon as one denies the existence of that evil spirit. If you deny the existence of the devil, you must also deny the fall of man into sin, original sin, therefore also the atonement, Christ, your baptism, yes, the whole Gospel; indeed, you must make liars of the holy prophets, the holy apostles, and Christ Himself.

Scripture tells us briefly this: God once created not only man, but also a countless host of higher spirits, namely angels, and gave them great glory, so that, gathered about His throne, they should serve Him and carry out His commands. But one of the most glorious and highest of these angels, fell away from God, and with him a whole multitude of heavenly spirits. That fallen angel could not keep his heavenly, princely status but, after he left his home, was cast out of heaven to hell in chains of darkness.

But this wicked enemy of God now decided to establish another kingdom in the place of the one he lost, and in this kingdom to destroy and bring to naught God's works everywhere. It was then that God made the first humans, holy and glorious, in His image in body and soul. The devil now sought to make them also disloyal to God and plunge them into sin. In the third chapter of his first book, Moses tells how Satan succeeded. Man permitted himself to be led astray, renounced obedience to God, fell into sin, and from a child of God became a subject of the kingdom of darkness. Sinful parents now keep begetting sinful children. Every human is now by nature not in the kingdom of God but in the kingdom of the enemy of God. With sin, God's kingdom vanished from the earth. Scripture says that the ruler and god of this world is Satan, and he now ceaselessly tries to spread more sin, error, blindness, darkness, misery, and misfortune on earth. It says:

He is the prince of the power of the air and prowls around like a roaring lion, seeking someone to devour. He is now at work in the sons of disobedience and has blinded the minds of the unbelievers, to keep them from seeing the light of the Gospel of the glory of Christ. For we are not contending against flesh and blood, but against principalities, against the powers, against the world rulers of this present darkness, against the spiritual hosts of wickedness in the heavenly places.

But God's Word reveals to us not only the depths of Satan, but also the depths of the Godhead, the depths of eternal love; it reveals to us not only the might and cunning of that evil spirit, but also that there is a much more powerful Lord of heaven and earth; it reveals to us not only our misery, how we all through sin have come into the kingdom of Satan, but also how Jesus Christ, the Son of God and Son of Man, conquered Satan, rescued us from his kingdom, saved us from the rule of darkness, and established through His blood a new kingdom of grace in which all who believe in Him find freedom and salvation.

Our Gospel lesson today places before our souls a great, important battle which our Savior fought for us against the prince of darkness. Let us in this hour consider this for the strengthening of our faith.

Text: Matthew 4:1-11

Under the guidance of the Gospel text just read, let us today center our attention on:

Christ's Battle with the Prince of Darkness and His Glorious Victory

In this connection we consider:

1. *how Christ here battled for all people and gloriously conquered;* and

2. *how a believing Christian should now follow the Captain of his salvation and also fight against Satan and overcome him through Christ's power.*

O Jesus, You faithful Savior, who once for us fought a difficult, hard battle, see, we are now assembled to consider it from Your precious Word. Let it be to the salvation of our souls; let Your believers among us be mightily strengthened by it in their faith, but let no one, no one among us leave here who is not mightily awakened to embrace You in faith. O dearest Lord Jesus, You alone know how many of us still lie in the power of darkness. O rise up, rise up, and fight also now for these souls. Make the dead living, raise the fallen, make the despondent happy, give the faint courage and zeal, and also today conquer again among us through Your Word. Yours, Yours shall be the glory, O Jesus, always and eternally. Amen.

42

I

My hearers, it is an altogether wonderful battle which is related in our Gospel for today. A short time before, Christ was baptized. Then heaven opened above Him as though it wanted to sink to earth. Now we see hell open up below Him and storm against Him with all its power. How wonderous! Once the almighty Son of God had hurled Satan out of heaven; here on earth He lets Himself be attacked, led around, laughed at, and mocked by him. And He conquers him not by the Word of His power, as He certainly could have, but through the written Word of God. He who is the eternal Light fights with the spirit of darkness, the eternal Truth with the spirit of lies, the All Holy with the spirit of uncleanness, the King of heaven with the powerless captive of hell. The Son of God permits Satan to place Him on the pinnacle of the temple. He permits him to demand that He worship him. What an amazing battle!

When the beginning of our Gospel reads: *"Then Jesus was led up by the Spirit into the wilderness to be tempted by the devil,"* we see that Christ's battle was not something accidental. It was arranged by God, the heavenly Father, Himself. It happened according to God's eternal, gracious counsel, the execution of which Christ had now willingly undertaken. If Christ had not wanted to, Satan would not have been permitted to appear before Him, let alone tempt and assail Him.

But Christ did not here fight for Himself. Christ here fought as Surety, as Mediator, as Substitute for the whole human race, for all people, also for us assembled here. Through sin all men sold themselves to Satan; through it they all became servants and subjects of his kingdom. Therefore, when Christ wanted to redeem and save people, He came as the real Owner of the souls of all men, to conquer Satan, to destroy his kingdom, to take his booty from him, to free us again from his sinister power, and to lead all humanity through the kingdom of grace into the kingdom of everlasting blessedness.

St. John says: "The reason the Son of God appeared was to destroy the works of the devil." Yes, the first prophecy of Christ, which the first human couple, led astray by the devil, received from God in Paradise reads: "The Seed of the woman," that is, Christ, the Son of the Virgin, "will crush the head of the serpent," that is, the devil. Of course, Christ did this chiefly through His bloody death on the cross as a reconciliation for all the sins of the world. Through that the serpent's head was totally crushed, and all humanity was completely redeemed. But the battle with the devil described in our Gospel for today was the beginning, the first assault, as it were, on the hellish robber's castle. This battle was the first engagement which the Captain of our salvation had to fight to tread Satan underfoot and to inflict on him the first deadly wounds. It was the first defeat the hellish army had to experience, to show them that now a Stronger One has come. Hardly had Jesus begun His public ministry but that He openly engaged Satan on the field of battle in the wilderness, and He did not leave until on the cross He also won the last battle for us and could cry out: "It is finished!" The resurrection which followed was the cry of victory of the Redeemer of the world, the great *Te Deum laudamus,* "We praise Thee, O God," and the descent into hell and the ascension were the glorious triumphal march of the heavenly Conqueror. But all of this could not have come to pass had not Christ in His first battle in the wilderness so gloriously conquered. Also this, therefore, was a necessary part of the work of our redemption.

In the Old Testament we find a splendid prototype of this battle of Christ. Under the rule of King Saul, the army of Israel stood opposite an army of Philistines. The battle was about to begin, and behold, a giant of awesome size and strength came forward out of the army of the enemy, ridiculed the people of God, and made the proposal that he was ready to engage an Israelite warrior in a one-to-one battle. If he fell, the Philistines would be the servants of Israel; if the Israelite fell, the Israelites would be the servants of the Philistines. Frightened by the unusual build of the giant, everyone fell back, anxiously awaiting the final outcome. For 40 days the giant repeated his threatening challenge, and no one wanted to volunteer for this dangerous fight.

But behold, a shepherd boy of Bethlehem Ephratha came forth, named David, a son of Jesse, and said: "Who is this uncircumcised Philistine, that he should defy the armies of the living God? . . . Let no man's heart fail because of him; your servant will go and fight with this Philistine." And David went out and said to the Philistine: "You come to me with a sword and with a spear and with a javelin; but I come to you in the name of the Lord of hosts, the God of the armies of Israel, whom you have defied. This day the Lord will deliver you into my hand . . . that all the earth may know that there is a God in Israel." Thereupon the lad slung a stone at the giant's forehead, and bleeding he fell to the ground; with this one victory all Israel was at once rescued, and they slew the fleeing enemy.

See, my beloved, as important and decisive as this battle of David was for the earthly freedom of all Israel, so important and decisive was the battle of Christ with the devil for the eternal salvation of all men. If we want to understand this battle properly, we must imagine the whole human race gathered in the wilderness on the one side, and on the other, the whole army of the spirits of hell, with the devil, the giant of hell, at its head. We must imagine that Satan challenged the human race to a duel; but there was no one who dared to attempt the frightful struggle for us; all sinners must quake and flee in fear before his strength; they could expect nothing except to be and remain the eternal slaves and bondservants of Satan. But see! The Son of God comes forward, the real David of Bethlehem, indeed of humble appearance, like a shepherd boy, but full of the invisible power of God, as we read in Luther's beautiful hymn, "Dear Christians One and All, Rejoice" [*The Lutheran Hymnal,* 387:6]:

> No garb of pomp or power He wore,
> A servant's form, like mine, He bore,
> To lead the devil captive.

Nothing less than the eternal freedom of all men was at stake; whether we should remain Satan's subjects or again become citizens of the heavenly kingdom and God's children and members of His household depended on this battle. If Christ had been *defeated* in the wilderness, pity us!—But well for us, Christ won, won gloriously, not for Himself but for us; the bonds are severed, and we are free.

Everything we lost in the fall in Paradise, Christ won for us again in the wilderness. Man ate of the forbidden tree; for that Christ hungered 40 days and 40 nights. Man wanted to be like God; for that the Son of God endured Satan skeptically and mockingly calling to Him: *"If You are the Son of God . . . If You are the Son of God . . ."* The serpent said to man: *"Did God say?"* and misled man by twisting God's Word; here Satan tried to do that to Christ, but He stood fast and said without wavering: *"It is written, it is written."* The serpent seduced man to pride and presumption by alluringly saying to him: "When you eat of it your eyes will be opened, and you will be like God, knowing good and evil"; here Satan tempted also Christ to pride when he said: *"All these I will give You, if You will fall down and worship me."* But Christ triumphed; Satan had to leave, and *"angels came and ministered to Him."*

Now, my beloved, if you want an eternal blessing from the battle of your Savior, your heavenly General and Commander-in-chief, nothing more is asked of you and of all humanity than that you act as believing spectators. The important thing is not that you learn from Christ's example to fight against sin and Satan, but the first, the most necessary, the most important is that you learn to believe that Christ fought for you, in your place, for your freedom and salvation. Whoever knows and feels his sin, whoever knows that hitherto he served the devil, that he was full of unbelief, despising God's Word, full of pride, vanity, lust, and love of the world, or that he did not properly fight against the world, flesh, and Satan, let him only look here upon his Savior; this Conqueror from David's tribe held the field for us; this lion of the tribe of Judah conquered

45

for us. O hearer, no matter how deeply you have fallen, even if you have asked the devil's pardon, renounce this awful tyrant of your soul; begin to hold to Christ. Then with Christ you are a conqueror over sin and hell, and so Christ will share with you the booty of battle, namely forgiveness of sins, righteousness, life, and salvation.

Ah, you who still serve sin joyfully, you despise the victory of your heavenly King and willfully remain with the infamous, defeated enemy. Once for all leave the army of the Philistines and come over to the believing Israel; under the Shepherd's staff of the true David is victory, life, and well-being.

But you who do not want to remain in sin, but remain timid and irresolute because of your poor battle against sin, do you not see the hellish giant lying in his blood on the battlefield, slain by the almighty stone-throw of your eternal General? Of what are you afraid? Just enlist in faith under the banner-of His cross. Then, no matter how weak you are, you will be standing on the side of the conquerors! All of believing Christendom joins St. Paul in exulting: "Death is swallowed up in victory. O death, where is thy victory? O death, where is thy sting? The sting of death is sin, and the power of sin is the Law. But thanks be to God, who gives us the victory through our Lord Jesus Christ." That is the way Christendom exults, and do you want to lament?

But you, beloved children of God, who already rejoice in the victory of your Prince of Life, who already exercise yourself in faith in Him, let me, your weakest fellow soldier in the Lord, now secondly speak with you about *how a believing Christian should follow the Captain of his salvation and also fight against Satan and overcome him through the Christ's power.*

II

I want to repeat that the first use we want to make of the battle of Christ with the prince of darkness is not that we be fellow soldiers but believing spectators, that we learn to believe that Christ fought for us, in our place. Whoever has learned to hold fast this truth in his heart can then also confidently and joyfully follow Christ in the battles of the Lord, armed with faith and the Word.

But this is also certain, that whoever has conquered with Christ should also fight at His side. If Satan ventured to try to tempt Christ, the Head, His members dare not remain secure. Christ is a general; therefore, all believers in Christ have been called to spiritual military service. The God of the spiritual Israel is called the Lord Sabaoth, that is, the Lord of hosts. Every little passage of the Bible is a battle trumpet, calling the Christian to battle. In baptism we all vowed "to renounce the devil and all

46

his works and all his ways," therefore also to fight against him. As Christ, immediately after His baptism, was led into the wilderness to be tempted, so all who have been baptized into Jesus Christ should expect nothing else.

Therefore, beloved Christian, if you have begun to hold to Christ and His Word in faith, and to comfort yourself in His victory, good for you, good for you! You have chosen the best part. But know, you are saved— but in hope. You are still in the world; you still have sin in you; you still have flesh and blood. But what is most significant is that you are still a foreigner in the land of death where Satan dwells; he is around you with his assistants and tools and is busy trying to rewin you, to make you tired and faint so that you forsake Christ, give yourself over to him again, and let yourself be brought under his scepter. Don't think Satan is far away from you. He is in his members, the countless spirits of darkness, wherever people are and most fiercely where Christians are. He is with you in your room when you pray, when you read God's Word; he is at your side when you work; he is near you when you go to church, listen to the sermon, and receive the sacrament. Wherever you go, he tries to tempt you and to fell you.

Therefore two things are necessary: that one know the treachery of Satan and, secondly, that one know how to conquer him. We learn both from the temptations of our Savior in the wilderness. Through three temptations Satan sought to conquer Christ. First, he showed Him the miserable wretched condition in which He found Himself, in order to lead Him to doubt whether He was the Son of God. He says: *"If You are the Son of God, command these stones to become loaves of bread."* He wants to say: How can You think You are the Son of God when You must live in hunger and distress?—When this temptation didn't succeed, Satan placed Christ on the pinnacle of the temple and said: *"If You are the Son of God, throw Yourself down; for it is written, 'He will give His angels charge of you,' and 'on their hands they will bear you up, lest you strike your foot against a stone.' "* Here the devil tried to mislead Christ by falsifying the Word of God, because, although he quoted a passage, he omitted important words, for in Psalm 91 the words are clearly added: "to guard you in all your ways." Christ should overlook these words and not remain in His way but, tempting God, throw Himself down in the air.—When also this temptation would not succeed for Satan, he became still more unashamed and placed Christ on *"a very high mountain, and showed Him all the kingdoms of the world and the glory of them; and he said to Him, 'All these will I give You, if You will fall down and worship me.' "* Satan finally wanted to blind and win Christ through the riches, honor, and lust of this world.

You see here, my beloved, the three chief temptations which also every Christian encounters. Satan either tries to make the Christian despair through poverty, want, trouble, misery, disgrace, mockery, and all kinds of misfortune; or he tries to move him through falsifying God's Word to all sorts of dangerous errors, heresies, and doubts concerning God's Word; or he tries to entangle his poor heart in his hellish nets again by painting pictures of good days, riches, honor, and the joy of the world.

Therefore, beloved Christians, learn to know the treachery of the evil foe. Satan is about you and tries all possible keys to open your heart again. If he can't open it with the key of need and misery, he tries it with the key of false doctrine; if that doesn't open it, he tries the key of lust and good days. Also today Satan often appears in a visible, assumed image, as öld and new examples incontestably prove, but Satan appears to Christians most often under the form of money, false doctrine, and honor and worldly joy.

Therefore note this well, dear Christians, if your earthly trouble tempts you to despair of God's goodness and help, if you begin to burden your hearts with earthly cares, you can be sure that the devil already stands before you and calls to you: "If you are a child of God, command these stones to become loaves of bread; so pray yourself well, sigh yourself out of your misery—let go of your faith; it is nothing." Or if you are tempted to doubt a precious doctrine of your Christian faith, and God's Word is even held before you in support of the error, do not doubt that Satan is standing before you saying: *"It is written, 'He will give His angels charge of you.' "* Therefore note this well: Through false teachers Satan cites the Word of God, but he garbles it; he tears it out of context in order to beguile you. This is Satan's method: He gives us one truth in order to bring in ten false teachings. Therefore be warned. First Satan tries to twist God's Word so that it gives false comfort for sins against conscience. But when the sin is committed, he tries to twist God's Word as though there were no grace for sin; then he knows how by lock and key to deprive the conscience of all comfort. Or Satan tries so to change God's Word that it seems contradictory to a poor human; in that way Satan tries to lead the heart to doubt and complete apostasy from the truth. But, finally, mark also this: As believers you will often face the temptation to injure your conscience, deny Christ, and leave God's Word for the sake of earthly advantage. Then consider nothing except that Satan stands before you and calls to you: "All these I will give you, if you will fall down and worship me." Yes, consider every proud thought that arises in you as nothing else than being placed by Satan on the pinnacle of the temple in order to cast you down.

From this you see, beloved, that Job is right when he says: "Has not man a hard service upon earth, and are not his days like the days of a

48

hireling?" Genuine Christianity is truly not an idle thing, no fun and games; it is a continuous fight with flesh, world, and Satan. Whoever dreams about rest, peace, and good days concerning his Christianity deceives himself. Satan is the enemy of all people, but he is a most dedicated enemy of the believer; he stalks him day and night to lure him out of his fortress and plunge him into darkness, blindness, sin, death, and destruction.

Now how shall a Christian arm himself against that? As Christ, the General, goes before, His own should follow Him. But how did Christ fight and win? Satan tempted Him to unbelief, and He answered: *"It is written."* Satan tempted Him to false doctrine, and He replied: *"Again it is written."* Satan tempted Him to pride, and He answered: *"It is written."* O great, important, golden, heavenly, eternal words of the Son of God! O that these words could be written in fiery script on the sky so that all men, all heretics, all doubters, all unbelievers, all despairing, all sinners would daily have to read them! O that these words could be engraved in the hearts of us all with an iron point and indelible letters! Oh, listen, you who still doubt whether God's Word in the Old and New Testaments is the eternal Word of the living God. Listen to this: When the Son of God was tempted by the power of Satan, He said only: *"It is written."* And with these few words from the Old Testament Scriptures He smashed all the entrenchments and bulwarks of the hellish spirit. How could Christ more clearly and incontestably have demonstrated before the whole world that the Bible is the imperishable Word of Him who made heaven and earth, that this Word stands fast when everything, everything else perishes!

Therefore see, dear Christian, let this be your weapon in all temptations. Learn from your Savior to answer all the attacks of Satan only with: *"It is written."* The Word of God is the sword of the Spirit; if you seize it in faith, you can fight, and all the flaming darts of the evil one will be quenched and broken by the shield of your faith. If need troubles you, take a promise and hold it to your heart: "It is written, 'I will never fail you nor forsake you.' " If false doctrine tempts you, just hold to the Word; do not depart from its letters; otherwise you are lost. And if false teachers hold up God's Word to you, place Scripture against Scripture, clear passages against dark, and say with your Savior, "Yes, that is written here, but again, again it is also written." If sin tempts you, if it entices you sweetly and lovingly, just hold before your heart: "It is written, 'He who commits sin is of the devil, for the devil has sinned from the beginning.' " If you are tempted to depart from the ways of God, say: "It is written, 'If he shrinks back, my soul has no pleasure in him.' " If you are tempted regarding your state of grace, say to your heart: "It is written, 'He who believes and is baptized will be saved. . . . This saying is sure and worthy of full acceptance,

49

that Christ Jesus came into the world to save sinners. . . . Come to Me, all who labor and are heavy laden, and I will give you rest . . . and you will find rest for your souls.' "

Learn from this that it was not stubbornness that Luther did not want to unite with those who departed from God's Word in anything. In 1529 there was a colloquy in Marburg between the Lutherans and the Reformed. On the one side Luther, Melanchthon, and others were present, on the other, Zwingli and others. They debated whether the true body and the true blood of Christ were in the Sacrament. At first Luther said nothing, but during the discussion just wrote with chalk on the table before him: "This is My body; this is My blood." As often as he now took part in the discussion, he referred to the words and said, "Here, read it: *It is written* 'This is My body, this is My blood' "; here is no wavering, here is no yielding. Zwingli himself was moved to tears at the sight of these honest men and said: "There are no people on earth with whom I would rather be one than with the Wittenbergers." But yet he persisted in his error, and Luther—in the truth. Blessed be Luther's memory among us always for this faithfulness; here he followed his Savior. Therefore the highest principle in the Lutheran Church has always been: *"It is written."* And that is the foundation upon which Christ built His church, which the gates of hell cannot prevail against.

So hear my last admonition, beloved hearers: Remain with the Word, and you remain with Christ; if you remain in Christ, you remain in grace; grace will lead you to eternal victory. Amen.

Palm Sunday Confirmation Address
John 6:66-69

Your Answer to Christ's Question:
"Do You Also Wish to Go Away?"
(Amerikanisch-Lutherische Evangelien Postille, pp. 140—145)

"Do you also wish to go away?" According to the sixth chapter of the Gospel of John, Christ with a sad countenance directed this question to His 12 apostles at a time when many other disciples left Him. And that is the question which I am urged now to ask also you, my dearly beloved children!

You have declared yourselves ready today to swear eternal faithfulness to your Savior. But ah, already many a child has knelt at this altar, wetting it with his tears, and with trembling voice and tear-filled eyes has said: Yes, I will remain with Jesus, with His word, with His grace, with His church; nothing, neither joys nor sorrows, neither honor nor shame, neither poverty nor riches, neither life nor death shall separate me from Him, and—before the next Palm Sunday the child had already left his Savior. Ah, with deep sadness I think today of so many dearly beloved confirmands upon whose head I have laid the hand of blessing in this holy place. They were the joy of my heart; they grew up in God's garden like green trees which now stood in full bloom; with joyous hopes I took leave of them; I thought that even if no one else remains faithful, surely these will, for I had often seen tears of emotion tremble in their eyes and roll over their cheeks! But what happened? Where are they now? The fire of faith and love kindled in them has died out; they are now cold and dead; like Demas, they have left Jesus and loved the world.

I must admit to you that the thought of these unfortunates has today entered my heart and wanted to change this day of joy into one of anxiety and grief. But as I wanted to give myself over to sorrow, I found in the Gospel of John that also the Savior had to once experience that many of His most hopeful disciples forsook Him. But what did the Savior do? Indeed, he looked sadly at those leaving Him, but He did not on that account give up on the others, who were still with Him. He rather turned trustingly to His beloved 12 apostles, who up to that point were still faithful, with the question: *"Do you also wish to go away?"* And what did these answer Him? Peter quickly spoke up, and deeply moved and with burning zeal cried out: *"Lord, to whom shall we go? You have the words of eternal life; and we have believed, and have come to know, that You are the Holy One of God."*

Now if Jesus would appear visibly among us, what question do you think He would lay before you? Surely He would ask you: *"Children, do you also wish to go away?"* And what would you answer Him? Would you perhaps say to Him: Dear Savior, we can no longer remain with You; the world is too inviting and sin is sweet, but Your yoke is too hard and Your burden too heavy! O no, no! I do not doubt that with one voice you would loudly repeat Peter's answer with your whole soul.

All right! So join me for a few moments as I present to you:

Your Answer to Christ's Question: "Do You Also Wish to Go Away?"

It is

1. this: *"Lord, to whom shall we go?"* and
2. this: *"You have the words of eternal life; and we have believed, and come to know, that You are the Holy One of God."*

I

"Lord, to whom shall we go?" With this new question Peter answered the question of Christ: *"Do you also wish to go away?"* Peter wanted to say: Lord, are You asking us? Even if it were possible that we would be so thankless, forgetting Your love, wiping out of our hearts and thoughts the benefits we have enjoyed with You, and leaving You, where would we then go? Where would we turn? Where would we look for the light of truth which we need? Where would we look to satisfy the hunger and thirst of our souls for the grace and peace of God? Where would we look for satisfaction of our longing for true happiness? Where would we look for comfort in our trouble and distress over our sins, for rescue from death, and for eternal life? In vain do we look about in all creation; we know no one in the world, no creature in heaven and on earth, to whom we can go to find what we are looking for.

Peter and all the apostles did not know where they would go if they wanted to leave Christ; do *you* perhaps know?

It is true, all those who have left Christ have thought they could find happiness elsewhere. One left Christ and sought happiness in the pursuit of money and other earthly goods; another left Christ and sought happiness in all sorts of lusts and pleasures; another left Christ and sought his happiness in the favor and friendship of the world; another forsook Christ and sought his happiness in honor and recognition among men; another forsook Christ and sought his happiness in the search after the wisdom of this world. But did they find what they sought? Ah, no! Either, recognizing their deception, they returned to Christ, or they had to confess in the hour of death that they sought in vain what they sought, that their heart had deceived them.

Judas forsook Christ to win earthly treasure; yes, he betrayed Him for 30 pieces of silver. But the money with which he sold Christ soon became a fire in his hands and in his heart; finally he despaired and had a fearful end. So little do earthly goods benefit anyone who seeks after them and forsakes Christ. Again, once David forsook his God and Savior and plunged himself into the lust of sin. But, ah! as sweet as it once was to him, so bitter it soon became. Listen how he complains and laments in his penitential psalm, how finally the lust of sin became arrows which pierced his heart and conscience and a heavy burden which like a mountain crushed him to the earth! With his lust of sin he did not *buy* his happiness but *sold* it; by night he bathed his bed with tears, by day he went about with fallen countenance, bent and bowed and sad. Gone was his previous blessed peace, gone the sweet rest of his soul. Again, Solomon left his God and Savior, began to love the world, and enjoyed all its joys. But hardly had he enjoyed them than he explained: "I said to myself, 'Come now, I will make a test of pleasure; enjoy yourself.' But behold, this also was vanity. I said of laughter, 'It is mad,' and of pleasure, 'What use is it?' " "Sorrow is better than laughter." Again, once even Peter, in spite of his promise, left his Savior for a short time in order to enjoy the favor and friendship of the world and in that way to save his life. But, ah! he soon found out that he thereby had only made himself inexpressibly unhappy; quickly he hurried outside, away from the company of the world, and wept bitterly. Again, once a famous German emperor at the time of the Reformation forsook Christ, in order to be and remain the mightiest and highest among men. But after he had enjoyed all the honor and glory of this world, he confessed that his crown with all its earthly honor had become only a burden for him; he laid his crown and scepter down and now in seclusion sought with Jesus the peace and happiness which he could not find in the whole world.[1] Finally, Paul, when he was still called Saul, forsook the Savior already proclaimed to him by the prophets and cast aside His Gospel and sought rest in the wisdom of the world and did not find it. But finally he turned to Christ, and now he not only confessed: "In whom are hid all the treasures of wisdom and knowledge," but he also testified: "To know the love of Christ . . . surpasses knowledge."

O my dear children, you see from this that all who forsook Christ and looked for happiness elsewhere, all without exception, finally had to admit that they deceived themselves. So tell me, what do you now want to do? How do you now want to answer your Savior, who lovingly asks you today: "Children, *do you also wish to go away?*"

Isn't it true that today all of you would answer Him: Lord Jesus, how could we leave You, since You have loved us from eternity, redeemed us in time, and bought us with Your blood and baptized us, from our birth carried us in Your arms and led us with Your gracious hand? We cannot express how much You have done for us! But could we be so unthankful to forget Your everlasting faithfulness and mercy toward us? Lord Jesus, if now we wanted to leave You, *"to whom shall we go?"* If You cannot make us happy here and saved there, who can? If in You we cannot find what our soul thirsts for, where can we find it? On the other hand, if we wanted to grub after gold and treasures, what would they help us? What would it help us if we gained the whole world and lost our own soul? We would be poor eternally. Or if we wanted to plunge ourselves in the lust of sin and the joys of the world, what would that help us? Here our heart would remain without peace, and there we would have to languish eternally. Or if we wanted to seek after the favor and friendship of the world, what would that help us, even if the whole world were our friend but the almighty God our enemy? Or if we wanted to seek honor and recognition among men, what would that help us, even if here we could boast the highest honor, and finally in eternity, cast down from our high position, would stand before God and His angels in shame? Or, finally, if we wanted to leave You and seek after the wisdom of this world alone, what would that help us? What would all the light for this life help us without the Light that shows us the way to yonder life, the way to heaven? See, Lord, where would we go if we wanted to leave You? We do not know.

II

Beloved children, Peter once answered Christ's question: *"do you also wish to go away?"* not only with the words: *"Lord, to whom shall we go?"* but he added: *"You have the words of eternal life; and we have believed, and have come to know, that You are the Holy One of God."*

With these words Peter wants to say: Lord, we cannot leave You, for You have words which, like no words of man, have penetrated marrow and bone and have breathed into our dead hearts a new life. You have words which have not only stirred and shaken our hearts, but which in a heavenly way have refreshed, brought joy, and comforted us. You have words which have not only shown us the way to eternal life, but which have enlightened us with the light of everlasting life and have filled our souls with the foretaste and the powers of the future world. You have words which have not only directed us from earth to heaven but have unlocked heaven and God's heart itself and have made us divinely certain that we have the forgiveness of our sins and a gracious God, that we are righteous before God and are His children, that we have a share in the glory of heaven and are heirs of eternal salvation. And in this way we have experienced it in our hearts that You truly are Christ, the only Savior of the world and the Son of the living God. Now if we would want to leave You, we would forsake life and choose death, we would leave heaven and choose damnation, we would leave heaven and choose hell.

See, my children, that is the way Peter, with flaming eyes and burning heart, once answered the Savior's question: *"Do you also wish to go away?"* Tell me, could you answer differently? Must you not also attest and confess before this congregation that you have already often discovered that Christ's words are not powerless human words but words of eternal life? Has not the hearing of Christ's Word often stirred something in your souls that you have not found in listening to human words? Have you not already often experienced how through the hearing of Christ's Word God Himself has mightily knocked on your hearts? Have you not often experienced how in the hearing of Christ's Word God's Holy Spirit has moved the foundation of your soul, how you began to sigh for grace, how you were mightily drawn to God, enlightened concerning your state of grace, rebuked on account of your sins, but also overwhelmed with comfort, hope, peace, and joy? Have you not already experienced it in your hearts that Christ's words are God's words, full of life and power, and that He Himself is the only Savior of sinners and the Son of the living God? Hasn't your heart already many times been disposed to call to the whole world: O you unbelievers, do not cast aside Christ and His Word; I can swear that He is truly God's Son and the Savior of the world! I have experienced it!?

If today the Savior asks: *"Do you also wish to go away?"* do you have to reflect long on what you will answer Him? No, no, like Peter, with flaming eyes and burning heart you will, you must say not only: *"Lord, to whom shall we go?"* you will, you must also add: Lord, if we left You, we would be like wanderers who left their guide and went into the dark forest on uncharted paths, only to perish helplessly; we would be like sheep who left their shepherd and his pasture and went into the barren desert, only to faint away; we would be like sailors who left their protecting ship and jumped into the raging sea, only to sink in it. No, no, we will remain with You, Lord Jesus: *"You have the words of eternal life; and we have believed, and have come to know, that You are the Holy One of God."*

O my dear children, say it not only today but as often as your sinful heart, your own flesh and blood, or the world tries to tempt you from Christ and His Word, namely as often as you are tempted to forsake Christ and either to strive after gold and earthly treasures, or to love the friendship of the world, or to participate in the vain lusts and joys of the world, or to seek honor and reputation among men, or even to join the manifest enemies of Christ and His Word. Ah, then consider, at that time as today Jesus stands before you and says: *"Do you also wish to go away?"* But you reply [*The Lutheran Hymnal,* 366:4]:

> Although all the world should forsake and forget Thee,
> In love I will follow Thee, ne'er will I quit Thee.
> Lord Jesus, both spirit and life is Thy Word;
> And is there a joy which Thou dost not afford?

[Walther quotes two more verses, from other hymns. Then came the confirmation ceremony.]

Closing Address and Prayer

So, my dear children, the great work has been completed. The heavenly Bridegroom has sought your souls, and you have given them to Him. The word of acceptance has been spoken, and therewith the bond of faithfulness has once more publicly been solemnized for eternity. He Himself was in our midst and heard your oath and is now ready to give you a friendly embrace. Now remain with Him to the last breath of your life.

For us, however, the hour for saying good-bye has come. We will not again be gathered as we were in the past months and today. Now at the end I therefore call to you from the bottom of my heart: Farewell, farewell, dear children! If God continues to give us life, I hope to see most of you again many times in this house of the Lord and at this, His altar. If all of you remain with Jesus, we will all see one another again *there,* in the temple of heaven, before the throne of the Lamb. Then you will all be dressed in white robes, wear crowns on your heads, and hold harps in your hands. Then you will really be confirmed. Then all temptation, all danger, all labor, all battle and strife will be at an end. Then you will no longer cry out: Lord, have mercy! but you will join in the eternal "Hallelujah!" of all the cherubim and seraphim, of all the angels and perfected saints. Oh, how glad you will then be that you endured until the end, that you remained faithful until death! Then you will bless this present day and give blessing and honor and thanksgiving and praise to the Lamb that was slain and has redeemed you with His blood and has kept you for salvation, from eternity to eternity. I call to you once more: Until then, dear children, farewell! farewell!

But you, dear congregation, and especially you fathers, mothers, godparents, brothers, sisters, friends, and relatives of these children, open the arms of your love and receive these children again from my hands, from the hands of their teachers and educators. Receive them as your brothers and sisters. Do not say like Cain: "Am I my brother's keeper?" Rather consider, you parents, that you remain the parents of these children until your death; from your hands God will someday require them. But you who are not so closely related to these children by ties of blood, think of the word of Jesus Christ: "When you have turned again, strengthen your brethren." If you therefore have yourselves been converted to Christ, strengthen these weak ones; watch over them. If you see them in danger, warn them; if you see them go astray, bring them back; if you see them in need, comfort and stand by them; if you see them fall, help them up again. If you do that faithfully, we will also someday with these children—oh, may it be all of them!—stand seeing before the throne of Christ just as we here stood with them hoping.

In order that this may come to pass, let us here at the conclusion of the service go down on our knees and bring the need of these children to the Savior in heartfelt devotion and firm faith.

Lord Jesus Christ, today You have asked these children: "Do you also wish to go away?" And they have answered you: "Lord, to whom shall we go? You have the words of eternal life; and we have believed, and have come to know, that You are the Holy One of God." With these words they have confessed to You that they know no other Savior but You, that only in You can they find rescue from sin, trouble, and death, only in You light, only in You grace, only in You righteousness, only in You comfort, only in You strength, only in You life and salvation. They therefore want to remain with You till death.

O Jesus, therefore remain also with them and do not reject them; yes, bind them fast to Your heart, for if You do not hold *them,* they cannot hold to *You.* Truly today their resolution and will are weak, but You have promised to be their Strength. Indeed they are unworthy sinners, but You have come into the world for the sake of sinners, as a Savior of sinners and not the righteous. Indeed, their souls are sick and weak, but You are a physician not for the well but for the weak and miserable. We know that none of these children will remain completely faithful to You; forgetting their vow they will often stumble and fall, but You have promised that You will remain faithful also when we are unfaithful. Finally, we know that also we are not worthy that you should hear our poor prayer for these children, but we do not lie here before You depending on our righteousness but on Your great mercy. We pray to You trusting only in Your command and Your promise; oh, therefore, hear us. These children are not our children; they are Yours. You have purchased them with Your blood. If they are lost, You lose them.

Oh, therefore, have mercy upon them. Preserve them in Your truth and grace; against all seductions be their Protection and Shield; against their sins, their Throne of grace; against trouble and temptation, their Comfort; against death, their Life; against judgment and damnation, their Savior and Intercessor.

O Jesus, *we* cannot guard them; therefore we herewith place them in Your lap and in Your arms. Herewith we give them over to You eternally. You watch over them; You help them in life and in death. You save them.

O You Lamb of God, who carries the sin of the world and also their sin, have mercy upon them.

O You Lamb of God, who carries the sin of the world and also their sin, have mercy upon them.

O You Lamb of God, who carries the sin of the world and also their sin, give them Your peace. Amen! Amen!

Maundy Thursday

1 Corinthians 11:23-32

How Important and Necessary It Is That We Also Henceforth Hold Fast to the Pure Doctrine of the Lord's Supper with Constant Faithfulness

(Amerikanisch-Lutherische Evangelien Postille, pp. 145—152)

Lord Jesus, true God and man in one person! You have indeed withdrawn Your visible presence from Your dear congregation because You here want to be believed in rather than seen; but yet You are and remain inseparable from it. You have not left us orphans. Although invisible, You are today really and truly with us, You Yourself with all Your grace. And in order that we may and can comfort ourselves in this truth without doubting, You in the night in which You were betrayed instituted a meal in which You give us to eat of Your body and drink of Your blood until You come. Oh, therefore help us that we do not let ourselves be robbed of this comfort but hold fast to it until with these eyes we finally see You, with these ears hear You, and with these our hands touch You and thus enjoy perfect fellowship with You in eternally blessed joy. Amen.

Beloved brothers and sisters in Christ Jesus!

The Lord's Supper, whose institution we celebrate today, is a *love-feast*, both according to its origin and its purpose. Out of inexpressible love for His own, Christ Himself first instituted it. When the holy evangelist John in his gospel comes to the report of the last supper which Christ had with His disciples, he begins with the words: "Having loved His own who were in the world, He loved them to the end." He wants to say: Even the nearness of His martyr's death did not prompt Christ to forget His disciples or even to weaken His love for them. Rather, at the very time of His leaving this world, His heart wanted to establish and leave behind for His own the greatest memorial to His love. Christ also said this Himself; for when He finally sat at table to eat the last meal with His disciples, as St. Luke reports, He said the memorable words: "I have earnestly desired to eat this passover with you before I suffer." As anxious as the dear Savior

59

was in the face of the baptism of blood with which He was now to be baptized, He at the same time looked forward to His last night of suffering with ardent longing because in this night He wanted to repeal the old covenant meal and institute the new.

Yet, the Lord's Supper is a feast of love not only because Christ Himself in ardent love for His own established it but, as mentioned, because of its purpose! Its purpose is that for Christians it should be the source and uniting bond of the most intimate brotherly love. For the holy apostle Paul writes: "The cup of blessing which we bless, is it not a participation in the blood of Christ? The bread which we break, is it not a participation in the body of Christ? Because there is one bread, we who are many are *one body,* for we all partake of the same bread." And further on the same apostle adds: "We have all been made to drink of one Spirit." He wants to say: Since we Christians together receive the blessed bread, which makes us partakers of the body of Christ, and since we together receive the blessed cup, which makes us partakers of the blood of Christ, we all thereby become one body and one spirit, like one man, a single person. Since all communicants do not divide themselves into Christ's body and blood, they do not each receive a piece of Christ's body and blood, but partake of the one and the same entire body of Christ and the one and the same entire blood of Christ, so by that act they are more intimately united and bound to one another than is their own body with their soul. Therefore is not the Lord's Supper truly a feast of love?—Without a doubt. As little as it is possible that a person should not love himself, so little is it possible that a communicant who from the heart believes in the mystery of the Lord's Supper should not love his fellow communicants, of whom he knows that the same body and the same blood of Christ is in them as in him. Therefore we read of the first Christians that, because they continued in the "breaking of bread," they were "one heart and one soul."

Yet, my beloved, has not since the Reformation just the Lord's Supper, instead of being a love-feast which should bind Christians together most intimately, become a subject for strife and battle, estrangement, separation, and division? Has not the church which left the papacy split particularly over the doctrine of the Lord's Supper into two warring parties and camps? And is it not especially our Evangelical Lutheran Church which wants to make no peace?

What? Is it right that our church wants positively to remain with her doctrine of the Lord's Supper and is willing to sacrifice the peace of the church rather than this doctrine? Should our church not rather yield on this point so that it can celebrate this feast of love in brotherly harmony with all who call themselves Christians? Would it not be in harmony with

Christian love if we Lutherans permitted everyone to believe and teach what he considers right concerning the Lord's Supper and appeared with him in peace at the table of the Lord? Should we not at least at the altar lay down our weapons and end all battle and strife at the meal of reconciliation?

Or is the pure doctrine of the Lord's Supper really so important that we cannot yield in this matter? that we must hold fast to it in unbroken faithfulness, no matter what the consequence? Yes, my beloved, we dare not, we cannot yield here, as dear as God's Word is to us, as dear as are Christ's majesty and honor, as dear as are our salvation and that of all people.

And that is what I want to lay on your hearts on this day of the institution of the highly reverenced Lord's Supper.

Text: 1 Corinthians 11:23-32

"For I received from the Lord what I also delivered to you." With this express assurance the holy apostle Paul in our text just read, begins his account of the institution of the Lord's Supper. This is highly noteworthy. From this we see that the holy apostle regarded the correct doctrine of the Lord's Supper as a matter of particular importance, so that he regarded it as necessary particularly to assure the Corinthians that he did not receive the right teaching about it from hearsay, nor through tradition, not from people at all, but through immediate revelation, namely from the mouth of the exalted Lord Himself. How important must a historical fact be which the Son of God, sitting at the right hand of the majesty on high, immediately reveals to His witness on earth, exactly, in every detail! How important must every word be concerning that event, each circumstance, even though apparently insignificant!—Today, therefore, let me present to you:

How Important and Necessary It Is That We Also Henceforth Hold Fast to the Pure Doctrine of the Lord's Supper with Constant Faithfulness

This is so important and necessary because it concerns itself with three incomparably important things:

1. *the reliability of the clear Word of God;*
2. *the real presence of Christ with His church;* and finally
3. *the precious and incontrovertible pledge of the forgiveness of our sins.*

61

I

All certainty of our faith and our salvation rests on the reliability of the clear Word of God. If we could not rely firmly on God's clear Word without having to fear in the least that we thereby could fall into error, our faith would be vain and our whole Christianity would be like a house built on sand.

To make God's Word dark and uncertain has therefore always been the trick Satan has used to deceive people concerning their salvation. Clearly God once said to Adam: "You may freely eat of every tree of the garden; but of the tree of the knowledge of good and evil you shall not eat." Now what did Satan do to ruin Adam and Eve? He sought to awaken doubt in them about this clear word of God and said: "Did God say, 'You shall not eat of any tree of the garden'?" And see, as soon as man let that clear word of God become uncertain, he fell and lost his salvation.

Furthermore, God called out clearly from heaven concerning His Son: "This is My beloved Son, with whom I am well pleased." Now what did Satan do, after he had already ruined man, now also to ruin the Redeemer of men? He sought to make that clear word of His heavenly Father uncertain also for Him. Immediately after the sound of that voice of the Father from heaven he said, tempting Him: "If You are the Son of God, command these stones to become loaves of bread." But far be it that Christ should let the clear word of His father become uncertain. Rather, he repulsed every attack of the tempter with the Word of God, as after each temptation He said: "It is written!"

Now say for yourselves, can there be a clearer and more explicit word of God than the words in the Lord's Supper: *"Take, eat, this is My body; take, drink, this is My blood"*? Do not these words say as clearly as the sunlight that in the Lord's Supper the body and blood of Christ are truly present and are received in, with, and under the bread and wine, so that it could not have been stated more clearly? Say, how else could Christ have spoken to express this mystery? Consider, if a person handed us a cup and said to us: "Take and drink; that is wine," could we understand this otherwise than that there is wine in the cup and that the wine is offered us with and under the cup and that we should drink it? Would not the one offering the cup be mocking us if it turned out that there was no wine in it?

Can we, dare we believe that the dying Savior only wanted to mock His disciples and His whole church when, handing the bread and wine and, according to His own explanation, establishing His covenant, He said: "Take, eat, this is My body; take, drink, this is My blood"? Far be it!

But those who do not want to believe this mystery appeal to this, that it is also written that Christ is a rock, a lamb, the door, the vine, and the

62

like. Dare not, yes, must not a person obviously take these words figuratively? Then why not also those words: "This is My body; this is My blood"? But this is an entirely empty subterfuge. That Christ is not an ordinary but a spiritual rock, not an ordinary but a spiritual lamb, not an ordinary but a spiritual door, not an ordinary but a spiritual, namely "the true," vine—this God's Word itself tells us. But where does Christ say of His body and blood of which He speaks that He means only a spiritual, figurative body and only a spiritual, figurative blood or only a sign of His body and blood? Rather, He says the very opposite when to the word *body* He adds: "which is broken for you," and to the word *blood:* "which is shed for you." But now it was not Christ's spiritual, figurative body, or a sign of it, but His real, true body which was given for us; and not Christ's spiritual, figurative blood, or a sign of it, but His real, true blood was shed for us!

So there is no doubt about it: All those who maintain that the bread and wine in the Lord's Supper *are* not, but only *represent,* Christ's body and blood; or that in the Lord's Supper not the *true* but only a figurative body and not the *true* but only a figurative blood of Christ are present; that both are absent and are therefore received only spiritually by the believers with the mouth of faith, as they should do at every common meal—all these willfully depart from Christ's clear word.

So I ask you who still regard Christ's Word as the Word of God, dare we, can we say yea and amen to this? Never! If the words of institution were dark, ambiguous, and enigmatic, then probably without danger one could interpret them this way, another that way, if only the interpretation agreed with the analogy of faith. But since the words of institution are so plain, so clear, and so simple that they could not be plainer, clearer, and simpler—so that a child can understand them—no man, no angel, in short, no creature has the power to take them other than they read.

If we would concede this, the reliability of the whole Word of God would thereby be lost. For if we can no longer rely on the clear words of institution, the testamentary words of the dying Son of God and Savior of the world, we can no longer rely on any word of God. If the clear words of institution no longer stand fast, then no word of God still stands fast. If we can depart from the clear words of institution only because they do not agree with our reason, we can depart from all the words of God which appear to be foolish to our reason. If we can interpret the clear words of Christ: "This is My body" to mean: "This only *represents* My body," then we can interpret also the clear words of God: "Christ *is* the Son of God, Christ *is* the Savior of the world" to mean: "Christ only *represents* the Son of God, Christ only *represents* the Savior of the world."

And that is what Satan has in mind with the overthrow of the clear words of institution. He wants to overthrow not only *these* words but the entire Word of God; he wants to make it wavering, unsure, and unreliable for us. Through this means Satan wants to bring matters to the point that no Christian can comfort himself in life and death or fight against flesh, world, and Satan with the words: "It is written!" This and nothing else was the first reason which once prompted Luther to hold so firmly to the pure doctrine of the Lord's Supper. Already in the year 1524 he writes:

> Even if someone in these days might try more persuasively to prove that only bread and wine are present, it would not be necessary that he attack me in bitter spirit—which I, unfortunately, am altogether inclined to do, if I assess the nature of the old Adam in me correctly. . . . *But I am a captive and cannot free myself. The text is too powerfully present, and will not allow itself to be torn from its meaning by mere verbiage* (*Luther's Works,* American Edition, 40, 68).

Melanchthon, too, writes:

> I find no reason why we should depart from this meaning, namely, that in the Lord's Supper Christ is present with His body and blood. It can be that such a meaning, in greater accordance with human reason, is more agreeable to an idle mind, especially when it is adorned and embellished with sharply contrived arguments; but how will it be in time of *temptation* when the conscience will argue what reason he had for departing from the accepted interpretation of the church? *Then these words: "This is My body" will be sheer thunderbolts.* What will a frightened mind then argue against it? With which Scripture and with which word of God will it protect itself and convince itself that Christ's words are to be taken in a figurative sense?

So far Melanchthon. Also he, therefore, realized that to reinterpret the words of institution according to reason and let them go is nothing else than giving up all words of God and letting no word of God stand fast.

Therefore, my beloved, as much as we love the sure comfort of the Word of God in general, with such constant faithfulness we must hold fast to the pure doctrine of the Lord's Supper also in the future.

II

But to do this is so necessary and important, in the second place, because it has to do *with the real presence of Christ with His church.*

Already during His earthly sojourn Christ gave the promise: "Where two or three are gathered in My name, there am I in the midst of them." And when Christ rose from the dead and was about to ascend into heaven, as He parted from His own, He comforted them once more with the promise: "Lo, I am with you always, to the close of the age."

From this we see that Christ did not belong to those founders of religions who merely give religious doctrines to their contemporaries, finally die, and then leave them nothing more than their teaching and their example. Furthermore, Christ did not belong to those friends and benefactors of humanity whose memory after their death lives on only in the hearts of a thankful posterity. Finally, Christ was not a mere prophet who, like John the Baptist, was not the Light itself but only bore witness to the Light, or who, like Elijah, at his ascension to heaven left his disciples only his mantle. No, Christ was God and man in one person and came into this world not in order to bring a new doctrine but to establish a kingdom of grace and glory in which He Himself would be Regent and King.

Therefore the Christian church distinguishes herself from all other religious organizations in this, that she not only has *the teaching of her founder* but also her *founder Himself* in her midst; that her Savior, her Redeemer, her Helper, her Protector is not absent from her but is really and truly present with her all the time and in every place. That is the highest, sweetest, most blessed, and strongest comfort the Christian church has. As long as the church holds fast to this comfort that Christ Himself is really and truly with her, she cannot despair.

Against nothing has Satan therefore always and ever raged and stormed more than against this most comforting doctrine. Against this doctrine the arch-heretic Arius arose in the fourth century, denying the deity of Christ. Still today all rationalists, who want to make Christ into a mere man, fight against this doctrine. They all want to take the comfort from the church that she has a living and present Savior who is always with her and in her midst. They all wanted to convince the church that Christ lives in her only in spirit, merely in memory.

But what else do all those do who do not want to believe that Christ is really and truly present in the holy sacrament with His body and blood? Also they thereby reject the greatest comfort the church has. They repeatedly say, of course, that they are far from denying this, for also they believe in their hearts that Christ, *according to His divinity,* is with His church even today; but they cannot believe that Christ is present also according to his *humanity.* But with that they either just want to deceive others, or they are only deceiving themselves by it. Is there a Christ who at any place is only God and not at the same time also man? Are there two Christs, one divine and one human?—No, if Christ is half present and not entirely, if He is not present with His church also according to His human nature, He is not with her at all; for Christ is God and man in one undivided person, which no heaven and no earth, yes, no death and no hell can separate from each other.

And that is precisely the comfort which the church has—not that He is merely the holy Son of God, who is only a consuming fire to sinners, but that He is the God-*man*, Jesus Christ; that the Son of God who became her *brother*, that the most gracious, friendly, lovely Savior of sinners is with her; that she has Him in her midst who once for her lay in the manger, who once lived for her, suffered, hung on the cross and died, who once was awakened from the dead for her justification, and who finally gloriously ascended into heaven for her eternal glorification. No other except this God-*man* has promised her that He Himself would be in her midst as often as she gathered together in His name; no other except this *Savior* has promised to be with her always, to the close of the age. Also the holy apostles bear witness of Christ as the *Head* of the church; that He has ascended, not only to heaven but far above all the heavens, that He might fill all things. Therefore she believes that also the man Christ is not enclosed in heaven like a mere human saint; but sitting at the right hand of God, which is everywhere, He is also as a man everywhere and therefore also with her with all the fullness of His power and grace.

But all this those deny who do not want to take as their stand the sunlight-clear, most holy words of the Lord's Supper: *"This is My body; this is My blood."* For just for this very reason they deny the presence of the body and blood of Christ in the holy sacrament, because they do not believe that Christ is bodily present in His church. They want to make the church into a school whose teacher has died and which now has nothing more of him than his teachings. Instead of a living and present Christ, they want to give the church only a dead and absent one, yes, only pictures in the memory and symbols of Him.

Know from this that when our church will not let the pure doctrine of the Lord's Supper be taken from us, we are not dealing with a mere word-battle of theologians, nor with a mere false interpretation of a Bible passage, yes, not even only with Christ's presence in the holy sacrament, but with Christ's real presence in His church generally. Woe to us if we want to weaken here and give in! By doing that we would surrender nothing less than the holy of holies of the Christian church, the ark of the covenant and the mercy seat of the new covenant. Therefore as dearer as Christ's true presence is to us than only His memory, as dearer as Christ Himself is to us than His mere silhouette, so faithfully we must hold fast to the pure doctrine concerning the most worthy Sacrament of the Altar.

III

Yet, my friends, for this we have a third reason, and it is this: because we are dealing with *the most precious and incontrovertible pledge of the forgiveness of our sins.*

It is true, my beloved, that in the Lord's Supper no other grace is given us than that which we already receive in Holy Baptism, in the preaching of the Gospel, and in the richly comforting absolution. When a person is baptized into Christ's death with water in the name of the Father and of the Son and of the Holy Spirit, God according to His promise thereby takes him into His covenant of grace, gives him everything Christ won by His suffering and death, and invisibly washes his soul from all its sins; and whoever believes that, has it. Further, when the Gospel is preached, the general pardon which God the Father has already festively proclaimed through the resurrection of our Savior is thereby made known to all sinners in the name of the great God. So the forgiveness of sins is offered and given to all hearers; and whoever believes it, has it. Finally, when a servant of Christ or a Christian in the name of God speaks the absolution to another Christian, it is, according to Christ's promise, no different than if God Himself spoke this absolution from heaven and in this way offered, gave, and sealed to him the forgiveness of all his sins. And whoever believes this, has it. From this it might appear that with these means every person is sufficiently provided with the treasure of the forgiveness of sins and it would matter little even if the Lord's Supper with its forgiveness of sins were shortened or entirely taken from him.

But this is in no way so. The Lord's Supper is rather the real crown of all the means of grace which Christ has conferred upon His dear Christendom. Consider this: In the Lord's Supper Christ gives the consecrated bread to His Christians with the words: *"Take and eat; this is My body which is broken for you,"* and the consecrated cup with the words: *"Take and drink; this is My blood which is shed for the forgiveness of your sins."* Hereby the Savior manifestly wants to say: There, take My body and eat it, but not as food for your body but as the body offered into death for your sins; there, take My blood and drink it, but not as drink for your body but as the reconciling blood shed on the cross for the forgiveness of your sins. Oh, who may express what a glorious, comforting, heavenly, sweet meal the Lord's Supper is? Here the forgiveness of sins is not only preached, proclaimed, promised, assured, and sealed, as in the other means of grace, but here at the same time Christ gives His Christians His very body and His blood as a *pledge* of it.

Tell me yourselves: Is that not so certain an assurance of the forgiveness of our sins that it could not be made more sure? Can a debtor still fear his creditor when his guarantor has not only paid his debt but gives into his hand the very sum with which he has already abundantly paid the debt? Certainly not! Can a person therefore still doubt that he has no more trouble with his debt of sin and that he has a share in Christ's reconciliation when the costly ransom money which God has already accepted as the full payment for the debt of all men has itself been put into his hands, into his mouth, and into his heart? No, there cannot be a more precious, more incontrovertible divine pledge.

But see, it is just this highest pledge of our redemption of which those want to rob Christianity who do not take Christ's words: *"This is My body; this is My blood"* as they read and who want to make of the Lord's Supper a mere empty memorial meal.

So tell me yourselves: Is not the pure teaching about the Lord's Supper worth it that we also in the future hold fast to it with unwavering faithfulness? Is it not worth fighting for with holy seriousness and zeal? Is it not worth suffering all disgrace and ridicule rather than surrendering it? Is it not worth it that we rather sacrifice earthly freedom and external unity among men than this highest treasure which the church has?

Yes, truly, my beloved! And since God in His grace has given our Evangelical Lutheran Church above all other churches the knowledge of the pure teaching about the Lord's Supper, He has also appointed it in His Christendom as guardian and steward of this heavenly treasure of the church; also all of us who are sons and daughters and servants of this church are therefore, out of His wonderful grace, likewise called to help guard that lofty treasure of His beloved Christendom. Therefore though all other Christians depart from this doctrine, though they in great blindness mock and slander this doctrine as an antiquated papistic superstition, let us also in these dreadful times of unbelief and apostasy all the more faithfully hold fast to it. Let us not be ashamed of this doctrine but confess it joyfully and openly praise it as the most precious treasure which has been entrusted to us. For—don't ever forget it! I repeat—we are dealing here not with small items but with three incomparably important things: the reliability of the clear Word of God, the real presence of Christ with His church, and finally the most precious and most incontrovertible pledge of the forgiveness of our sins.

But, above all, let us ourselves diligently draw near to this table of grace in faith to pluck the heavenly fruit from this new tree of life which Christ has transplanted from paradise into the garden of the church, and let us draw the water of eternal life from this divine source. In this way we will be strengthened and preserved in true faith unto eternal life. There we with Christ will then celebrate the true, eternal Lord's Supper, when we will drink of the fruit of the vine with Him in His Father's kingdom. To that end help us, Jesus Christ, true God and true man in one undivided person, blessed in time and eternity. Amen.

Good Friday, 1846

Luke 23:27-48

There Is Nothing Which So Strongly and Compellingly Urges Us to Turn to God with All Our Heart as the Death of the Son of God for Our Sins on the Cross

(*Amerikanisch-Lutherische Epistel Postille,* pp. 187-192)

> O Christ, Thou Lamb of God,
> that takest away the sin of the world,
> have mercy upon us!
> O Christ, Thou Lamb of God,
> that takest away the sin of the world,
> have mercy upon us!
> O Christ, Thou Lamb of God,
> that takest away the sin of the world,
> grant us Thy peace!

In Christ, the Lamb of God, slain for us, dearly beloved hearers!

On the sixth day, namely on Friday, God created man in His image and therewith completed the great work of *creation.* But, through the temptation of Satan, man fell away from his Creator, fell into sin, and with that into misery, into temporal and spiritual death and eternal damnation. But what happened? Again on the sixth day, namely on Good Friday, man's Creator died on the cross out of love for people, earned for them their lost life, and thereby completed the great work of *redemption.* "It is finished!" cried the Lord of Glory at the end of His suffering as He bowed His head and died.

Oh, what a sad day, on which God dies! Life dies with Him. But oh, what a blessed day, on which God dies *for us!* His death is our life.

Today is the day on which we celebrate this great event. Oh, that this holy day and this holy hour may be for all of us truly a day and an hour of our second creation and of a new life! Without Jesus we can indeed live physically and biologically, but not spiritually, not eternally. Without Christ we are dead while living. "Flesh and blood," says the holy apostle,

69

"cannot inherit the kingdom of God"; and Christ says: "That which is born of the flesh is flesh." This means that whoever has had only a human birth is still fleshly, no matter how pious his appearance may be.

All of us, therefore, must experience a great change; otherwise we will not see the kingdom of God. We must first be spirit, born of the Spirit. Just as in the first creation God had to breathe into man, made from earth, the breath of life so that man could be a living soul, so we participate in the second creation of God, namely the redemption, only when the life from God is breathed into us again through the breath of the Almighty. Therefore if this day comes to a close without our being renewed in the image of God, God will until today have died in vain for us.

O hearer, if today the greatness and severity of the suffering and death of your Redeemer comes to life in your soul, if today your spirit is wrapped in sorrow because of it, if today your eyes fill with hot tears of sadness, if your heart bleeds at the sight of the bleeding, blameless Lamb of God bleeding for you, good!—But do not be secure; you can still remain without the one true fruit of the death of God for you. This death has brought forth fruit only when your flesh has died with Christ and when His death has worked life in you.

Oh, that God may have mercy upon us all; and today, as in spirit we go to Golgotha and stand beneath the cross of dying love, may God give us to drink of the spring of the water of life opened for us on Golgotha and flowing from the heart of the Crucified; may He make His cross a tree of life for us! Let us now once more together call upon Him on our knees for this, after we have sung: "O Christ, Thou Lamb of God, etc."

Text: Luke 23:27-48

Three things my beloved, are set before me in the portion of the passion history just read; first, how Christ is led to Golgotha, to the cross; then, how for six hours He languishes on the cross; and finally, how on the cross He commends His spirit into the hands of His Father and dies. But each of these three portions tells us about nothing else than the necessity of our repentance and conversion. It is a sermon on repentance that Christ preaches on His journey to the cross; and as He hangs on the cross we hear that a malefactor hanging at His side genuinely repents at the sight of His final suffering; and when He finally dies, we hear that even the heathen centurion and his rough soldiers on duty suddenly turn to God and that all the frightened people, moved by God's hand, beat their breast. You see, the day of Christ's death is for us a day of repentance. Therefore, let us now ponder the truth given in our text:

There Is Nothing Which So Strongly and Compellingly Urges Us to Turn to God with All Our Heart As the Death of the Son of God for Our Sins on the Cross

The reasons are:
1. *because nothing reveals to us so clearly the offense of our sins;* and
2. *because nothing shows us so irrefutably God's willingness to pardon and save even the greatest sinners.*

I

From the story of our text, beloved, we see clearly what the characteristics of true repentance and conversion are. In the first place, Christ preaches repentance to the women accompanying Him, in these words: *"Daughters of Jerusalem, do not weep for Me, but weep for yourselves and for your children."* Of the penitent malefactor we hear first the confession over against his partner in crime when the latter mocked Christ: *"Do you not fear God, since you are under the same sentence of condemnation? And we indeed justly; for we are receiving the due reward of our deeds."* Finally, according to the report of St. Matthew, we hear that the centurion and his soldiers "were filled with awe" before they in faith declared Christ to be the Son of God.

The first part of a genuine conversion is therefore a painful acknowledgment of our sins and a heartfelt anxiety on account of them. Without these experiences no one comes to a genuine conversion. But since everyone who wants to be saved must first be converted, because without conversion no member of our fallen race can return to God, everyone must first of all realize that he truly is such a great sinner, lost without Christ, as God describes all people; filled with fear, anxiety, and terror, he must be bowed down, humbled, and softened thereby.

Now, is it not important to know how and where one can best have these experiences so necessary for the work of our salvation? Ah, yes! And see, just today on the deathday of our Savior we are reminded of this in a living way. For there is no better or more appropriate place for us sinners to come to true repentance, by first coming to a living knowledge of our sin, than the hill of Golgotha which today we are climbing in spirit and the cross under which we stand in spirit today. Nowhere, nowhere else are we so strongly and compellingly summoned to turn to God from the heart as right here. If you ask: "Why that?" I reply: Because we here see human sinfulness in its highest degree, further because we here see the most fearful

71

consequences of sin, and finally because we here see sin as an unbearable burden.

If we want to know what heights the sinfulness of the human race has attained, we must go to Golgotha. For who hangs there between heaven and earth, between two criminals, with arms outstretched, naked and bare, with blood spattering his whole body? Who is it who here is mocked and ridiculed, given vinegar and gall to drink? Who is He who here is slowly being tortured to death?—It is not a criminal who is there suffering for his deeds; for He calls to His Father in heaven on behalf of those who are crucifying Him: *"Father, forgive them, for they know not what they do."* One of the criminals himself confesses: *"This man has done nothing wrong."* And after His death the centurion on duty cries with a quaking heart: *"Certainly this man was innocent."*

If the Crucified had been only an innocent man, we would still be shocked at the malice of men, that they could bring him to such an agonizing death. But the Crucified is more than an innocent man, yes, more than all the angels and archangels: He is the Son of the Most High God, He is the Lord of glory, the Creator of the world, the Lord and God of all men, who out of eternal love took human nature into the unity of His person in order to redeem mankind. He traveled about, preached the truth, did good, and healed all who were overcome by the devil—this is the One whom people took, hanged on the cross, and killed.

That was the most shameful, wicked, and cursed deed that has ever been conceived in human hearts and carried out by human hands. Here we see human sinfulness and malice in its highest degree, its greatest enormity, and its most horrid form. Here we see: The human heart is capable of the most fearful thing imaginable, namely capable of killing its own Creator, capable of killing eternal Love. When the sun saw this, it lost its light, as if it could not bear the sight of this fearful drama. And when this deed was done, the earth quaked and the rocks split as though they rebelled against any longer bearing those guilty of such a crime against their Creator. How? Shall we not be appalled that we are human beings and that we belong to a race that has made itself guilty of such a crime of rebellion against the Almighty? When we have seen the Son of God crucified by men, can we still doubt that we humans have fallen away from God and become subjects of the kingdom of darkness? Must we not also beat upon our breast and sigh: "Ah, God, be merciful to us sinners"?

Yet at Golgotha we see sin not only in its highest degree but also see its most fearful consequences. For what we here see Christ suffer He endures not for *His* sins but, willingly, for *ours*. As Isaiah says: "He has borne *our* griefs and carried *our* sorrows. He was wounded for *our* transgressions; He was bruised for *our* iniquities." What we see Christ suffering today is what we should have suffered eternally on account of our sin. He endured the most terrible pains; from this we see that our sins have deserved eternal pains. He hangs there naked and bare, full of disgrace, ridicule, and shame; from this we see that our sins have deserved eternal disgrace, ridicule, and shame. He thirsts and is not refreshed; from this we see that our sins have deserved eternal thirst without refreshment, and eternal languishing. He hangs there in disgrace among robbers and murderers; from this we see that our sins have deserved our exclusion from the fellowship of all holy creatures, and instead eternal fellowship with the children of wickedness and damnation. But Christ was also forsaken by *God;* from this we see that our sins have deserved eternal rejection also by God. He hangs there in fearful darkness; from this we see that our sins have deserved the darkness of hell, without light and glimmer of grace. Christ, the Life, dies; from this we see that our sins have deserved eternal death and damnation. If we do not want to believe the fearful threats of the Law against sin, on Golgotha God has written them before our eyes in bloody letters so legible that all excuses for our doubts are removed. At the cross of Christ is written before the eyes of all people: God carries out what He threatens; sinner! you must die.

But still more! At Golgotha we also see sin as an unbearable burden. How? If it had been possible for any creature to bear and atone for the sins of humanity, would God have given His only begotten Son into death to atone for them and blot them out? If God could have had mercy on people and saved them without such an offering which He Himself brought, would He not have spared His own Son?—Therefore, what an insult against God sin must be, what a violation of His law, what an incitement to His wrath, since God could not be reconciled unless God's Son Himself shed His blood since God Himself must die if the sinner is to live! How unbearable must be the burden of the sin of the fallen world, since no creature but only the Creator could bear it!

See, the death of the Son of God on the cross for our sins preaches all this. Therefore nothing else so strongly and compellingly urges us to turn to God with our whole heart, because nothing else reveals to us so clearly the horror of our sins.

Whoever among us still has not been persuaded by anything to recognize himself as a lost sinner, to be terrified by it in his heart, and to fall at the feet of God with remorse and sorrow—ah, let him finally learn today, as in spirit he stands at the cross of the Son of God bleeding for his sins, that, even if up to now he has lived honorably before the world, also *his* sins are truly no joke. May he let the suffering which God's Son took upon Himself also for his sins finally shake and break his heart. If the Law's thunder and lightening from Sinai could not frighten him, ah, let him not also be hardened against the blood of the Son of God that once on this day had to flow on Golgotha so that God could be reconciled to him again and which therefore still louder, still more penetrating to marrow and bone, calls: Man, repent! Whoever can see Christ die and even then remain secure in his sins and peaceful in his miserable outward uprightness, and who even then does not become anxious and tremble—nothing will arouse such a heart from its slumber, nothing will bring such a person to repentance and conversion.

II

Still, my beloved, true repentance and conversion does not consist only in terror over our sins, but also, and indeed above all, in a firm faith in God's grace. Through nothing are we so strongly and compellingly urged to this faith as through the death of God's Son on the cross for our sins, for, secondly, *nothing shows us so irrefutably God's willingness to pardon and save even the greatest sinners.*

My beloved, if God had done nothing more to assure us of His grace than to reveal the decision to be gracious to us sinners to someone who certified by God, would now have to preach that to us, should we not believe such a person and let that give us peace? If now God besides had sent an angel from heaven to proclaim His grace to us, should we then not much more comfort ourselves in the grace of God revealed to us by a heavenly messenger? And, finally, should we not much less doubt God's grace when God's Son Himself announces it to us? Oh, surely!

But see, God did infinitely more than all this to assure us of His grace when in the knowledge of our fall we want to return to Him as lost sons and daughters; for God gave His Son into death for His reconciliation and for our assurance.

O man, you who gaze upon Jesus, the Crucified, and fall before His cross terrified by your sins, be comforted; your sins are forgiven you! Do not ask: What more shall I do? when your sins trouble you. Christ has already done everything; you should only believe in Him. If you are anxious because you know that your sins are as many as the hairs of your head, more than the sands on the seashore, more than the stars of the firmament—see, your Savior has endured afflictions without number; with that everything has been paid down to the last farthing.

If you are anxious because you know that your sins are great and terrible, great as mountains reaching to heaven—see, infinitely greater still is the grace which has been won for you; for the Most High, the infinite, the

74

Lord of the world Himself has become an eternally valid offering for your sins.

If you are anxious because you have sinned, because you let yourself be called without hearing God's voice, because you let yourself be awakened from your sleep in sin without getting up, because you began to hold to Christ but did not remain faithful—see, God's Son carried this sin of yours; for He, the Eternal and Infinite, remained obedient unto death, yes, death on the cross. Therefore His eternal faithfulness swallows all your temporal unfaithfulness and opens also to you the gates of paradise as to a poor malefactor who in the eleventh hour seeks grace.

If you are anxious because you cannot weep as much and find as much remorse and pain as you would wish—see, God Himself in your place offered so many tears, with strong crying and fear of hell, that also you who must complain about the hardness of your heart and your lack of tears can find grace and forgiveness.

If you are anxious because you have drawn near to God and have sighed for grace but have not found rest, anxious because you feel nothing within yourself but doubt, fear, and anxiety of conscience—be comforted! You should not seek rest in *your* heart but in the heart of the Crucified; that is why He let it be opened even after His death. Flee into it with your trembling heart! After the battle and fighting, you will finally go into everlasting rest with Christ.

But realize this also: As the death of the Son of God is in vain for the person who does not learn to see in it the abominableness of his sins, so it is in vain for the one who does not accept in faith the grace which through it was earned also for him. On the cross the words stand clearly for the secure sinner: Repent, for you shall die! But just as clearly shine the words for the terrified heart: Be reconciled to God; you shall live!

Oh, let none of us therefore leave today burdened with the load of his sins. Let each one say: Lord Jesus, "All sins Thou borest for me; else had despair reigned o'er me." Therefore I lay at Your cross the burden of my sins. Oh, take it with You into Your grave and bury it there. But I will wait in faith for the great day of resurrection, when I will awake with You, in Your likeness, and, completely clean, will triumph with You.

Oh, that none may be left behind! Today God raised His Son between heaven and earth, and He now calls heaven and earth as witnesses that He does not will the death of the sinner, but that he turn and live, He calls heaven and earth to witness that He has excluded no one from His grace. He calls heaven and earth to witness that He has done everything to woo sinners to Himself, that He has opened heaven to all, that He has stretched out His arms to all. Amen.

Easter Sunday, 1852
1 Corinthians 15:55-57

True Freedom, the Glorious Fruit
of the Resurrection of Our Lord Jesus Christ
(Amerikanisch-Lutherische Epistel Postille, pp. 198—205)

Lord Jesus, only a few days ago we beheld You with tears. For we saw You bound, bleeding, dying on the altar of the cross as the Lamb of God who takes away the sin of the world. And what do we see today? Oh, marvelous change! Oh, blessed sight! We see Your cross transformed into a banner of victory, Your death into life, Your disgrace into glory, your weakness into strength, Your bonds into freedom, Your silent soul's struggle into loud triumph. Oh, You Conqueror; oh, You dear Redeemer! So it is no deception if we trust in You! So it is no deception when we pray to You as our God, when we hope to receive our salvation from You as our Savior! No, for you *have* accomplished the great work of our salvation— mightily, magnificently, gloriously. Yes, now through You we are redeemed; through You we are rescued; through You we are snatched away from all our misery. In You we can now rejoice and be happy; in You we can now glorify and praise; in You we can defy sin, death, and hell. Ah, now let the Word of Your victory, which today rings in our ears, also sink down into the depth of our hearts. Through it burst all chains of unbelief with which we are still bound; through it open all graves of worry and sadness in which we still languish; through it tear away all bonds of sin and love of the world which still hold us captive; and through the message of Your resurrection make all of us here happy and free; but there take us in to be with the hosts who rejoice in You before Your throne and serve You from eternity to eternity. Amen.

In Christ, our victorious Redeemer, dearly beloved hearers!

"Freedom!" this is the general watchword of our time. "Freedom!" that is the word which now fires all hearts with bewitching power as often as it is expressed by mouth or in print. "Freedom at any price!" reverberates almost throughout the world, from land to land, from city to city, from village to village, from mouth to mouth, from husband and wife,

76

from young man and young woman, from the child and the aged.

Until now we Christians have been silent about this celebration of freedom. But behold! today a day has come on which also we must finally join in the cry. Yes, what do I say?—"Freedom!""Freedom!"that is today the watchword of all Christians, whatever language they speak and wherever on earth they live. Today we Christians go to meet a great hero of war, who comes from the field of battle crowned with victory and upon whose banner is written in flaming words: To all captives, pardon; to all who are bound, release; to all who are subjugated and oppressed, freedom! Those are songs of freedom we are singing today in full, jubilant tones; all our festival garments stand for freedom; freedom is the theme of all our evangelical sermons, for with the festival of Easter the great universal festival of freedom of Christians has come.

But now, shall we Christians declare that also we have finally been conquered by the spirit of our times? Shall also we Christians finally convert our churches into temples of freedom and instead of worshiping the great God who created heaven and earth, worship rather the idol of our day, the goddess of freedom? Shall we Christians join the cry of the drunken mob which now, in the intoxication of freedom, filled with fury and rage, raises the murderous cry: Down with the tyrants! and those who see in the overthrow of the existing order the salvation of the world and the advent of the golden age?—Far be it!

It is an altogether different freedom which we celebrate today, a freedom which gives *all* people, also temporal rulers, the palm of *peace;* a freedom which is not dependent on outward circumstances and can be perfectly enjoyed under emperors, kings, and princes, yes, under the oppression of the most brutal dictators and tyrants, as in the freest of republics; a freedom which also he can enjoy who, in chains and bonds, lies in a dark subterranean prison cell; a freedom which did not first climb over the corpses of the slaughtered and over the smoking ruins of destroyed cities, which need not first *be* gained by blood and tears, by trouble and misfortune of whole races and nations, but which 1800 years ago *was* dearly fought for and won for all. It is the freedom which Christ, the Prince of Peace, brought from his grave for all of subjugated humanity, for the entire enslaved world.

This is indeed not a physical but a spiritual freedom; but as much as our immortal soul is of more importance than our mortal, frail body, so much more important, glorious, noble, and honorable is the freedom of the Resurrected. It is indeed no freedom for this earthly life, no political, civil freedom from kings and princes, but a freedom for yonder life; but as much as eternal life is more important than temporal life (these few fleeting hours, which fly away like a dream), so much more important, precious, and worthy of the struggle is the freedom of the Resurrected. Without the freedom which Christ brought, even every king is really only a slave; but with it, every human being, also the slave, is a king. Without the freedom which Christ brought, every free citizen of a republic is still the most obedient subject and most contemptible servant of the most dishonorable and brutal of all princes, the prince of this world; with this freedom, however, the Christian can trample underfoot as his captive even this great and mighty world ruler.

Poor, deceived world! With uproarious joy it celebrates a freedom which is no freedom, and delights itself on its empty shadows, and does not see the banner of true freedom that flutters over the empty tomb of the Resurrected. But blessed, again blessed are we Christians, whom God has given open eyes to see the banner of Freedom which God's hand itself has planted! Come, then, come, you Christians; let us now gather about this banner and hear about our freedom. But first let us turn in silent prayer to the hero of David's stem who so bitterly fought for our freedom, after we have sung a hymn verse.

Text: 1 Corinthians 15:55-57

All the individual details in the story of our Savior's resurrection are so lovely, so comforting, and so full of power to awaken, that on the present festival one almost feels compelled to dwell upon each of these individual details. The fact of the resurrection of Jesus Christ is so great, so important, so powerful, so overflowingly rich, that it is impossible for us today to dwell upon other thoughts than the consideration of this divine deed itself and its inexpressibly glorious fruit. Therefore let me present to you today:

True Freedom, the Glorious Fruit of the Resurrection of Our Lord Jesus Christ

1. *freedom from the* right *of sin to* torment *and* condemn *us;* and
2. *freedom from the* power *of sin to* coerce *and* rule *us.*

I

Beloved, we human beings were created for freedom. But through the fall of the first people, humanity has gotten into slavery under the power of a fearful, body and soul destroying tyrant. And this tyrant is—sin.

I would try in vain to describe all the craftiness and cruelty with which sin carries out its fearful rule over humanity. Human language is too poor to describe it fully. There are indeed millions who imagine that sin is a gentle mistress who seeks only to provide fun and laughing among people; indeed, precisely these thoughts of countless persons show how cunningly sin has entangled people in its net and chained them to its throne. Now I do not want to remark about how sin once changed the paradise-like earth into a vale of tears and the social life of mankind into a constant lacerating battle; I want only to remind you what sin brings to everyone.

Indeed, sin always sends out friendly messengers who promise only good fortune to those who want to serve it; but the consequences are misery and heartache, temporal and eternal ruin. Sin instills a sweet poison into people, but after it is enjoyed, it tortures and torments the soul. It gives a person a friendly Judas kiss in order to betray him to the lurking bitterest remorse. Like a Delilah, it talks fondly to him in the hour of temptation, in order to betray him into the hands of the enemy of souls. It promises a person, if he will yield to it, all the kingdoms of the world, fulfillment of his most burning desires, help in his need, joy, bliss, good days, riches, and honor; but if one yields to its service, it rewards him finally with all misfortune, with grief and sorrow, with poverty, with shame and disgrace, with a sickly body and an empty soul. Yes, the more faithful a servant of sin a person has become, the more dreadful is the reward it gives him; it smites him with blindness, so that he can no longer realize what belongs to his peace; it calls upon the aid of the conscience, which like an evil worm in his heart gnaws and stings him; it feeds him with unrest, gives him the drink of despair, and finally plunges him unprepared into death.

First, sin always reminds a person only of God's great love, grace, patience, and longsuffering, and so rocks him into the sleep of security; but once it has brought him to a serious fall, it preaches about nothing except God's justice, holiness, wrath, and vengeance. At first it tries to convince a person that sin is only a trivial matter which one can soon enough again pray away; but when one has permitted himself to be convinced, then it takes off its mask and shouts: Your sin is so great that it cannot be forgiven; keep on sinning; you are lost anyway. First it says: Remain my servant for only this year, for only this week, for only this time; there is always time for repentance. But if one permits himself to be fooled that way, it finally calls: It is too late; there is no help for you. In life sin often accompanies a person only as a friendly guardian angel of light; but when the faithful servant of sin finally lies in the throes of death, then all sins of the past, like spirits of hell, stand around his deathbed, grin at him, and call to him: You are lost! And, ah! when the servant of sin has breathed his last, often with a foretaste of damnation, even then the host of his sins does not leave his side. Speedily they drag him before the judgment of a wrathful God, accuse him with heated voices, and, now when he is judged, cast him down into the dark abyss of hell and damnation.

Beloved, this is a small picture of the fearful rule which sin exercises over man, sometimes secretly, sometimes openly. But the most fearful thing about it all is that not until eternity do most people come to realize that sin has so shamefully betrayed them and that, on account of the holy law of God, sin has a right to reward all its servants with that kind of pay. For according to God's law the wages of sin is—death, namely temporal, spiritual, and eternal death.

Now if we ask all the wise men of the world how humanity can be freed of this tyranny of sin and how sin's *right* to torment and damn can be removed, they would all have to remain silent; they would all have to admit that they know no remedy against this fearful power.

Only Almighty God knew a remedy and—praised be His holy name!—He pitied us as He saw us in this fearful servitude; and He had a plan. Namely, He sent His only begotten Son Himself into the sin-enslaved world, and laid on Him the sins of all sinners, to battle with sin and to overcome it. And what happened? The sin of the world, which God's Son carried, indeed soon pressed also Him down into unutterable fear and distress; it damned Him, nailed Him to the cross, killed Him, and at last buried His body in the grave.—It appeared as though the all-destroying tyrant, sin, had swallowed up and conquered also our Savior from sin; but no!

The single power of sin is, as the apostle in our text writes, the *Law*. But Christ, who for His own sake was not obliged to keep the Law, had just now as the God-man fulfilled it through His now completed holy life and innocent suffering and death for all people. Therefore when Christ, swallowed up by sin, reached the realm of the dead, the Law suddenly had to be silent, because now it was fulfilled. Therefore Christ was not conquered by sin, but sin by Christ; sin lost the storm and the battle, and now its right to accuse, torment, and damn a sinner came to an end forever.

Now a wonderful sight opened up before the eyes of the holy angels. They saw the gates of hell broken down by the hand of Christ; and sin, together with its consequences, death and Satan, under Christ's feet. And while death lay there bound, and Satan with a crushed head was writhing in the dust like a trampled worm, Christ dragged out all the princes and mighty ones of the kingdom of hell, disarmed them, made a public display of them, and triumphed over them.

Since the work of Christ was not so much for angels as for human beings, Christ did not remain in the realm of the dead, or go invisibly from hell to heaven, but returned to earth, gloriously rising from the dead. What then is the meaning of the resurrection of Jesus Christ?—It is the triumphal march of Christ, as substitute for all people, held on earth after His victorious battle with the sin of the whole world, and therefore it is the triumphal procession of the whole redeemed and freed world of sinners. It is the uncontrovertible revelation before heaven and earth that, through the death of Christ, the power of sin has been removed, and therefore likewise the sting of death and the victory of hell. It is God's actual witness that the Savior of humanity has conquered, that the sin of men has really been atoned for, and that therefore their death has really been put to death and their hell has really been destroyed. It is the loud cry to all people from the throne of the Father, the Judge of the whole world Himself: "Leave, men, your captivity; your tyrant, sin, is dethroned; your executioners, death and hell, are conquered; their right to torment and denounce you has been taken from them; *you are free!"*

Perhaps you will say: Doesn't sin even now still exercise its right to torment and damn those who have sinned? But I reply: No! Of course, millions still experience unrest, fear, and torment after they have sinned, and many finally still go to eternal darkness in their sins. But that is now not really the work of their sins, but of their unbelief. After Christ's resurrection complete freedom from all distress on account of sin has been brought to all sinners, also to the greatest sinners. When, therefore, a sinner is still harassed and damned by his sins, the fault is only that he did not believe God, who through the glorious resurrection of His Son, the Savior of all sinners, has proclaimed and given pàrdon to all prisoners, an open door to all captives, and freedom to all sinners, freedom forever.

O sweet, blessed fruit of the resurrection of Jesus Christ! Freedom from the guilt, fear, and misery of sin!—On whose heart among you my hearers, shall I lay and strongly recommend this freedom? It applies to all people, also to you assembled here. But what will *you* think of the freedom from the misery of sin, you who do not consider yourselves sinners, or who do not yet feel the misery of sin, yes, who perhaps even serve sin with jokes and laughing? May God have mercy on you and, before it is too late, lead you to feel what a fearful tyranny sin exercises over you.

But to you who from the bottom of your heart not only join in the general complaint: "There is no distinction, since all have sinned and fall short of the glory of God," but also feel the weight of the chains of your sins and long for freedom from their right to accuse, torment, and damn you—to you I cry today the blessed word of Easter: Freedom!

Oh, do not think that because you are conscious of many sins you must now fear their threatenings. Let sin threaten you; if in faith you place yourselves under the protection of the Resurrected, they are empty threatenings because sin has been dethroned and you now live in the free country of the church of the Resurrected. What attention does a free citizen of a republic pay to the threats of a dethroned tyrant?

Do not think that, because you have often transgressed the law of God, you must fear the hour when the Law as your promissory note will be opened and the payment of your debt will be demanded of you. When the Lord hung upon the cross, He fastened on the cross the promissory note of the Law, cancelled it with His blood, and tore it up; and now He has come forth from His grave with the pardon of grace and forgiveness. How could a promissory note unnerve you now, one which the creditor Himself has torn up and destroyed and in its place has handed you a receipt solemnly signed with His blood?

Furthermore, do not think that, because your conscience still warns you, witnesses against you, and accuses you, you cannot be confident. Let your conscience, let the whole world, let the devil and his whole host continue to accuse you before God; they are false witnesses, they are rejected accusers. If they witness *against* you, the resurrected Son of God witnesses *for* you; if they *accuse* you, your Substitute declares you *free;* if they appeal to God's *righteousness,* the Resurrected appeals to His all-sufficient *death* and to the *resurrection* and *acquittal* arranged by the Father Himself.

Finally, do not think that only when you have completely freed yourself from sin or at least have become *better* than formerly, that only then can and should and will you also believe that you are free from the right of sin to torment and damn you. No, you do not first have to earn this freedom, nor first fight for it; it *is* already earned; it *has* already *been* fought for. Look back to the garden of Joseph of Arimathea; there the captain of your salvation is holding his triumphal procession after victory in battle.

Therefore do not weep, do not be sad, fear nothing. Do only this one thing: In faith join this triumphal procession which first the holy apostles and thereafter a countless host of confessors of Jesus Christ joined; follow the banner of freedom which flutters among this host, and never leave this triumphal army. Then in this life sin will always lie helpless under your feet, your whole life on earth will become a happy journey of victory, and death will finally vault over you as a rainbow of triumph through which you will enter with Christ from the conquered land of sin into the eternally free city of God, the heavenly Jerusalem.

II

Finally, my beloved, true freedom is also therefore the blessed fruit of the resurrection of our Lord Jesus Christ because, secondly, this freedom delivers us from the *power* of sin to *coerce* and *rule* over us.

82

Through the Fall we mortals have not only come under the awful tyranny of sin but also into willing obedience to it. To serve sin is our natural desire. Particularly, everyone by nature serves particular sins, which have full power over him and which he follows like a bound sacrificial animal wherever they lead him. One is ruled especially by avarice and greed; another is especially under the rule of drink or gluttony; a third is bound by the cords of lust and unchastity, or at least of vanity and love of pleasure; a fourth is ruled by anger and desire for revenge or envy and jealousy; a fifth is under the rule of hypocrisy, lies, or slander; a sixth is under the power of the love of honor and pride and the like. Without resistance people by nature obey the commands of these shameful tyrants and often knowingly and willfully offer them property, honor, rest, and peace of heart and conscience, yes, body and soul, God's grace and eternal salvation.

The most fearful thing about this is that even though a person by nature often wants to free himself from this or that sin because he sees that it is hurling him into misery and misfortune, he cannot. All his resolutions come to naught. Indeed, a person can at times guard against the *outbreak* of his sin, but to dethrone it from his *heart,* to remove the love and lust for a certain sin—that he cannot do. By nature sin lives in man's heart like a well-fortified army camp, like a high, strongly fortified, unconquerable castle. The garrison which defends this castle consists of the indwelling evil inclinations and lusts, and the troops which from the outside daily and hourly come to its aid are the enticements and threats of the world. That man by nature has a free will to choose the good and to reject the evil is an empty dream from which a person is awakened in every temptation.

As little as the wise of this world know a means by which the *right* of sin to torment and damn mankind can be taken away, so little do the wise of the world know a means by which man can be freed from the *power* of sin to coerce and rule him. The wise of this world themselves lie in the disgraceful servitude of sin—most of all the sin of ambition. As this or also other sins command their heart, thus they must do. What Peter writes applies to the wise of this world: "They promise them freedom, but they themselves are slaves of corruption."

But—hail to poor, captured humanity!—as God knew and created a way to free mankind from the *right* of sin to torment and damn, so God knew and created a way to set us free also from the *power* of sin to coerce and rule us. And also this remedy is nothing else than the resurrection of Jesus Christ from the dead. For as soon as a person believes with his heart that through the resurrection of the Son of God, his Savior, he is declared righteous from the guilt of sin, so soon sin is also toppled from its throne in his heart and its power in his soul is broken; the desire and joy of the heart, which previously was centered on sin and the world, is now centered on Christ and His precious freedom and grace. Yes, Christ Himself enters the heart of such a person and brings with Him a new heavenly fire and life; from now on He sits in his heart on the throne vacated by sin and now rules in it through the impulse of the Holy Spirit. Whoever in his heart believes that in the resurrection of Christ sin has lost its power to accuse him, he not only will be filled with peace and joy in the Holy Spirit, but such a person need not first be told: But now you must also give up obedience to sin; now you must also serve Christ as your only lawful Lord. Before one has said this to such a person, he has already begun to do it, driven by a free, willing compulsion now dwelling in him. The living faith that he has risen with Christ to his salvation urges him to walk with Christ in a new life.

O, precious, sweet freedom which Christ from His grave has brought us poor humans, captured and enslaved by sin! It makes us lords over sin, death, and hell; greatest of all, it makes us lords over our own heart. It makes us free citizens, yes, priests and kings who do not let themselves be ruled by any sin and who, even if they subject themselves to men, do it only for God's sake and therefore are really subject to no man, yes, no creature, but only to the great God, whom to serve is not a disgraceful slavery but true freedom, honor, and salvation.

Therefore, Christians, you are the real sovereign people, a people of only kings and priests. Therefore stand fast in the liberty with which Christ has made you free and do not be entangled again in the yoke of bondage. Do not deny the kingly Spirit who has been planted in you by faith, and never again be slaves to any sin.

Take an example from the world. How much the world spends to achieve a mere bodily, earthly, temporal freedom! For this purpose people band together and form organizations; there all without exception are busy, men and women, young men and girls, children and the aged; they tax one another; they buy weapons; they are concerned not only to assure freedom for themselves, but strive after it also for others; therefore they send speakers all over to extol freedom, and spread writings in order to awaken and cultivate the love of freedom everywhere; they claim that freedom is the inalienable blessing of all human beings; and leaving house and home, wife and child, as a last resort they fight for it in dangerous battle. I repeat, take an example from this, you Christians. What the world does is only for a shadow of freedom and is rebellion against God's ordinance. Besides, it is laughable that the world plumes itself with its freedom when it succeeds in abolishing the rule of a weak human being, while the world quietly and patiently, yes, eagerly and joyfully suffers the worst possible rule, the rule of sin and vice.

Up then, Christians, let the world have its childish game with freedom; you are assigned to a greater, holier battle for freedom, the battle against the mightiest tyrants, against the rulers of this whole world, against sin and the devil. The revolution in the kingdom of these tyrants is a just, honorable, God-pleasing revolution. To this end you do not have to form a union; it is already established. In Holy Baptism all of you have already joined in the great covenant of freedom to enlist as volunteers under God; you have sworn allegiance to the banner of the Resurrected; you have declared irreconcilable enmity and unending war against the kingdom of darkness, the devil and all his works and all his ways. Therefore let no trouble or sacrifice be too great. Clothed in the armor of God, girded with the sword of the Spirit, the Word of God, on your head the helmet of salvation, on your breast the breastplate of righteousness, on your arm the shield of faith, enter the battle with holy martial music and hurl to the ground every sin which would take you captive. Give no pardon, and fight on until you hold the field and gain the victory; help to overthrow the disgraceful tyranny of sin in the whole world and to establish everywhere the blessed free country of the church of grace. This battle for freedom will not end in shame and disgrace, for God Himself is in the confederacy; its end must be victory, must be eternal triumph.

But you who do not want to take part in the battle, know this: You will not share in the eternal feast of victory. You miserable slave of your sin and vice, your talk about freedom is miserable chatter, by which you make yourself a joke to the devil who leads you around. You miserable worldling, who because of your concern for your daily livelihood can hardly think of the freedom in Christ, let alone fight for it; you vain maiden, chained to the empty glories of the world, turning your back on your kingly Bridegroom, and even on the Easter festival of freedom dancing about the golden calf of worldly joys; you miserable slave of gold, like a mole desiring to roam over the whole world and to burrow through it, only to gather a little more of such glittering filth and then to let yourself be buried in this filth and forgotten—none of you consider yourselves worthy of the freedom with which Christ has made you free. May God have mercy on you and awaken you from your fearful, dangerous dream, and at last let also you come to know the blessed freedom for which on your behalf the Resurrected fought and which from His grave He brought to light.

But you, beloved Christians, who dearly want to be free of every chain of sin but complain that you still fight so poorly against it and so seldom overcome it—just don't lose your courage. Your comfort is not your own incomplete victory, but the complete victory of your eternal General, who for the whole world fought the great duel to the finish. Your freedom according to your justification is complete; your freedom according to your sanctification is incomplete, and it will remain incomplete. Only fight; do not leave the field of battle; just don't lay your weapons down. Then you will die as victors, enter the free port of heaven on the waves of death, be crowned, and on the last day awaken to the totally complete, glorious liberty of the children of God. For today we sing of our resurrected Victor [*The Lutheran Hymnal*, 192:6, 8]:

> Now I will cling forever
> To Christ, my Savior true;
> My Lord will leave me never,
> Whate'er He passeth through.
> He rends Death's iron chain,
> He breaks through sin and pain,
> He shatters hell's dark thrall—
> I follow Him through all.
>
> He brings me to the portal
> That leads to bliss untold,
> Whereon this rime immortal
> Is found in script of gold:
> "Who there (on earth) My cross hath shared
> Finds here (in heaven) a crown prepared;
> Who there with Me hath died
> Shall here be glorified." Amen.

Ascension
Mark 16:14-20

The Ascension of Christ, a Sure Foundation of a Joyous Faith
(*Amerikanisch-Lutherische Evangelien Postille,* pp. 193—98)

How glorious, O Jesus, is Your name in all the earth! For our salvation You not only descended to the lowest part of the earth, but also finally in divine majesty ascended far above all heavens. Just as You did not come into this world poor and miserable for Your own sake, so You also did not leave it in glory and honor for Your own sake; as You did not do battle and fight for Your own sake, so You did not conquer and triumph for Yourself but for us whose sins You bore and whose righteousness You have become.

Therefore You still let Your great deeds be proclaimed to humankind; therefore You have today again given us the great grace to assemble and to hear of Your great victory.

Oh, therefore, You gracious, universal, and glorious Savior, let not today's proclamation of Your glory fall upon our hearts in vain. Let every one of us realize that he is involved in Your being received into heaven and Your sitting at the right hand of the Father.

O Lord Jesus, all of us have already triumphed with You, for You are our Head and the Captain of our salvation. Therefore drive away our unbelief, which reasons that Your ascension does not concern us, and give us the faith which says not only when You hung on the cross but also now that You are sitting on Your throne: You are mine! For Your own sake hear us, King of heaven and King of all sinners. Amen.

In Christ, the Ascended, beloved hearers!

We have gathered here quietly before God to commemorate a great, precious, and glorious deed. For today we are celebrating the coronation day or the festival marking the beginning of the royal session of our King of grace, Jesus Christ; I mean the festival of His glorious ascension.

Rightly, therefore, everyone who knows he has been baptized into this great Lord and Savior should enter the courts of the Lord with you, and

87

with still greater joy should leave this place where he has heard about it from God's Word. Yes, rightly it should be thus, for we find that already the believers of the old covenant were full of the most joyous praise of God when in spirit they saw this day, which then lay in the dark future. Among others, David cries out: "Clap your hands, all peoples! Shout to God with loud songs of joy! . . . God has gone up with a shout, the Lord with the sound of a trumpet. Sing praises to God, sing praises! Sing praises to our King, sing praises! For God is the king of all the earth; sing praises with a psalm!" Similarly the author of Psalm 68 rejoices and says:

> With mighty chariotry, twice ten thousand, thousands upon thousands, the Lord came from Sinai into the holy place. Thou didst ascend the high mount, leading captives in Thy train, and receiving gifts among men, even among the rebellious, that the Lord God may dwell there. Blessed be the Lord, who daily bears us up; God is our salvation. Our God is a God of salvation; and to God, the Lord, belongs escape from death. . . . Sing to God, O kingdoms of the earth; sing praises to the Lord, to Him who rides in the heavens, the ancient heavens. . . . Ascribe power to God, whose majesty is over Israel, and His power is in the skies. . . . Blessed be God!"

See, my beloved, thus the believing Israelites already rejoiced when they thought of the day of the Messiah's ascension, which for them still lay in the future. The church of the Old Testament therefore had a living faith that His ascension was something that concerns not only Him, Christ, but all the redeemed, namely that it is the precious final stone and the sparkling crown of the entire work of redemption.

And so it is. If we view Christ's ascension only as the happy occasion on which Christ was taken from all suffering, all shame, all imperfections, and all persecutions and thus, so to speak, received the reward for His faithfulness unto death, then we are still viewing it without its real use. We must follow the Ascending One with our eyes as our *Redeemer*, we must see ourselves in Him as the triumphing ones, and we must make His whole work the foundation of a joyful faith; then, only then, will we enjoy the blessed fruit which His word is to bring us.

Text: Mark 16:14-20

The Gospel just read tells in a few words the story about Christ from His last appearance on Easter day until His entrance into His glory. Mark indicates the following as the heart of all commissions which the Lord gave His apostles during this time: *"Go into all the world and preach the Gospel to the whole creation. He who believes and is baptized will be saved; but he who does not believe will be condemned."* "Believe in Me"; that is, as it were, the last will Christ at His leaving left for all people, and which He confirmed and sealed by His glorious ascension. Accordingly, consider with me:

The Ascension of Christ, a Sure Foundation of a Joyous Faith

1. *It bases our faith on the completeness of our redemption from all enemies;* and

2. *It bases our faith on the continuous gracious presence of Christ with His congregation.*

I

Through the fall of our first parents, my friends, all humanity came under the power of three great enemies; and these are sin, the law, and death. Namely, through the Fall human beings, first, became subject to the lordship of sin; on account of which, second, the Law speaks the sentence of damnation; and, finally, death received the right to swallow them up. These three enemies stand in the closest relationship with one another and so bind people with an iron chain of destruction, as the apostle describes this in the words: "The sting of *death* is *sin,* and the power of *sin* is the *Law*"; that is, sin turns death into a king of terrors, but the Law makes sin powerful to damn us.

No human power was in a position to conquer these enemies; man had become their powerless, defenseless servant and captive. If *God* had not had pity on men, they would have been created in vain and would have had to be lost, without possibility of salvation. But the Son of God undertook the astounding work of freeing them from their prison. And what did He do? He became sin for us, in our place became subject to the Law, and for us sprang into the jaws of death. The sin of all the world's people He took upon Himself, bore their punishments, and was the reconciliation for them. He fulfilled the Law and by that act won for us a complete righteousness. He permitted death to swallow Him up and conquered it through the power of His almighty life.

Therefore when Christ victoriously arose from the dead, the whole fallen world conquered with Him; the sins of all people were atoned for; a righteousness that avails before God was won for all; hell was destroyed; death was disarmed; life and immortality were brought to light; and the redemption of all men was gloriously sealed by God the Father. All our enemies already then lay at the feet of Him who for us entered the battle.

Only one thing remained in order that Christ might be a complete Savior for us: After He had defeated all our enemies, He had to be installed as their absolute Lord; the scepter of power had to be given into His hands; the crown of heavenly glory had to be placed upon Him; and He had to mount the throne of divine majesty. The prophecy of the second Psalm had to be fulfilled in Him, where the heavenly Father says: "I have set My king on Zion, My holy hill. . . . Ask of Me, and I will make the nations Your heritage, and the ends of the earth Your possession. You shall break them with a rod of iron, and dash them to pieces like a potter's vessel."

And this happened through the glorious ascension of Christ and through what followed it and was bound up with it: His session at the right hand of the Father. There Christ as Conqueror not only held a public triumphal march through the gates of heaven and as God-man and Reconciler received the homage of all angels and archangels, but by it He also became the absolute Lord over sin, Law, death, the devil, and hell. Therefore He ascended in divine splendor from the same place where in bloody sweat He fought the hardest battle against these enemies, namely the Mount of Olives.

If we want to consider the ascension of Christ properly, the main point consists in this, that we see Christ in His ascension not only as the head but also as the substitute and forerunner of the whole human race. David was a prototype when he killed the giant Goliath. Just as through the victory of that one individual, David, all Israel was saved from the power of the hostile Philistines, so through the triumphal ascension of Christ all Christians with Him have become lords over sin, the Law, and death. Already Psalm 68 speaks of this, where, as already mentioned, we are told: "Thou didst ascend the high mount, leading captives in Thy train, and receiving gifts among men, even among the rebellious. . . . " St. Paul tells us the same thing in Ephesians 2 when he says: "But God, who is rich in mercy, out of the great love with which He loved us, even when we were dead through our trespasses, made us alive together with Christ (by grace you have been saved), and raised us up with Him, and made us sit with Him in the heavenly places in Christ Jesus. . . . " Just as we all have already risen with Christ and in Him have been justified by God, so we have already ascended to heaven with Christ and thus in Him are already lords over all our enemies; and as surely as now no sin can harm Christ, no Law damn Him, and no death rule over Him, so certainly are also we freed from their captivity and already translated into the heavenly life with Him, if only with all our heart we believe it.

Learn from this what a sure foundation for a joyous faith we have in the ascension of Christ. If we do not want to believe that sin, Law, and death lie under our feet, we must entirely deny the ascension of Christ, or at least deny that the one who ascended into heaven is our Savior, our Redeemer, our Brother, our Head, our Captain, and that His fight for us has won so blessed an outcome. Therefore if our sin wants to make us afraid, we should not let it bring us to despair, but in faith look to the ascension of Christ and say in our heart: Sin, you are conquered; you shall not conquer me anew, but as my captive you shall serve me for this, that I cling all the more firmly to my Savior. He has ascended into heaven, and I with Him, for I clasp Him with the hand of my faith, and in His name I have been baptized. If the Law wants to damn us, we should not submit to its judgment, but say in our heart: You are fulfilled; your demands have been completely satisfied; God's Son subjected Himself to you for me; thereby you have lost all your right to me, for Him you cannot reproach with anything; yes, He sits on the highest chair and is now, Law, your Lord; not from you, but from Him I therefore receive my verdict, and that reads: "Grace, mercy, forgiveness!" If death wants to frighten us and hell wants to open its jaws against us, we do not now have to be afraid; now through Christ's ascension they have become empty phantoms; confidently we can and should therefore now ridicule them and say: "Death is swallowed up in victory. O death, where is thy victory? O death, where is thy sting? . . . But thanks be to God, who gives us the victory through or Lord Jesus Christ." [Here we have omitted a hymn verse.]

II

Yet the ascension of Christ is also the foundation of our faith in the continuous gracious presence of Christ with His church. And that is the second point I want to present to you now.

In our day especially it is very generally believed that after His ascension Christ with His humanity is no longer on earth and in the world in general. Therefore some, after the manner of Zwingli, still misuse the doctrine of the ascension to deny that Christ's body and blood are truly present in the Lord's Supper.

But this error rests upon an entirely false conception of the real nature of the ascension of Jesus Christ, Son of God and Son of man. It is entirely mistaken to think that Christ went to heaven in no other way than an Enoch or Elijah and that He now lives in a specific place, as it is believed of all other saints.

In this connection it is to be observed, first, that we are much too weak to grasp and to discern the real nature of Christ's ascension. Time-bound as we are, we do not even have an idea of what Scripture calls heaven, for it says that there time and space cease; but our mind has no conception of something that is not bounded by time and space. But Holy Scripture does not even say of Christ that He only went to heaven, but rather St. Paul, among others, says in Ephesians 4: "He who descended is He who also ascended *far above all* the heavens, that He might fill all things." Which human heart can grasp this mystery? I will be silent about which human tongue can describe it. Therefore consider this: The ascension of Christ is like the sun—the more intently one wants to look into it, the more blinded our eyes become, so that at last we cannot see anything at all; this work therefore belongs to those which are not to be *fathomed* but simply *believed* in childlike faith, according to what Scripture says about it. The more simply we hold to what Scripture says about it, however, the more strengthening to our faith this mysterious article of Christian belief will become.

But what do the Scriptures tell us about it?—They do not tell us that Christ is now confined or circumscribed by heaven as the other saints are, but on the contrary, that *He* fills all things; not that He *was* taken up by heaven but rather that He *has received* heaven, yes, that He "ascended *far above* all the heavens,"as our Gospel says, and "*sat down at the right hand of God.*"

What does that mean? If we do not want to go astray on this point, we must ask Scripture for counsel. It says, among other things, that with His right hand God led Israel out of Egypt and hurled Pharaoh with his army into the sea. It says further, in Psalm 77:10: "It is my grief that the right hand of the Most High has changed." It says: "If I take the wings of the morning and dwell in the uttermost parts of the sea, even there Thy hand shall lead me, and Thy right hand shall hold me." From this it is clear that by God's right hand Scripture understands nothing else but His omnipotence, omnipresence, rule, and His eternal, divine majesty and glory.

And Scripture shows us again that we are not mistaken in the application of this interpretation to Christ's sitting at the right hand of God; for St. Paul says in Ephesians 1: " . . . which He accomplished in Christ when he raised Him from the dead and made Him sit at His right hand in the heavenly places, far above all rule and authority and power and dominion, and above every name that is named, not only in this age but also in that which is to come; and He has put all things under His feet and has made Him the head over all things for the church, which is His body, the fullness of Him who fills all in all." And already in Psalm 110 we read: "The Lord says to my lord: 'Sit at My right hand, till I make Your enemies Your footstool.' . . . Rule in the midst of your foes!"

Now, naturally, all of this is not said about Christ's divinity, but of the nature according to which he previously went about in a servant's form, namely about His human nature. For the divine nature could neither be humbled nor exalted; it could experience neither a diminishing nor increase of its glory, as Psalm 102 says expressly about the divine nature: "Thou art the same."

From this judge for yourself whether according to Holy Scripture Christ is no longer with us according to His human nature. Far be it! It is true, He left the world in the sense that He no longer walks among us as a mortal man, visible, touchable, and occupying space, as once He did with His disciples. Therefore Christ in this sense could say: "I came from the Father and have come into the world; again, I am leaving the world and going to the Father." Therefore also the angel, pointing to Christ's empty grave, in this sense could say: "*He is not here;* see the place where they laid Him." Therefore also in this sense we read at the close of the second article of the creed: "From thence He shall come to judge the quick and the dead."

But far be it from us therefore to believe, that what Abraham said to the rich man in hell applies also to Christ: "And besides all this, between us and you a great chasm has been fixed, in order that those who would pass from here to you may not be able, and none may pass from there to us." Far be it from us therefore to believe that Christ is King in a kingdom from which He is separated and that He can rule only from afar. No, Christ took a spatial departure from His disciples; with His glorified body He truly lifted Himself higher and higher, as far as the eyes of the disciples could reach. But that was to be only an assurance of the genuineness of the great change which was now taking place in the state of the man Jesus. We must not think that, when the cloud like a chariot of triumph took Christ up and away from the eyes of His disciples, He now slowly continued to rise, farther and farther removed from the earth, and raised Himself up beyond the starry heavens. No, as soon as the cloudy gate of this earth closed behind Him, in that moment He entered the state of divine majesty, appeared full of glory to all the angels and saints amid their ringing songs of triumph, and now, also as man, took part in the omnipotent and omniscient rule over heaven and earth and all creatures.

When we thus consider the ascension of Christ according to the clear testimonies of Holy Scripture, oh, what a sure foundation for a joyous faith we find in it! Far be it that Christ should have withdrawn Himself from His congregation; rather through His ascension He has come to be very near to it. We do not need to go to Judea to find Him; rather, shortly before His ascension He promised: "Lo, I am with you always, to the close of the age." And through His visible entrance into His invisible glory He confirmed this and set it in motion. In all places he is now near us as God and man, with His grace, with His help, with His protection. When He

C. F. W. Walther and his wife Emilie *nee* Buenger (courtesy Concordia Historical Institute).

Walther's carriage, presently located at Concordia Historical Institute. An illustration of this carriage serves as the logo for this series.

94

Georg Stoeckhardt, teacher of Biblical theology at Concordia Seminary, St. Louis, from 1881 until his death in 1913. A friend and colleague of Walther, Stoeckhardt was the preeminent Missouri Synod exegete at the turn of this century (courtesy Concordia Historical Institute). See p. 164 in this volume.

Ottomar Fuerbringer, Walther's brother-in-law and one of the Saxon immigrants who played a key role in the founding and early history of the Missouri Synod (courtesy Concordia Historical Institute).

95

Another view of Walther's study, where many of his works were produced (courtesy Concordia Historical Institute).

Christ Episcopal Church on Fifth and Chestnut Streets in St. Louis, where Walther's Trinity Congregation worshiped until the church below was dedicated in 1842 (courtesy Concordia Publishing House Library).

The first house of worship of Trinity Evangelical Lutheran Church, St. Louis, dedicated in 1842 (courtesy Concordia Publishing House Library).

walked on this earth, Christ dealt chiefly with His Father for us; now His own attention is upon us, His redeemed, in order through the Gospel to give us knowledge of Him, to bring us to faith in Him, to keep us in faith, and to carry out the good work in us until the day when we shall see Him as He is. Christ has not ceased to carry out His work on behalf of sinners; He does not rest from His labor in the enjoyment of salvation, as do those who have fallen asleep in Him; but He has appeared for us before God in the Holy of Holies. As Aaron on his breastplate bore the names of the tribes of Israel when he entered the Holy of Holies, so Christ there carries on His heart the names of all believers as He appears before God in heaven as the true high priest; there without interruption He pleads for His own and rules them, is concerned about them, and protects them, so that even the gates of hell cannot prevail against them.

Oh, therefore, let everyone today be awakened to faith in Christ and be strengthened in it through the consideration of His glorious ascension. Let no one say: What does that concern me? For as you are a captive of sin, the Law, and death, which you cannot deny, the ascension of Christ concerns you as much as eternal salvation, the rescue and redemption of your soul, for by His ascension Christ has led captivity captive. Now if at your death you do not want to go down into that eternal captivity, hold fast in faith to the Ascended; then already here you are free, and one day you will follow Him into His glory. For He thought also of you when before His ascension He gave His disciples, yes, the whole church, the command: *"Preach the Gospel to the whole creation. He who believes and is baptized will be saved; but he who does not believe will be condemned."*

Now if you in the meantime, before your Savior takes you home to your Father's house, experience much trouble, many trials and danger to your soul, just do not give up holding to Him who today entered the kingdom of His Father. For your sake all power has been given Him in heaven and on earth; He will let nothing tear you from His hand, and will be your Shield and Protection until He has placed you among the host of the saved who sing to Him an everlasting Hallelujah in the temple of heaven.

To Him be glory and praise here and there from eternity to eternity. Amen.

Trinity Sunday, 1844

John 3:1-15

Baptism, the Powerful Means of Regeneration

(*Gnadenjahr*, pp. 312—22)

Triune God, Father, Son, and Holy Ghost, we were all once baptized into You. Then Your most holy name was placed upon us, and then You again became our dear Father and we Your dear children. Then You gave us the forgiveness of all our sins, washed our souls, made us Your temples, regenerated us to eternal life, and received us into a new kingdom of grace and salvation. Therefore, O You faithful covenant God, look upon us all in grace today. Show those among us who until now have attached little value to their baptism what an incomparable and unsurpassed blessing they have despised, and prevail upon them to return with remorse and shame to the spring of salvation which You have opened up. Through the word about Your sacraments, so rich in grace, awaken in us all a soul-thirst and the courage of faith from now on daily in the face of our sin and uncleanness to draw near to the free, open well which You have promised and given to all the citizens of the New Testament Jerusalem and also to us. Hear us, O Triune God. Amen.

Beloved brothers and sisters in Christ Jesus!

As you know, it is chiefly the doctrine of the holy sacraments which now for more than 300 years has separated the orthodox Evangelical Lutheran Church from all other so-called Protestant churches, apparently forever. Many, for whom truth is more or less a matter of indifference, see this point of separation as such an indifferent and small matter that they counsel that one should completely give up the fight over the holy sacraments, disregard it, let everyone believe about this matter what seems best to him, and, since the "Protestant" churches agree in many other important points, unite in one great "evangelical" church.

Now if the separation rested upon an insignificant difference of certain human opinions and views, who would then not with overwhelming joy accept the proposal to unite? But, my beloved, the teaching concerning the holy sacraments deals not with human opinions, also not with nonfundamental doctrines, but with *chief parts* of the Christian faith. Therefore the points on which we are not united are considerations of the highest importance.

We Lutherans know from the Word of God, and therefore we also believe, teach, and confess, that the holy sacraments, Baptism and the Lord's Supper, are *means of grace,* through which that is really offered and given us which God has promised to those who use them in faith. On the other hand, the other so-called Protestant churches teach—some explicitly, some essentially—that the holy sacraments are only *signs and seals* of grace, through which a person does not receive the blessings of grace, but which only make him sure and seal to him that which he must already have. In a few words, that is what it is all about; it is that which separates us from those heterodox churches.

In this connection perhaps some, who do not have a clear understanding of the relationship among Christian doctrines, will ask: Is it so important whether a person looks upon the holy sacraments as true *means* of grace or whether he regards them merely as *signs* of grace? To this I must answer: By all means! This difference concerns the true heart of the Gospel, or the doctrine concerning the way of salvation. For it concerns the doctrine about how a person is justified before God, whether through *his* works or through *God's* works; whether a *human being* himself can lay the first stone of the building of his salvation or whether *God* must lay it; whether a person can raise himself up to God or whether God must descend to him in order to help him; whether God gives us poor beggars everything free and for nothing or whether He merely approves and puts His seal on the good which we ourselves have achieved.

That this is the case with Holy Baptism, among other doctrines, we see clearly from a declaration of the holy apostle Paul. For he says in Titus 3:5-7: "He saved us, not because of deeds done by us in righteousness, but in virtue of His own mercy, by the washing of regeneration and renewal in the Holy Spirit, which he poured out upon us richly through Jesus Christ our Savior, so that we might be justified by His grace and become heirs in hope of eternal life." See, in this precious passage the dear apostle sets the achievement of salvation through our works and its achievement through the washing of regeneration, namely through Holy Baptism, in opposition to each other. Here you therefore have an irrefutable proof that whoever denies the saving power of Baptism bases salvation on human works and so undermines the chief pillar of Christianity, namely our justification alone through faith by grace. Is such an error such a small one that we as believing Christians can easily overlook it? Oh, indeed not—unless we wanted to regard the basis of our salvation as an insignificant matter.

Now since our today's Gospel lesson directs us to the important article of Holy Baptism, let me now speak to you of that in greater detail.

Text: John 3:1-15

The chief sentence in the Gospel lesson just read, about which everything in it moves as a circle around its center, is this: *"Unless one is born of water and the Spirit, he cannot enter the kingdom of God."* As you heard, these words lead us today on the festival of the Holy Trinity to consider Baptism, which all of us have already received in the name of the Father, the Son, and the Holy Spirit—namely how through it we have been born anew. Accordingly, I want to speak to you about:

Baptism, the Powerful Means of Regeneration

1. *how it always is that;* and
2. *how it becomes that also for us.*

I

Nicodemus, about whom our Gospel tells, was, my friends, indeed a Pharisee, but he distinguished himself in many ways above the members of his sect. For, although Christ attacked the Pharisees severely, Nicodemus showed himself to be just; therefore he did not hate Christ, did not reject Him untried, but (although he was of high standing and learned while Jesus was lowly and despised) he sought Him out in the night in order to discuss religion with Him. And he admitted: *"Rabbi, we know that You are a teacher come from God; for no one can do these signs that You do, unless God is with him."* Manifestly he was an honest, honorable, and irreprovable man.

But yet he was of the opinion that Christ was only a teacher of the Law, that such a man was all he *needed,* and that through a strict observance of the Old Testament law he could and must be pleasing to God. Therefore without a doubt he belonged to those of whom it is written in Luke 7: "But the Pharisees and the lawyers rejected the purpose of God for themselves, not having been baptized by [John]." For he baptized for repentance and remission of sins.

Now what is the first word with which Christ returns his greeting? He says to him: *"Truly, truly, I say to you, unless one is born anew, he cannot see the kingdom of God."* Truly a hard saying! With these words Christ not only roundly denies salvation to Nicodemus in his present condition, but also assures him that it cannot be gained by works of the Law; they would not help at all; a change must take place not only in his life but in his whole *person;* in a word, he must be born again.

Never did Nicodemus expect an answer like that from Christ. It appears that he felt that he had not heard correctly; therefore, very much surprised, he asks: *"How can a man be born when he is old? Can he enter a second time into his mother's womb and be born?"* Since Nicodemus knew of no other birth except the natural one, the Savior explained the matter more clearly and said: *"Truly, truly, I say to you, unless one is born of water and the Spirit, he cannot enter the kingdom of God."* Here the Savior says that Baptism works the miracle of regeneration. This means nothing else except that through it a natural man becomes a spiritual man; that from a child of wrath he becomes a child of grace, from a child of darkness, sin, death, hell, damnation, and Satan he becomes a child of light, righteousness, life, heaven, salvation, and God; that Baptism is the door into the kingdom of God and that it transfers and regenerates from the earthly into the heavenly, eternal life.

"How can this be?" Nicodemus called out in amazement, and that is the cry of thousands upon thousands when they hear this teaching. "How can water do such great things?" they all cry with one voice.

We can answer in no better way than to quote the fourth chief part of Luther's Small Catechism: "It is not the water indeed that does them, but the Word of God which is in and with the water." If God had not commanded it and attached to it His dear promise, we could sprinkle a person with water a thousand times, using the name of the triune God, and our undertaking would be useless. But as surely as God's Word and command are connected with Baptism, so surely it effects the great, ineffable blessing that "it works forgiveness of sins, delivers from death and the devil, and gives eternal salvation to all who believe this, as the words and promises of God declare." The Word of God connected with the water makes the water so precious, so divinely powerful, that it is medicine for the soul, a heavenly stream which flows from the sea of divine grace and mercy.

Therefore Christ further says to Nicodemus: *"Do not marvel that I said to you, 'You must be born anew.' The wind blows where it wills, and you hear the sound of it, but you do not know whence it comes or whither it goes; so it is with everyone who is born of the Spirit."* Christ wants to say: Just as a person does not understand anything about the mightiest storm winds except the sound, so in Holy Baptism nothing is perceived by the senses except the water and the Word; this is the audible sound, but the moving of the Spirit accompanying it is beyond our natural senses.

But, says one, "How can I believe that natural water cleanses the soul? Nothing earthly has this power." But, my beloved, here we cannot ask counsel of our mind. Indeed, reason must be offended at God's mysteries;

here God's Word alone can decide. But, among other things, it says clearly: "Baptism, which corresponds to this, now saves you, not as a removal of dirt from the body but as an appeal to God for a clear conscience." Accordingly, the water of Baptism is not to cleanse our flesh but our soul, and to place us in the covenant of grace with God. Therefore Ananias says to Saul: "Rise and be baptized, and wash away your sins." It is indeed true: Mere water could not do that. For that very reason Christ says in our Gospel lesson: "of water *and the Spirit.*" Through the Word the Holy Spirit is joined to the water, as He was joined to the fiery tongues which on the first Pentecost hovered visibly over the heads of the holy apostles; therefore the blessed Luther calls it a water permeated by God.

If we find that unbelievable, let us only look at the workings in nature; there we find a similar situation. Why does bread strengthen and nourish our vitality? It happens only because God has placed His Word of blessing into the bread; for if, according to God's counsel, the hour of death has come, bread no longer helps to keep the living flow of blood from running cold. Further, why is the bosom of the earth so fruitful that unbidden it brings forth bread and all sorts of precious fruits? It happens only because God said: "Let the earth put forth vegetation, plants yielding seed, and fruit trees bearing fruit." In vain would the sun send its life-giving rays to the earth had not the only fruitful sun of the divine word of blessing first arisen over the globe. Just as the word of God: "Let the earth put forth" still in this moment unceasingly works and vivifies and creates in the realm of nature, so in the kingdom of grace the water of Baptism is still a living and powerful water of regeneration and renewal because of those words of Christ: "Go therefore and make disciples of all nations, baptizing them in the name of the Father and of the Son and of the Holy Spirit. . . . He who believes and is baptized will be saved." Therefore when today a servant of the church says: "I baptize thee in the name of the triune God," that means: What I do now, I do only as an instrument; I am really not the one who performs this work of grace; it is God who does it through me and thereby snatches you out of sin, death, and hell and transfers you into His kingdom of grace.

Therefore, my beloved, do not let yourselves be led astray by those who say: All these blessings are not worked through Baptism, but it is only a sign and seal of all these. They say: Do not the Holy Scriptures clearly say that God gave Abraham the sacrament of circumcision as a sign of the covenant and as a seal of the righteousness of faith? But I ask you, what sort of conclusion is that? In the Holy Scriptures a sacrament is called a sign and seal of the covenant, but is it *only* a sign and seal? Can there be a more senseless conclusion? It would be just as if I wanted to draw this conclusion: In the Holy Scripture man is called earth and ashes; therefore he is only earth and ashes; therefore he has no mind, no soul, and is not immortal. Would you not find such a line of argument laughable, whose wrongness even a schoolchild could point out? But see, that's the way the false teachers must present their proofs in order at least apparently to ground their errors in the Scriptures. Is it not a crime when they say that, because Scripture calls the holy sacraments signs and seals, therefore it counts for nothing when Scripture calls Holy Baptism a washing of regeneration, a washing away of sins, a Baptism unto salvation? Pitiable men! *With* God's Word they want to fight *against* God's Word!

It is indeed true that the sacraments are also signs and seals, but on that account they are not empty hulls without kernels, not empty ceremonies without gifts of grace. God does not jest with us by the appointment of outward rites which do not help us. God does things which no human can do; but when people establish a society they can also give signs by which they are known. Therefore do not let yourselves be led astray but consider this: Noah's ark was also a sign of God's grace, but not only that; it served to rescue from the universal flood, and this was a prototype of Baptism. So also the burning bush was a sign of the presence of God, but not only that; God was truly present in this fire. Again, the cloud and fiery pillar were for Israel a sign of the gracious guidance of God, but not only that; God was in it. Finally, the dove over Christ was a sign of the Holy Spirit, but not simply that; the Holy Spirit was truly present in the dove.

"Do not marvel at this," Christ says to Nicodemus and to every one of us. Indeed, Baptism appears much too simple for the great works it is to carry out; but we dare not look upon what we are to do, but to the One who has commanded us to do it and who has attached such wonderful promises thereto. God alone wants the honor and praise for our salvation; therefore He prescribed means in whose use we can in no way praise ourselves. If God had commanded us to do great, difficult works, we would much more easily believe in their power; but since He says: "Be washed with water in My name, and you will be saved," that is too humbling for us. Then in self-righteousness we cry out: "Is that all God demands? Should that do such great things?"—If we persist in this proud contempt, we will inevitably be lost.

In this connection we find an excellent example in the fifth chapter of the Second Book of Kings. There we are told that Naaman, the Syrian general, came to Elisha the prophet to be healed of his leprosy, which no one could heal. Elisha commanded him to wash in the Jordan seven times. When Naaman heard this, he was angry and said: "Are not Abana and

Pharpar, the rivers of Damascus, better than all the waters of Israel? Could I not wash in them, and be clean?" and he wanted to return home, feeling that he had received useless advice. But his servants said to him: "If the prophet had commanded you to do some great thing, would you not have done it? How much rather, then, when he says to you, 'Wash, and be clean'?" Naaman did that, and behold! in a moment he became well and, brought to faith, he cried: "There is no God in all the earth but in Israel." See, Naaman thought at first: Water is water; yes, he thought, if it depended on the water, the Syrian waters were more healthful than those in Israel. But finally he experienced what a difference there is between water connected with God's Word and that which does not have His promise. That's the way it is also with Baptism. If one asks: "How can water do such great things?" the answer is: "Without the Word of God the water is simple water and no Baptism; but with the Word of God it is a Baptism, that is, a gracious water of life and a washing of regeneration in the Holy Ghost." It is always that.

II

Let us now, in the second place, in a few words hear how Baptism becomes this also for us.

Christ talks about this at the end of the Gospel lesson when He adds: *"No one has ascended into heaven but He who descended from heaven, the Son of man."* With these words the Lord says first how Holy Baptism, this ladder to heaven, gets its saving power, namely not from men but from Him; for He came from heaven and through His life, suffering, and death alone won and opened heaven for us. From there all the treasures of grace have flowed forth and have been placed into Holy Baptism; so this well of salvation was actually dug on Golgotha.

Now Christ continues: *"And as Moses lifted up the serpent in the wilderness, so must the Son of man be lifted up, that whoever believes in Him may have eternal life."* With these words He explains that through *faith* Baptism is for us a washing of regeneration.

For it is the same with Holy Baptism as with the Word of God. Scripture says clearly that without faith the Word is "a fragrance from death to death." The Letter to the Hebrews tells us concerning many Israelites: "The message which they heard did not benefit them, because it did not meet with faith in the hearers." And again we are told: "Faith comes from what is heard, and what is heard comes by the preaching of Christ." Thus it is also with Baptism; it is a powerful means of regeneration, and yet without faith we are not partakers of this benefit.

My beloved, this gives you an explanation of the objection so often made: "If Baptism saves, then faith alone does not save." This is no different from a person's saying: If the sword has killed this or that person, the soldier did not do it!—The sword is the instrument with which the soldier does his deeds. So it is Baptism with its treasures which faith seizes and on account of which it saves; for faith must have promises of God upon which it rests.

At the same time another reproach is rejected which is frequently raised against those who on the basis of Christ's and the apostle's clear sayings declare that Baptism is the means of regeneration. For some say: "Do you maintain that every baptized person is born again? Are all baptized persons children of God, no matter how ungodly their lives are? Oh, what a soft pillow Baptism is even for the most insolent servant of sin!"

So some twist the pure doctrine only in order to make it hated; for the orthodox church has never taught that. It is indeed true that every child is regenerated when it is baptized, for children do not yet resist in willful wickedness; therefore without doubt God can work faith and regeneration in their hearts in Baptism. But it is different with grown-ups; if they resist and do not let themselves be brought to faith, they are not born again through Baptism. But as certainly as the Word of God remains the powerful seed of regeneration even though many hearers are not regenerated, so it is with Baptism when a rogue in his unbelief and wickedness receives it in vain.

But now, how does it come that one notices so little in children that through Baptism they have been born again? It comes from this, that regeneration can also be lost. How many adults are converted only to fall away again! So there are many more who as children are transferred through Baptism to the kingdom of God but only too soon lose again what they received. How can it be otherwise, since most children never experience what precious blessings Baptism has given them? What does it help children when parents bring them to Baptism but do not at an early age instill the Word of God in them to preserve and strengthen their faith? For where faith in the benefits of Baptism dies out, there also these benefits are taken from their hands, for Christ says: "If a man does not abide in Me, he is cast forth as a branch and withers; and the branches are gathered, thrown into the fire and burned."

Yet, my beloved, Baptism itself is not lost on that account. On God's part this covenant of grace stands fast. "If we are faithless, He remains faithful—for He cannot deny Himself." Therefore when a person is again awakened from his lost condition, when through God's Word he comes to a knowledge of his misery, and he again stretches out the hand of his faith for the blessings he received in Baptism, then Baptism is for him anew the powerful means of the regeneration of his soul. Repentance is not, as the Romanists say, the saving plank after the foundering of the ship of Baptism. No, it is rather the ladder on which a person again climbs aboard the ship of Baptism, which never breaks.

Oh, that every one of us would therefore let himself be brought to faith in the promises once given him in his Baptism! Oh, you who do not believe though you have been baptized, what riches of grace and salvation God has given you already and you do not consider or desire them! You belong in God's kingdom and yet willfully want to remain in the kingdom of darkness! The dove of the Holy Spirit has brought you like an olive branch of peace into the ark of the Christian church, but you would rather wither and fade. Oh, open your eyes and return to your baptism; then God will be your God and Father again, your sins will be drowned in the sea of grace, and your Baptism will be the door to heaven.

But you who indeed believe, although in weakness, know this: You have in your Baptism a glorious means of strengthening. Consider this: even if everything becomes doubtful and uncertain, your Baptism stands fast; it happened once, and God does not go back on His word. God has there, so to say, made Himself your captive. Only do not let Him go; do not let your hand of faith go from His covenant of grace. *He* cannot leave you. [Here we have omitted a hymn verse.] Amen.

Tenth Sunday After Trinity, 1847

Luke 19:41-48

God Does Not Desire the Death of Any Sinner, Even Though So Many Perish Eternally

(Licht des Lebens, pp. 496—504)

"May grace and peace be multiplied to you in the knowledge of God and of Jesus our Lord." Amen.

Beloved brothers and sisters in Christ Jesus!

The most fearful revelation contained in Holy Scripture is the revelation of the future fate of most people. For Holy Scripture tells us that all those will be lost who remain in their sins until death and who do not from the heart believe in Christ, in short, all who leave this world without being regenerated by the Holy Spirit. Since the number of those who remain in their sins is always greater than those who truly turn from their sins to God, and since the number of those who do not believe in Christ from the heart is always greater than those who have true faith, therefore it is unfortunately only too certain that according to Holy Scripture more people will be lost than saved. Therefore Christ says expressly: "Many are called, but few are chosen." "The gate is wide and the way is easy, that leads to destruction, and those who enter by it are many. For the gate is narrow and the way is hard, that leads to life, and those who find it are few."

No man can fully perceive the fearful truth that lies in this doctrine, much less describe it completely in words. Whoever does not pass over this doctrine carelessly and indifferently, but takes it to heart, for him from that moment on the whole beautiful world appears to be covered with a mourning-crepe; before his eyes the whole world is changed into a vestibule of an eternal prison, and he sees millions pass by as sheep led to the slaughter. Then this earthly life appears as something of utmost seriousness and importance, for he sees that eternal life or eternal death depend on it. Oh, fearful thought: Every day death, as a busy messenger of the holy Judge, carries hosts of immortal human souls to an unsaved eternity! Oh, fearful thought: There is no land, no city, yes, hardly a house where people are not born who one day will die eternally—millions will one day die eternally! When this thought becomes real to a person, all the vain joy of the world comes to an end forever; when a person meditates deeply on this thought, it becomes unbearable.

Now what do most people do when this revelation of the Holy Scripture is preached to them? Instead of everyone's realizing with fear what a terrible thing sin is, into which we human beings have fallen, and instead of murmuring against sin, people rather murmur against God. When one hears how many will be lost, instead of thinking with much greater seriousness about the salvation of his immortal soul, so that one day he will not be among the host of the lost but rather among the small number of the saved, he rather complains against God and says that a God who lets so many die eternally cannot be a God of love but must be a cruel God who takes pleasure in plunging into eternal damnation those whom He has created.

But, beloved, even though blind human reason accuses God, He has already sufficiently justified Himself through words and works of eternal love, and on that great day of general revelation He will more clearly justify Himself before all amazed creatures—that He does not desire the death of a single sinner, that He is not to blame for the death of a single person, but rather that His serious will was that all, all without exception, should be saved, and that the lost have themselves bound the saving hands of God's eternal mercy which He stretched out also to them. Our Gospel lesson today leads us to this truth, as comforting as it is awakening; it therefore shall occupy us in our meditation.

Text: Luke 19:41-48

In the Gospel just read the Son of God announces temporal and eternal misfortune to the citizens of Jerusalem, but with tears of pity. This permits me to present to you this truth:

God Does Not Desire the Death of Any Sinner, Even Though So Many Perish Eternally

In this connection we shall answer these two questions:
1. *Does God really not desire the death of any sinner?*
2. *How is it possible that so many nevertheless die eternally?*

O Lord God and Father, You "who desire all men to be saved and to come to the knowledge of the truth," help us to realize in a living way this Your love to all sinners; but also awaken us so that we walk on the way by which You want to save everyone, also us. Help us to remain steadfast to the end; then we will there praise Your love in Christ for all eternity. Amen.

I

Does God really not desire the death of any sinner? Oh, well for us that I can most confidently and surely answer yes to this question. Already in the 33rd chapter of the prophet Ezekiel we read God's solemn declaration to all the world: "As I live, says the Lord God, I have no pleasure in the death of the wicked, but that the wicked turn from his way and *live*. . . . Why will you die, O house of Israel?" Here God swears by Himself and speaks the solemn affirmation that He would not be the living God if He took pleasure in the death of any ungodly person. However, when God adds: "Why will you die, O house of Israel?" He wants to say that it lies with a person alone whether he wants to be lost or not; no sin is so great that God cannot forgive it; no man is so deeply fallen and corrupted that God does not desire to save him. Therefore whoever dies eternally has himself chosen death; he has *wanted* to die; he is willfully lost.

Thus God spoke already under the Old Covenant; but how does He explain Himself in the New? We find God's clearest declaration in our Gospel lesson for today. For there Christ, the Son of God, with hot tears laments the temporal and eternal death of the citizens of Jerusalem. Do not say: True, Christ, who came to receive sinners, indeed did that; but what does that show about God's attitude? Consider this: Christ came into the world for the very purpose of revealing the Father to us. In Christ the inscrutable God has come out of His hiddenness. In Him the proper image of God and man is manifested. Whoever sees Him sees the Father. From Christ, therefore, we can and should draw the conclusion about how the Father is disposed. Yes, God now does not want to be known or prayed to except in Christ; whoever pictures God differently than He has manifested Himself in Christ has no God but prays to a dream-picture of his own fantasy. Therefore believing Christians are fortunate; in Christ they see God as in a clear mirror with His face uncovered.

Who can therefore doubt that God does not desire the death of a single sinner? Indeed, no one can look into the heart of God, but in Christ bursting into tears we at the same time see the love in the Father's heart like a sea of undulating love. Christ's tears over the misfortune of the sinners who persecuted Him and were even planning to murder Him—these tears are witnesses that speak louder than words concerning God's heartfelt pity also for the most deeply fallen. In the weeping eyes of the Son of God everyone can clearly read the words: "God really does not desire the death of any sinner!" For how could He weep over a death in which He took pleasure?

Yet, as proof that God does not desire the death of any sinner, we have not only God's own clear declaration and the great pledge of the tears of

His own Son; God has shown this also in deed. Consider this: God made man in His image and not only gave him the choice to remain in His kingdom or to leave it, but also the power to remain faithful to Him and to conquer all temptations. But still man let himself be led into apostasy from God, plunged himself into the abyss of sin, and with that into death and eternal separation from God, the only source of salvation. After this happened, we human beings have no power to rise up from our fall; with our sins we have angered God and have nothing with which to reconcile the offended God to us. Even the angels and archangels cannot help us. If we were to be helped, God Himself had to cast Himself in the middle. And— oh love!—He did that. He sent into the world His own, only begotten Son, with whom He had made this decision already in eternity, and let Him become a human being like us in order that as a human being He might fulfill the Law for us, suffer for our sins, and die on the pole of the cross as the offering of reconciliation.

How? Should God offer more than heaven and earth to save humanity fallen into sin, should God offer His only begotten Son Himself and permit Him to become a man so that He could suffer, bleed, and die for humanity—and shall we still doubt that God does not desire the death of any sinner? Now consider this: When the Son of God shed His blood, God Himself paid a price which is infinitely greater than all the debts of all sinners; for if millions of worlds with their sins had sold themselves into Satan's slavery, a single drop of blood which the Son of God Himself shed would be sufficient to purchase freedom for them all.

No! Until the end of the world Golgotha stands there as a herald who cries throughout the world: Rejoice, you sinners; yes, hear this, heaven and earth: God does not desire the death of any sinner!

It is indeed true, one could still be in doubt about it if God had established great, weighty, and unfulfillable conditions, on the basis of which alone a person could partake of the reconciliation of the Son of God. But also in this, God's love for sinners is revealed as a cloudless, rising sun of mercy. For what are the conditions which God has established for a person who wants to be saved? They are none other than these: He should realize that he is a lost sinner, and should believe in the Son of God crucified for him. What easier way could God have devised so that people could find their way to heaven? See, also this is a clear evidence for the truth: God does not desire the death of any sinner.

Still another question deserves to be answered, and that is this: Has God also done everything so that people may come to know the way on which they can easily flee death and gain life? Has He given all people the means by which they can easily come to the knowledge of their fall and to faith in His Son? Also to this I can joyfully respond: Yes, beloved, already in paradise God revealed to fallen human beings their deep fall and promised them that one day a Savior would come who would atone for their sins and thus redeem them from sin and death and bring them back to the lost salvation. God repeated this Gospel through many prophets in century after century. But in the time of the New Testament, Christ not only sent His apostles into all the world to preach the Gospel to every creature, but he also established the office of the ministry, through which repentance and remission of sins should be preached until the end of days. True, some nations cast aside the Word of God completely and thus deprived also their descendants of it, but God always made provision so that the sound of the saving Gospel might penetrate the farthest corner of the world. Also, God gave everyone a conscience to remind him that he is a sinner and in need of reconciliation with God. If the heathen did not in willful malice stop their ears to the shouting voice of their conscience, they would soon cry out with longing: Oh, that we knew of a source of help to be rescued from the misery of our sins! Wherever the hearts of the heathen sighed in this fashion, God always, often in the most wonderful ways, sent them a herald of His Gospel, yes, entire hosts of evangelists.

God proceeds in the same fashion with the souls who were reared in the midst of so-called Christendom but heard little or nothing of the pure Gospel. God often leads them in a wonderful way so that also they finally find the way to salvation. But who is able to tell all the wonderful ways through which God seeks to bring every single person to the knowledge of his sin and to faith in His Son? Who is able sufficiently to describe the patience and long-suffering with which God pursues even the greatest sinners in order still to rescue and to save them? Ah yes, God shows clearly that He really does not desire the death of any sinner; He keeps His oath. Indeed, there remain some blind spots before our short-sighted eyes, but on judgment day all sinners before the throne of God will have to acknowledge loudly: God did not desire my death; God wanted to save also me. He is and remains just, and all sinners must turn silent before Him.

II

Yet, beloved, if it is really true that God does not desire the death of any sinner, *how is it possible that so many nevertheless die eternally?* Let me now, in the second place, speak to you about that.

Truly, it strikes us strange that, according to the report of our text, the Son of God wept over Jerusalem; for, we think, was it not in His power to avert the misfortune of Jerusalem over which He wept? Yes, was it not He Himself who as a punishment brought about the destruction of Jerusalem in which hundreds of thousands died in their sins? If Christ truly loved Jerusalem so much that the misfortune of the city moved Him to tears, why did He not show His love, instead of through tears, by a merciful rescue of the city?

Beloved, the basis for Christ's action does not lie far afield. It lies in this, that God is not only Love, according to which He does not desire the sinner's death, but is also implacably just and holy, according to which He hates sin, detests it, and will and must punish it in time and eternity. In God there is no contradiction in His attributes as among humans; but His love is also no greater than His justice.

According to His love, therefore, Christ offered His grace to the city of Jerusalem so richly, and with so many convincing signs and wonders, as to no other city in the world. If the inhabitants of Jerusalem had listened to Christ's gracious voice and turned to Him in faith as poor, lost sinners, Christ could have saved them for time and eternity, and surely would have. However, since they, proud and self-righteous, relied on the fact that they kept the law of Moses, and therefore turned their back on their only Savior, yes, mocked Him, persecuted Him, and did not rest until they nailed Him to the cross, God's justice demanded the punishment of the godless despisers. Because they despised the *grace* which alone could give them forgiveness, not even grace could speak for them any longer; it could only weep and give the willfully lost over to the inevitable punishment of justice. Therefore Christ says: *"Would that even today you knew the things that make for peace! But now they are hid from your eyes. For the days shall come upon you, when your enemies will cast up a bank about you and surround you, and hem you in on every side, and dash you to the ground, you and your children within you, and they will not leave one stone upon another in you; because you did not know the time of your visitation."*

In the example of Jerusalem, my beloved, we also see why *in general* so many sinners die eternally, although God does not desire any sinner's death.

For if Christ had not died for sinners, God's love, as great as it is, could not save any sinner, because if God wanted to do that, God would by that action cease to be a good and just God. But after Christ did and suffered everything for the human race that God's justice demanded of them, God's love can save all those who in faith take Christ as their Savior and Mediator. For if God's justice wanted to damn a believing sinner, the Son of God would stand up for him and say: I have paid for him.

But whoever, like the citizens of Jerusalem, will not hear the call of grace in the Gospel; whoever will not let himself be persuaded by the Law and by his conscience that he is a lost sinner, or whoever wants to remain in his sins and does not want to be redeemed from them through Christ; or whoever in pride and self-righteousness despises the grace of Christ and wants to stand before God with his own miserable righteousness, with his virtue and so-called good works; or whoever does not want to confess Christ because of fear and shame before the world: God *cannot* save such a person, although He *wants* to save Him. Sadly God says to him, as it were: "O Israel, thou hast destroyed thyself, but in Me is thine help"[Hosea 13:9 KJV]. "Why will you die, O house of Israel?"[Ezekiel 18:31; 33:11]. Yes, over the sinner's eternal death God's love sheds tears of pity while God's justice inexorably gives him over to it.

What is therefore, briefly, the reason that so many sinners perish eternally even though God does not desire the death of any sinner? It is this: because so many despise the only means of rescue which eternal Love in Christ has prepared for them and offered to them.

Therefore, oh how foolish are all those who go along without true faith in Christ, and at the same time trust in God's love! They do not know the things that make for their peace; they do not know the time of their visitation. They act like those who have fallen into a river and do not want to grab hold of the outstretched, saving hands of their friends and yet hope for help in their love. Just as these must sink even if thousands of hands stretch out to them in love, so must also those who do not believe in Christ perish eternally although God has loved them from eternity and also for them has offered His Son on the altar of the cross. On judgment day these all will acknowledge: God wanted to save us, but we did not want to let ourselves be saved; He knocked, but we did not open to Him; He sought us, but we did not permit ourselves to be found; God opened the door to us, but we did not enter. God wanted to give us life, but we chose death.

Ah, therefore, whoever wants someday to go to heaven, let him hurry to Christ; He is the right, but only, door to heaven. Whoever fears God's justice, let him go to Christ; Christ gives him everything that God's justice can demand. Whoever does not someday want to perish eternally, when the prelude of the destruction of Jerusalem is followed by the terrible postlude of the destruction of the world, let him hold to Christ. He indeed atoned for sin, took the power of death, and conquered hell; in Him all sinners find righteousness, life, and salvation. Without Him no one can escape eternal death; but in Him and with Him no sinner, not even the greatest sinner, can die. For God does not will the death of any sinner. Whoever believes on His Son shall live, though he dies. Amen.

Eleventh Sunday After Trinity
Luke 18:9-14

The Justification of a Poor Sinner Before God According to the Gospel
(Amerikanisch-Lutherische Evangelien Postille, pp. 274—79)

God give all of you much grace and peace through the knowledge of God and of Jesus Christ our Lord. Amen.

In the same, our dear Savior, beloved hearers!

If a man is to be saved at all, he must first be righteous before God. That is an entirely undeniable and irrefutable truth. God is not a God who is pleased with godless ways; anyone who is evil cannot stand before Him. God would have to cease to be God, that is, the eternally and perfectly good Being, if He willed to be united eternally with an unrighteous creature. Therefore, as little as fire can have fellowship with water or light with darkness, so little can God, the Fire that destroys sin, and the pure, eternal Light, have fellowship with the unrighteous.

In addition, God once gave man the Law and in it said: "You shall be holy, for I the Lord your God am holy." There the matter must rest in time and eternity. Already in Creation, God wrote the Law in man's heart; for that reason, when a man does wrong, his conscience accuses him, strongly or weakly, and tells him that he has displeased God. However, because after the Fall the Law in the man's heart was darkened, indeed for the most part wiped out, God through Moses on Sinai again revealed the Law publicly and solemnly and through all His prophets and apostles caused it to be repeated, confirmed, and explained. As surely, therefore, as God must remain God, so surely does He not want to, will not, and cannot recall His law.

Even Christ, the Savior, did not come to repeal the Law. He Himself says in the Sermon on the Mount: "Think not that I have come to abolish the law and the prophets; I have come not to abolish them but to fulfill them. For truly, I say to you, till heaven and earth pass away, not an iota, not a dot, will pass from the law until all is accomplished. Whoever then relaxes one of the least of these commandments and teaches men so, shall be called least in the kingdom of heaven; but he who does them and teaches them shall be called great in the kingdom of heaven." There is no doubt, therefore, that unless a person has a righteousness that conforms entirely to God's holy law, he cannot be saved.

Now it is indeed true that God is Love, Goodness, Patience, Long-Suffering, and Mercy itself; but God is also Holiness and Righteousness itself. All of these qualities are God's very essence, and therefore he has them all in the same high degree. Human beings, can, indeed, do something out of love and thereby violate righteousness; but with God that is impossible. God is not a God who gives a law and is satisfied even if it is not completely kept. No, what He demands and what He threatens must come to pass; heaven and earth would sooner be destroyed! All people who think that God is like a weak human father who is not always serious about His demands and threats, all these thereby only blaspheme God's inviolable majesty, and the god they carry in their thoughts is nothing else than an imaginary, self-made god, nothing but an idol. All who do not have a complete righteousness according to God's law and yet rely on God's love therefore have an empty hope and will surely be lost eternally, as surely as God is a holy and righteous God.

But what am I saying? Beloved, is it possible for a person ever to achieve a truly valid righteousness before God? Are not all human beings from birth full of sinful thoughts and desires? And when God's commands are placed before him, what adult can say without lying: "All these I have observed from my youth," or "I have made my heart clean; I am pure from my sin"? Must not everyone, also the most pious, much more acknowledge: "All have sinned and fall short of the glory of God"?

What am I saying? Must all men therefore be lost because God must remain righteous? No, no, my beloved—praised be God for His eternal mercy—there is a way by which everyone, also a sinner, indeed, also the greatest sinner, can be righteous before God and therefore be saved without God's ceasing to be a righteous God. This is a mystery which could never have come into the heart of man, had not God Himself revealed it to us human beings in His Gospel. Today's Gospel lesson also treats of this mysterious justification of a poor sinner before God.

Text: Luke 18:9-14

The most significant sentence in the passage just read is what the Lord says about the publican: *"This man went down to his house justified rather than the other."* From this we see that through the parable of the Pharisee and the publican God wants to show how also a poor sinner can become righteous before God. On the basis of this parable let me now speak to you about

116

The Justification of a Poor Sinner Before God According to the Gospel

In this connection I will show you three things:
1. *in what it consists;*
2. *what a firm foundation it has;*
3. *by what means alone it is received.*

O Lord God, who Yourself have prepared a way to righteousness and salvation for us sinners and have revealed it in Your Gospel, a clear, bright way, on which even fools will not be led astray, we pray You, give us grace, that all of us may not only know this way but also walk in it and continue in it until our final, eternally blessed goal is reached. Oh, enlighten our understanding so that this way may not be foolishness to us, and rule our hearts that it may not be an offense to us. Ah, on this way You have already filled millions of sinners with comfort in life and death and have finally permitted them to arrive in Your eternal kingdom. Do that also to us sinners, and to that end bless Your Word also in this hour, for the sake of Jesus Christ, Your beloved Son, our Lord and Savior. Amen.

I

Beloved, there is no religion which does not want to show man a way to become righteous before God and be saved. But now, which way do the various religions propose? The heathen says: If you want to be righteous, give everyone his due; but if you have not always fulfilled this duty, bring an offering to the gods. The Jew says: If you want to be righteous, be circumcised and keep the Law of Moses and the writings of our elders. The Mohammedan says: If you want to be righteous, acknowledge that there is only one god and Mohammed is his prophet, and conform to the rules of the Koran. The papist says: If you want to be righteous, keep the commandments of God and of the church; and if in that way you want to be real certain of your salvation, leave the world, go into a cloister, and there keep the threefold vow of poverty, chastity, and obedience. The enthusiast says: If you want to be righteous, pray, wrestle, and struggle until you receive a different heart and feeling; and if you want to be real sure, do not rest until you are perfect and sin no more. Finally, the rationalist or the one who believes in reason says: If you want to be righteous, exercise yourself in virtue and do honorable works; but if you have failed, feel sorry for it and better yourself.

From this you can see that, as different as are the answers which the various religions give to the question of how a man becomes righteous before God, yet all finally come out to this, that a man should and can

117

become righteous before God and be saved in part through outward good works, in part through inner moral improvement.

But what does our today's Gospel say to this? In it we find the exact opposite of all these.

In it a Pharisee and a publican are placed before our eyes. The Pharisee is described to us as a man full of so-called good works; the publican, on the other hand, as a poor sinner without any good works. Of the Pharisee we are told that he went into the temple to pray and here spoke thus to God in his heart: *"God, I thank Thee that I am not like other men, extortioners, unjust, adulterers, or even like this tax collector. I fast twice a week, I give tithes of all that I get."* But of the publican we are told that he could not boast any of these things, but that, on the contrary, he had to be ashamed before God and man because of his previous unrighteousness, so that he did not lift up his eyes, but smote upon his breast and sighed: *"God, be merciful to me, a sinner!"*

And yet—how wonderful!—Christ says that the publican went down to his house justified rather than the other, that therefore, on the contrary, the Pharisee, with all his righteousness before men, was not righteous before God.

So, according to the Gospel, in what does the justification of a poor sinner before God consist? You see, it obviously does not consist in this, that a person through outward, so-called good works or through an achieved or infused inner holiness has made himself righteous before God, but rather in this, that God in grace does not charge his sins to man, who is and remains a sinner, but in spite of them regards, looks upon, and declares him righteous. A person's justification before God according to the Gospel, therefore, is not a deed which man himself does but a deed done by God to him. It is not something that goes on in a person's heart, but something which goes on *outside* of man, namely in the heart of God. It is not to be compared to the activity of a doctor who actually frees the sick person of his sickness and restores him to health again, but it is like the activity of a judge who acquits an indicted and convicted criminal, not only releasing him from all punishment, but even in spite of his crimes awarding him all the rights of a citizen in good standing. A person's justification before God according to the Gospel is not to be compared to an actual cleansing of stains but to the putting on of a nice white garment by which the stains are covered. In a word, it is the *forgiveness* of sins, and indeed of a kind according to which God views a person as though he had never committed a sin, but as though he had always been so completely holy and righteous as God's law demands of all people.

Even David and all the saints of the Old Testament understood well

118

the mystery of this justification. Therefore David in Psalm 32 does not write: Blessed is the man who has committed no sins and who is clean of all sins, but: "Blessed is he whose transgression is *forgiven,* whose sin is *covered.* Blessed is the man to whom the Lord *imputes* no iniquity."

II

We have now seen briefly in what the justification of a poor sinner according to the Gospel consists; the important question immediately arises whether it has a sure foundation. Let me speak of that as the second point.

Beloved, whoever is a sinner and still for this reason hopes to be saved that he trusts in God's goodness—his hope, as we have heard, is without any firm foundation because God is not only Love but also Holiness itself, is not only good, gracious, patient, and long-suffering, but also inviolably just. Consequently it would appear that also the justification of a poor sinner before God according to the Gospel no less lacks a sure foundation. For what does it help a sinner, one might think, if God's grace considers, sees, and declares him righteous, if at the same time God's holiness and righteousness must condemn and damn him? Does not the justification according to the Gospel stand in the same contradiction with God's being, attributes, will and unchangeable law as does the justification which all *false* religions teach?

Indeed, it appears that way; but praise God! it only appears so. The justification according to the Gospel has such a sure foundation that nothing either in heaven or on earth or in hell can overthrow it.

To be sure, in our Gospel this is not extensively set forth, but yet it points it out most clearly. Our text reports that the publican who went down to his house justified had sighed: *"God, be merciful to me, a sinner!"* If one examines in the original language what these words really mean, one sees that the publican intended to say: "God, be *reconciled* to me, a sinner!" Therefore the publican took refuge not in the goodness and grace of God in general, but in His *reconciling* grace; he grounded his hope on the grace which through the Savior's work of reconciliation would be won for mankind.

Here you have the sure foundation on which justification according to the Gospel rests. In a word, it rests on the work and word of the reconciliation of Jesus Christ.

Consider this. When we human beings fell into the guilt of sin, there was no help for us from ourselves, from angels, or from any other creature. Yes, it appeared as if God Himself could not help us. For if God wanted to forgive us sinners out of His grace, His severe, implacable righteousness

119

would eternally object to it. As impossible as it was for all creatures to give advice and to discover means of help, it was not impossible for God's eternal wisdom. It knew and made a way. And what did God do? Since we human beings could not pay the overwhelming debt of our sin and God's justice could not declare us righteous without payment, behold!—O wonder of wonders!—God let His only begotten Son become man and imputed our guilt of sin to Him; and He, the only begotten Son, Jesus Christ, paid our debt in our place through His holy life and through His bitter suffering and death. And when He had paid our debt to the last farthing, God the Father awakened Him again from the dead and gave Him authority to have the completed payment of their debt proclaimed, offered, and given to all people, and with it forgiveness, righteousness, life, and salvation.

See here the basis of the justification of a poor sinner before God according to the Gospel! How? Is this foundation not sure enough? Tell me, can there still be any doubt whether a debtor's debt can no longer be charged to him when another has already paid his debt for him to the last farthing? Can the righteousness of God still hinder grace from declaring such a debtor free of debt? Must not righteousness itself then pass the sentence of grace? Yes, beloved, that's the way it is. Therefore also John in his First Letter in a wonderful way attributes the justification according to the Gospel or the forgiveness of sins not to the grace of God but to His faithfulness and righteousness and says: "If we confess our sins, He is faithful and just, and will forgive our sins and cleanse us from all unrighteousness."

Therefore it is certain, beloved, that the justification of a poor sinner before God according to the Gospel stands unshakable, for it rests on God's righteousness, holiness, and faithfulness as well as on His goodness and mercy. Its foundation is that God's Son has already reconciled all people, has already paid the debt of their sin, and has already won and offered them forgiveness and righteousness.

III

Beloved, now that we know wherein the justification of a poor sinner before God according to the Gospel consists and which firm foundation it has, let us, in the third place, seek to learn also how it is acquired.

According to our text, the Pharisee did not receive it. Why not? Not because he was free of gross sins and was an honorable man before the world, but because he belonged to those described at the beginning of our text as *"some who trusted in themselves that they were righteous and despised others."* In a word, he was self-righteous.

But why did the publican go down to his house justified before God rather than the other? By what means did just he receive this highest and best of all gifts? As we see from our text, he did not even think about doing something in order to achieve justification before God, something about which he could boast before God. On the contrary, he went into the temple as he was, a poor, lost, damned sinner, burdened and bent low by the load of his great guilt, despairing of his own righteousness and piety. Here was the mercy seat, which prefigured the Messiah's reconciliation. Here he sought the help which he could not find in himself, smote upon his breast, and only sighed: *"God, be merciful to me, a sinner!"* or, as we read more clearly in the original, *"God, be reconciled to me, a sinner!"* Casting aside all other comfort, he made the Savior's reconciliation his only comfort. What was to take place for all sinners, that he considered as applying particularly to him; that he laid hold of in faith, and behold!—as our Lord expressly says in our text, he went down to his house justified.

Tell me, according to our text how is justification according to the Gospel received? In a word, it is nothing else except faith, and faith alone.

It cannot be otherwise. What does a debtor have to do to be free of debt when another has paid his bill? He must accept the payment made for him. What must the offending party do to be reconciled when the offended party already has been reconciled? He must accept the reconciliation. What must the prisoner do to enjoy freedom when his prison has been opened for him? He must take the freedom given him and leave the opened prison. What must the indicted and convicted criminal, who has already been pardoned, do in order to enjoy the pardon? He must accept the pardon.

Look, now the sin of all people has been paid by Christ; God is reconciled with them; the prison of God's wrath and hell has been opened; the amnesty with all humanity has been accomplished and through the Gospel is announced and offered to all people. Therefore, what should and can a person do in order to enjoy all this with gladness? Nothing, absolutely nothing, except to take all this. But this is nothing else than *believing.*

Yes, my beloved, believing, believing, that is the only way by which justification according to the Gospel is achieved. Not because faith is such a good work or such an excellent condition of the heart, so that God on that account would and must consider a person righteous; also not because man must do something toward it, even if only a little; but because man cannot and need not do anything toward his justification, because his righteousness has already been won by Christ and in the Gospel is offered, given, and distributed to all who hear it. Therefore St. Paul says: "Christ is

121

the end of the Law, that everyone who has faith may be justified." "For we hold that a man is justified by faith apart from works of law." "To one who does not work but trusts Him who justifies the ungodly, his faith is reckoned as righteousness."

Beloved, is that not an inexpressibly sweet, a heavenly sweet doctrine for us poor sinners? Can there be a hell deep enough and painful enough for those who in enmity against God, pride, and self-righteousness despise this doctrine and do not want to become righteous before God and be saved as poor sinners? Oh, may there be no one among us for whom this doctrine is foolishness and an offense! This teaching is the sun in heaven of the Christian religion, which distinguishes it from all other religions as light from darkness. This teaching is also the treasure which only our Evangelical Lutheran Church, as opposed to all sects, has kept pure and holds fast. Hold fast to this doctrine, my dear Lutheran brothers and sisters! If you do that, you will always have here on earth the right ladder to heaven; then in the darkness of all trials you will always have a brilliant light from heaven; then even in the deep waves of death you will have the right anchor of heaven, which will not let you sink.

Ah, beloved, just now when the pestilence of cholera has again opened wide its deadly maw against us, just now we so much need the pure teaching of justification! It is the best, indeed the only sure preservative and remedy. If you use this means, no fear of death will torment you; and when death finally embraces you with its ice-cold arms, you will not despair but with the publican will call out in faith: *"God, be merciful to me, a sinner!"* And when your ear and eye and mouth close in death, all the angels in heaven and God Himself will open their mouths and say about you: *"This man went justified,"* not *"down,"* but up, yes, up *"to his house,"* to the house of heaven.

To this end may Jesus Christ, our Reconciler, our eternal Righteousness, praised in time and eternity, help us all. Amen.

Twelfth Sunday After Trinity
Mark 7:31-37

The Daily Renewal of a Justified Christian
(Amerikanisch-Lutherische Evangelien Postille, pp. 279—84)

The grace of the Lord Jesus Christ and the love of God and the fellowship of the Holy Spirit be with you all. Amen.
Beloved brothers and sisters in Christ!
Last Sunday we considered a most comforting story; namely, how the deeply fallen publican became justified before God. That story tells us: It is not our righteousness and piety, it is not our good works through which we are justified before God; it is all *grace,* which God gladly gives to all who need it and long for it. From that story we see that God does not reject even the greatest sinner but gladly receives him in grace. If a person is destitute of everything, if a person can produce no good before God, if he sees in himself nothing but sin and therefore can only cry out, "God, be merciful to me, a sinner," God will hear his anxious sighing and will give him the righteousness of His Son, Jesus Christ. [Here we have omitted a hymn verse.]
With such a Gospel, who is there who should not take courage and hope that one day he will be among those at the right hand of God? Whoever knows this Gospel cannot ever despair as long as he still regards it as true and does not deliberately throw it away.
Oh, may this precious doctrine be taken to heart by all who hear it! But the majority gladly let it be preached to them once; they listen with pleasure; they rejoice that heaven so readily stands open to all people; but with this pleasure it also remains. The majority who still seek a church approve this doctrine, but that is also all they do, all that goes on in them; for the open heaven they have no open heart.
Yes, there are such hearers who severely misuse the doctrine of justification by grace through faith and turn this costly medicine for the soul into a poison to the soul; they willfully misuse grace. When they hear that God forgives also the greatest sins, they consider the greatest sins as insignificant. When they hear that the publican was justified when he cried, "God, be merciful to me, a sinner," they think that if they repeat these

words with their tongue and with a pious mien, the work of conversion has been accomplished in them, even though their old disposition remains. Also, many delay their repentance until the hour of their death because they think that there is still time to beat on their breast as did the publican. They talk the way it says in that hymn: [Here Walther inserts a hymn verse which speaks of how a secure sinner thinks]. When such people hear that a man is not justified before God by his works, they draw the conclusion that it is unnecessary to pursue holiness with all seriousness and zeal.

From all of these one sees clearly: The Gospel is a doctrine only for the troubled, those weighed down with sin, and for souls sated with the world. Also today the important message of Isaiah 26 is confirmed: "If favor is shown to the wicked, he does not learn righteousness; in the land of uprightness he deals perversely and does not see the majesty of the Lord."

My beloved hearers, since a week ago I showed how a person is justified before God by grace through faith, let me today show how a justified person should walk in holiness and godliness.

Text: Mark 7:31-37

My hearers, the wonderful cures which Christ effected in the physically sick are pictures of what Christ through His grace works inwardly in souls; Christ confirmed thereby that it is indeed so when He says of Himself: "I am a physician not for the well but for the sick," namely in their soul.

On the basis of the story of our Gospel lesson for today, let me therefore now speak to you about

The Daily Renewal of a Justified Christian

1. *that it is genuine;*
2. *that it is never completely perfect.*
[Here we have omitted a hymn verse.]

I

That not only the doctrine of justification but also the doctrine of sanctification is of great importance to us, we see from the way the Holy Scriptures speak of the latter work. For example, in the Letter to the Hebrews we read: "Strive for holiness ... without which no one will see the Lord." Agreeing, St. Paul says: "Any one who does not have the spirit of Christ does not belong to him. If anyone is in Christ, he is a new creation; the old has passed away, behold, the new has come." Therefore, according to God's Word sanctification is not an appendage which can be considered a part of Christianity or not considered a part of it, but something without which no one can be a Christian.

But perhaps some will immediately think in their heart: If that is true, is not the doctrine of justification by grace alone through faith again being overthrown? If a person becomes righteous and saved by grace, why is sanctification necessary?

My beloved, that is only an apparent contradiction. It is and remains eternally true for the complete comfort of all poor sinners that we do not earn our salvation through our works but that it is given us when we believe in Christ. Now when we talk about sanctification, the question is not how a person becomes a Christian and justified before God but how a person who already is a Christian and justified before God then lives. We are not asking today what the publican had to do in order to go down to his house justified but how the publican afterwards lived in his house when he returned home after being justified.

All this will become clearer when we consider the example of the deaf-mute in our Gospel. He was first a miserable creature and was thereby a picture of all people as they are by nature according to the soul. But this deaf-mute was brought to Christ in order that He should help him, and Christ received him graciously and friendly. See, that is a picture of how a person becomes justified before God. For if a person realizes from God's Word his misery in sin; if with sorrow he sees that previously he was deaf over against God's command and dumb in praising God; if he realizes that the rottenness of his heart is so unspeakably great that he cannot rescue himself from God's wrath and eternal damnation; now, if there arises in such a person terrified by his sin a heartfelt longing after grace, if he sighs after it and turns in this his need to Christ because he hears in the Gospel that Christ is the Savior of all sinners, if the sinner begins to implore: O Jesus, you suffered and died for all, will You not have mercy upon me also? Oh, help me also; O Jesus, be merciful to me, a sinner!—if it comes to that point, Christ receives such a poor sinner in a friendly manner and in God's judgment he is now absolved of all his sins, Christ's righteousness is credited to him, and he is received and adopted as a child of God. That is justification.

O blessed, blessed is the person who goes this way; his salvation is eternally sure. Such a person, who with pain and sorrow over his sins turns to Christ, should hold fast to the Word of the Gospel and firmly believe that he is accepted in grace, even he feels nothing of it in his heart, yes, notices nothing in it but death and damnation. "Though our flesh cry ever: Nay! Be Thy Word to us still Yea!" [*The Lutheran Hymnal*, 226:8].

But we hear not only, my beloved, that Christ received the deaf-mute in a friendly manner, but we read further: *"He put his fingers into his ears, and he spat and touched his tongue; and looking up to heaven, he sighed, and said to him, 'Ephphatha,' that is, 'Be opened.' And his ears were opened, his tongue was released, and he spoke plainly."* Here we have a picture of sanctification. For as the Savior, after having received the deaf-mute in grace, now also healed his infirmities, so the Savior treats the soul of every person who has found grace in Him.

Justification happens in heaven; yes, a poor man, mourning over his sins, often does not know that he has already been justified; often he still weeps tears of repentance on earth, while in heaven all angels are already rejoicing over him. But justification does not remain without its influence upon a person; on the contrary, its first fruit is that a person is *born again,* that is, he receives the Holy Spirit, he receives a new heart and a new disposition, so that he no longer loves sin but has love for God, His Word, and His will, and desires to live piously and godly.

In justification the sun of grace arises in a person's heart; but then it also begins to shine, spreading light, life, and warmth more and more in it, and causes the most beautiful blooms and fruits of a holy life and good works to come forth and to ripen.

When in justification the heavenly Father declares a person to be His child for the sake of Christ, the Holy Spirit also begins His work of sanctification in his heart; even though it begins weakly, it is still genuine. This sanctification does not consist in this, that a person no longer curses, no longer commits adultery and lives in gross works of uncleanness, no longer gets drunk, no longer openly deceives and lies; even a heathen can keep himself from such manifest vices. But sanctification consists in this, that the one justified becomes an altogether different person. He begins to live not to himself but to the Lord Jesus; he does not go to church only now and then, hearing God's Word out of custom or curiosity, but a sanctified person considers God's Word more important than anything in the whole world; such a person has God's Word in mind day and night; he arises with it and goes to bed with it; the concern for his soul's salvation busies his heart constantly; therefore such a person loves to speak of nothing more than the heavenly and godly, of the one thing needful; even when he carries on his earthly business, he does that with a disposition directed to God. Such a person begins also to keep watch over his thoughts and desires; no longer can he so indifferently let evil thoughts pass through his mind; if they arise, he sighs and prays against them. He is an enemy of sin; he doesn't nurse and foster it anymore; he does not let it rule over his will; rather, he fights against sin, also against his dearest pet sin. If he falls into a sin because of rashness or weakness, he does not become hardened in it, but is ashamed of himself, confesses it to God with heartfelt humility of soul and asks for forgiveness; he also lets his fall serve him as a warning and now becomes all the more humble and watchful over himself.

A sanctified person sees the pleasures of the world as vanities; he is therefore no longer on a par with the world; he prefers the pleasure of the Word of God and the edifying fellowship of zealous Christians.

If such a Christian has a day of joy, he seeks to enjoy it *in the Lord;* if he possesses earthly riches, he takes care that his heart does not cling to them but that it clings to God alone. If suffering befalls him, he prays God for patience, guards against murmurings against God, and comforts himself with the glory of heaven which awaits him.

A sanctified person is concerned to offer up his whole life for his neighbor. He looks not on his own things but on the things of others. He loves his neighbor from the heart, not only in appearance, not only with his tongue, but in deed and in truth; he likes to help him in need; he rejoices over his good fortune and has sympathy for his misfortune; he gladly covers his neighbor's sins and is eagerly reconciled with one who has offended him; he has concern for his neighbor's soul's salvation. Finally, what is most noble about the sanctified person is that he more and more sees what he lacks rather than the good which God's grace works in him; therefore, he considers himself as nothing before God and humbly condescends to the lowly.

See, my beloved, this is the form of the new heart and the new life which the Holy Ghost begins to work in those who have been justified, but let me ask each of you: After your justification which you think you have experienced, have you become a new person? Have you received a new heart? Are you now impelled by a new spirit, namely, the Holy Spirit? Has your whole disposition now turned from the earthly toward the heavenly? Have you become an enemy of sin? Do you consider that as vanity in which the world seeks its peace? Do you rejoice as though you did not rejoice? Do you own as though you did not possess? Are you prepared, if it is God's will, to go the way of the cross? Is your heart no longer so cold but warmed by the fire of love? Do you find that the words of Paul apply to you: "If anyone is in Christ, he is a new creation; the old has passed away, behold, the new has come"? Or have you only for the sake of appearance repeated after the publican: "God, be merciful to me, a sinner"? Do you think that in that way you have taken care of the matter of your salvation? Do you want to remain sitting quietly in the lap of the church and think that, although you remain the same old person, you will arrive in the new Jerusalem?

Ah, how many, what a countless number, will one day find themselves deceived who here considered themselves to be Christians! For without sanctification no one will see the Lord. Not for the reason that through sanctification one must first receive grace, but because the person who accepts the grace of God from his heart then also is sanctified by the Spirit of Christ. As soon as the publican Zacchaeus experienced salvation, he immediately wanted to give half of his goods to the poor and to repay those fourfold whom he had deceived. When the woman who was a great sinner was forgiven much, she also loved much.

II

Ah, my dear hearers, as sweet and incomparably comforting as the article of forgiveness and of righteousness and salvation by grace is, so easily one can forfeit this comfort; therefore let no one willfully deceive himself, but let everyone be earnestly concerned about his soul's salvation.

Yet it is a common experience: Those who should be afraid for the most part remain secure and think they certainly have salvation; but those who should not be afraid easily become dependent and fear that one day they will find themselves deceived.

For the sake of these last I must add, in the second place, that the sanctification of justified Christians truly is genuine but will never be entirely complete.

We find an indication of this in our Gospel lesson. Those who brought the deaf-mute to Jesus were, as we can hope, already justified, and therefore God had already begun in their hearts the work of sanctification through His Spirit. Christ forbade them to tell anyone about the miracle that happened. But we read: *"But the more he charged them, the more zealously they proclaimed it. And they were astonished beyond measure, saying, 'He has done all things well; he even makes the deaf hear and the dumb speak.'"* Without doubt these people had good intentions in openly praising this wonderful miracle, but yet in so doing they sinned; their zeal. was not completely pure because thereby they transgressed a command of Christ; their otherwise good deed was spotted with willfullness and disobedience. They acted without a call. Yet they did all this not out of malice but out of weakness.

In this connection, we ought to note this: Justification happens in a moment; as soon as a sinner with sorrow realizes his sin, and desires grace and redemption, God speaks a word in heaven and justification has taken place; sanctification, on the contrary, does not happen so suddenly, but proceeds by degrees and continues to the end of life. Justification is at once complete; in it everyone immediately receives full forgiveness of his sins, the entire righteousness of Christ, and everyone there becomes as much a child of God as St. Peter, Paul, and all the great saints; on the other hand, sanctification first begins weakly after justification and should grow until death, but never comes to perfection. According to justification all Christians are alike, equally clean, holy, and righteous; but according to sanctification there is a great difference. There one is farther ahead, the other farther behind; one is strong, the other is weak. One has more love, more humility, more zeal, more knowledge, more self-denial and self-control than another. Not everyone reaches Paul's level of sanctification, who could say: "I worked harder than any of them"; not everyone reaches the patience of Job, the zeal of Peter, the love of John, the openness of Daniel, the strength of faith of Abraham, or the joy in death of the holy martyrs. And yet *all* of these had to confess again and again: "Not that I have already obtained this or am already perfect; but I press on to make it my own, because Christ Jesus has made me His own." The question is not whether we have already reached the goal, for in this life that is impossible; the question is only whether we are among those who really pursue the goal of sanctification or whether we are still secure in the death of sin. If we are among the spiritual runners, if we run after the treasure, good for us! That is a sign that we have been made alive by grace.

Sad to say today there are enthusiasts who say that a person can become completely sanctified; that is easy to say, but in this life the doing will always fall short. Only a hypocrite or one who has blinded himself, only one who is not ashamed to exalt himself over all apostles and prophets can say of himself that he is completely sanctified. Whoever thinks he is completely sanctified can no longer pray the fifth petition of the Lord's Prayer; consequently, he no longer needs a Savior and the Gospel. Oh, immense blindness! Oh, what a frightful despising of the merit of Jesus Christ and His dearly won grace! Indeed, the holy apostle Paul speaks of those who are perfect, but read the passage itself in Philippians 3. There the apostle says: "Let those of us who are mature be *thus* minded." Minded how? Just as the apostle had said: "Not that I have already obtained this or am already perfect." Therefore Christian perfection consists chiefly in this, that in a really vital way one realizes his imperfection and regards himself as perfect in Christ Jesus.

Not a few doubt that they have the right marks of their state of grace because they still find so much of the life of sin in their hearts. They think: If I stood in grace, I would also have such a powerful feeling of grace in my soul that I could always victoriously and joyfully conquer sin, the flesh, the world, and the devil. Instead of that I must daily fight it out with sin, and I feel so little that it appears that my faith has no victorious power over the world and sin. I cannot say with Paul Gerhard: "The world against me rageth, Its fury I disdain" [*The Lutheran Hymnal,* 192:5].

129

In this connection we should consider this: When a person is justified, God in the beginning ordinarily lets him taste many sweet things of His grace in order thereby to draw him from the world and to Himself. Therefore especially a beginner in Christianity often thinks he has progressed beyond the world, sin, and Satan. If things remained that way, the person would soon become secure and proud. Therefore the faithful God in most cases again withdraws the sweet feeling of grace and power and gives it to them sparingly and trains them more in humility; now one first becomes really poor, must beg everything from God daily, and must more and more hold to Jesus' word of grace so that one is not lost. Whether God's work of sanctifying grace is active within a person, one can tell especially by whether there is still a battle between the flesh and the spirit within him. If a person experiences that, although sin rages within him, there is within him another something that restrains him from the rule of sin, that drives him again and again to prayer and God's Word, that when sin takes him by surprise drives him to go to Jesus and to pray for forgiveness—it is absolutely certain that such a person is not dead, because a dead heart does not fight.

Now, my beloved, you who are already in this fight, fight on courageously and do not spare yourselves; but do not fight in your own strength; draw it daily from the well of divine grace in Jesus Christ, and you will surely not fall mortally, but finally you will hold the field and obtain the victory. [Here we have omitted a hymn verse.] Amen.

Thirteenth Sunday After Trinity, 1846

Luke 10:23-37

Love for the Neighbor—a Fruit of Faith

(Licht des Lebens, pp. 522—34)

"May grace and peace be multiplied to you in the knowledge of God and of Jesus our Lord." Amen.

In the same, our Lord, heartily beloved hearers!

The ways by which most people want to be saved are chiefly two. For they either want to do good works but not believe, or they want to believe but then do no good works.

The class of those who want to do good works but not believe is in our day particularly large. Very many think that our present time is one of great enlightenment. They feel that the realization has finally come that most of the articles of the Christian faith oppose the laws of reason. Therefore, in their view, an enlightened man cannot accept such articles of faith; much less dare he still espouse the old prejudice that in the matter of salvation everything depends on faith. Rather, they hold that it is an entirely indifferent matter what sort of faith or religion a person has; good works are the right key to heaven now and in eternity; whoever lives properly already now carries salvation in his breast, and in eternity he will stand on nothing else except the blessed knowledge that he was a good person on earth.

As large as is the number of those who preserve these principles, still there are also a great number of baptized Christians who, on the contrary, indeed believe, but then do not want to do any good works. They think that, according to Holy Scripture, whoever believes and is baptized will be saved, and therefore it is now unnecessary for a person to be troubled and anxious about good works and sanctification. Christ has done everything for us; therefore they feel there is nothing further for us to do. Christ has suffered all for us; therefore they hold that it is superfluous to want to suffer for the sake of Christ and to crucify the flesh with its affections and lusts. Christ, they say, made the way to heaven so easy for us that a person

131

can get to heaven without his own works; therefore why should one want to make this way needlessly difficult?

Now as different as these two classes appear to be, they really travel the same road. For we dare not think that the first indeed have good works, but without faith, and the others indeed have the right faith, but without good works; rather, both groups lack the one as well as the other. With all their bragging about good works, the first are without true good works; and the others, with all their bragging about faith, are without the true, proper faith. For whoever casts faith aside does not have good works either, and whoever casts aside good works surely does not have the true faith. For, in the first place, Scripture clearly says: "Whatever does not proceed from faith is sin." Therefore all the works of an unbeliever however glorious their appearance, are before God nothing but sins. But Scripture also says further: "Faith by itself, if it has no works, is dead." Therefore a faith without works is nothing; it is powerless, useless, a shadow-faith which can save no one.

But perhaps some will ask: Do *both* save, faith *and* works? Does not Holy Scripture say clearly that faith *alone* saves?—That is indeed true; and it *remains* eternally true for the comfort of all sinners. But also this is certain and true: If a person does not have a heart that is full of the desire and love for all good works, he does not *believe* in Christ. For whoever comforts himself in Christ from the heart, into his heart Christ Himself enters and fills him with love toward God and his neighbor and with a heartfelt desire for holiness in body and spirit. As little as heat and light can be separated from a fire, so little can good works be separated from true faith. It is not that faith first becomes good and saving through good works; but when faith is good, it brings forth good works as a good tree surely brings forth good fruit.

Oh, faith is a different thing than most people imagine. It is a mysterious work of the Holy Spirit, who works it only in those souls who can find comfort neither in themselves nor in the whole world. It is a heavenly light and a divine power which makes the heart alive and renewed and a spring of love and all good works.

It is well known that our Luther writes about this beautifully in his *Preface to the Letter to the Romans*. Furthermore, he writes about this in his *Lectures on Genesis* (on 12:4): "Faith is a vigorous and powerful thing; it is not idle speculation, nor does it float on the heart like a goose on the water. But just as water that has been heated, even though it remains water, is no longer cold but is hot and an altogether different water, so faith, the work of the Holy Spirit, fashions a different mind and different attitude, and makes an altogether new human being" [*Luther's Works,* American Edition, Vol. 2, pp. 266—67].

We are shown this also in our today's Gospel lesson. Therefore let us consider it in this hour.

Text: Luke 10:23-37

On the basis of this Gospel lesson, let the object of our present consideration be:

Love for the Neighbor—a Fruit of Faith

In this connection we shall consider:
1. *that without faith there is no true love;* and
2. *that without love there is no true faith.*

I

Our today's Gospel appears at first glance flatly to contradict many other places in Holy Scripture; for what in other places is ascribed to faith, Christ here appears to ascribe to love of God and the neighbor, hence to good works. In other places the answer to the question: "What must I do to be saved?" is: "Believe on the Lord Jesus, and you will be saved." But in our Gospel lesson we hear that as a lawyer once asked Christ: *"Teacher, what shall I do to inherit eternal life?"* Christ directed the inquirer not to the Gospel but to the law and said: *"What is written in the Law? How do you read?"* Thereupon the lawyer answered: *"You shall love the Lord your God with all your heart, and with all your soul, and with all your strength, and with all your mind; and your neighbor as yourself."* And what judgment did Jesus make on the basis of these words? He said: *"You have answered right; do this, and you will live."* Is that not strange? Can a person really keep the Law completely and in that way be saved or achieve eternal life? According to our today's Gospel lesson, are not the preachers of works in our day absolutely right when they teach that not faith but deeds save?—It really appears so, but let us consider the whole thing in its connection; then everything will soon appear entirely different.

As we hear in the beginning of our Gospel lesson, Christ called His disciples and all those who saw and heard Him blessed. As the lawyer heard this, he may have been highly provoked. How, he might have thought, and why should just these who see and hear this rabbi be so blessed? Can He teach something better than the Law that God gave us through Moses? Are not all Jews already saved if they only keep this? Will this Jesus perhaps reject God's law? All right, he thought, I'm soon going to be behind this mystery. Therefore he asked Christ what he must do in order to achieve eternal life. Luke says explicitly that the lawyer thereby only wanted to *"put"* Christ *"to the test."* He was not concerned about finding the way to salvation. But Christ, who saw into the lawyer's heart and knew that he was self-righteous and labored under the delusion that he could keep the Law, yes, that he had kept it, now answered this fool according to his foolishness and said to him: You are entirely right; keep the Law completely and you will surely be saved.

Christ dealt with him here as a wise doctor. If a deathly sick person tells his doctor that he is entirely well, that he should spare him his medicine, that he could, if he wanted to, get up and do what a well person does, then perhaps the doctor would say to the sick one: If you really are so well, get up from your bed; take this burden and carry it up this mountain. Just as the doctor says this not because he believes that the sick person is really able to do this, but only by advising such an attempt wants to bring the sick one to the realization of his deathly sickness and his complete powerlessness, so also Christ said to the self-righteous lawyer: *"Do this, and you will live "*—not because He thought the lawyer could really do this, but to bring him to the realization that although the Law shows a way to heaven, a human being fallen into sin cannot go that way. Christ wanted to say: Beloved friend, just try once to love God above everything in deed and in truth and your neighbor as yourself; then your courage will soon sink, and you will soon ask about another way to salvation.

That this is the right explanation we see clearly from what follows. For we are told that the lawyer *"desiring to justify himself"* asked further: *"And who is my neighbor?"* From this we see incontrovertibly that through His answer Christ did not want to strengthen the lawyer in his self-righteousness, but wanted to dissuade him from it and persuade him that he could not keep the Law and that it was impossible to gain eternal life through love and good works.

This explains also why Christ, after the lawyer's last question, told the story of the good Samaritan. Christ thereby wanted to teach the lawyer that until now he had in no way truly loved his neighbor—that as a poor sinner, as a transgressor of God's commands, he first had to believe in Him, namely in Christ, and so receive a new heart; only then would he be able truly to love his neighbor. In a word, through the example of the good Samaritan Christ wanted to show that true love does not dwell in the heart of any natural man, that without true faith there is also no true love. Let us also now *learn* that from this example.

As is well known, Jews and Samaritans at Christ's time lived in extremely bitter enmity; particularly, there was among the Jews a deep-seated hatred and great contempt of the Samaritans. When, therefore, the Pharisees wanted to really disgrace Christ before the Jews, they said: "Are we not right in saying that You are a Samaritan and have a demon?" Now our text tells us about a Samaritan, hated and despised by the Jews.

Once a Jew journeyed from Jerusalem to Jericho and on this trip fell among robbers. They *"stripped him and beat him, and departed, leaving him half dead. Now by chance a priest was going down that road; and when he saw him, he passed by on the other side. So likewise a Levite, when he came to the place and saw him, passed by on the other side."* So the priest and the Levite, although they knew the Law well, had no love for their brother lying in misery. They saw him lying in his blood, but their heart remained unmoved. They did not even speak a word of comfort to the poor man, let alone help him with deeds. They thought: Who knows who the man is; who knows whether he would thank you; to help here would also make us too much toil and trouble. They passed by.

But behold! Soon after, a Samaritan came; and when he saw him who had fallen among the thieves *"he had compassion."* Although he was a Jew, although he was an enemy, yet the Samaritan's heart was deeply moved over his enemy's misfortune. And what does he do? He goes to him, binds up his wounds and pours in oil and wine which he had brought for his own refreshment. Ah, he thinks, you are well, you can sooner do without this refreshment than this miserable person. But more, the Jew is so badly maltreated that by himself he can go no farther. The Samaritan does not consult long with flesh and blood, but resolves to cover the difficult and dangerous way on foot, lifts the wounded man on his beast and brings him to the nearest inn. Here, full of love, he himself takes the responsibility of caring for the sick man, remains with him all night, and when on the next morning duty calls him to continue his journey, even now his love does not grow tired. He does not think: You have now done your duty; others may now do something also. No, he regards himself as the one called by God to help this unfortunate man; and therefore, as he leaves, he gives the innkeeper several pieces of gold and says to him: *"Take care of him; and whatever more you spend, I will repay you when I come back."*

See, there is an example of what true love to the neighbor is. From this we see that true love does not first ask whom it should help; it helps everyone, even the bitterest enemy, when he is in need. And it does not only help him, and does not only not rejoice over the enemy's misfortune, and is not only not filled with thoughts of revenge, but it is also inwardly moved with pity, and takes the enemy's trouble to heart as its own. True love also does not wait until one is asked; it also does not first ask: "What's in it for me? It acts even when the one helped does not know who helped him, yes, even when no one knows, and even when perhaps one can expect nothing except ingratitude. Furthermore, true love does not give only from what is left over; it denies itself refreshment and ease if only it can help another who needs it more, for it seeks not its own but that of another. It places itself in danger of life for the sake of the neighbor, yes, it is ready, if necessary, actually to give its life for the sake of the brethren. Finally, true love does not tire out. As long as it sees need, so long it has an open, gentle hand; as long as wounds give pain, so long its assuaging oil flows; as long as the miserable person returns asking, so often its willingness is renewed, to advise, to give, and to help.

Now what person can say that by nature such a love lives in his heart? Indeed, the unbelievers brag that their religion is a religion of love, but which unbeliever loves people without exception as himself? Indeed, also unbelievers out of proud generosity can do something good even to their enemy and thereby "heap burning coals upon his head." But where is there even one who truly like the Samaritan is troubled in his heart over the misfortune also of his bitterest enemy and who in his heart rejoices when things go well with his enemy? Furthermore, where is the unbeliever who would rather do good when no one knows, yes, who even then does not cease to love and do good when he reaps only ingratitude for it? Which unbeliever, if he once does a good deed, does not soon become tired when there seems to be no end to the giving and helping? Which unbeliever would rather suffer injury than that another suffer? Which unbeliever is not ruled by selfishness? Which one looks as intently after the benefit of his neighbor as he does after his own advantage? Which one does not in most cases follow the common saying: Everyone is his own neighbor? Which one follows the principle that in this world a person should not live for himself but for his neighbor? Which one does not above all seek his own honor, his own advantage, his own well-being? Which unbeliever carries out his business only so that he may serve others and not so that he may serve himself?—None, not even one; all, without exception, *seek after themselves;* the *chief guiding principle* in all they do in their whole life, in their buying and selling, in their trade and traffic, in their work and activity, is—their own advantage. All without exception go through the world like the priest and Levite, seek their own advantage, and pass by their neighbor. All their love is only a fake love. For where there is no true faith, there no true love can be either.

But it is equally true that *without true love there is also no true faith;* let us now, in the second place, consider this.

II

My beloved, as impossible as it is for natural man truly to love his neighbor, so impossible is it for a believer not to love his neighbor.

Although all of us are born with self-love and self-seeking, although like a poison it has spread through humanity's every vein, although, so to speak, it has become second nature for us, faith has the wonderful power to kill this poisonous snake in our bosom, to free us from our natural self-love, and to create a new spirit within us, namely the impulse to love our neighbor as ourself. As cold and stone-hard as is our heart by nature toward the need and welfare of our neighbor, particularly when our own advantage comes into play, still our heart is warmed and softened by the fire of God's love as soon as true faith enters in.

Indeed, if faith were nothing more than regarding the Holy Scriptures as true; if it were nothing more than being intellectually persuaded that Christ is the Son of God and Savior of the world; further, if it were nothing more than a self-generated thought or delusion of the heart which says: I believe—then, indeed, faith would not have the power to transform human beings permeated with self-love in all their powers and desires and to make their barren, stony heart green and blooming with true love.

But what then is true faith? It is such a living knowledge of Christ and His grace that one places in Him the trust of his whole heart; it is such a living conviction that the Gospel of Christ is God's voice, Word, and promise that one relies on it with his whole heart, seizes the Word of grace as his only anchor of hope, builds on it as on a rock, and holds fast to it as to the gracious, outstretched hand of God Himself. True faith is such a living, bold trust that what Christ did and suffered for all happened also for our benefit, that one becomes so sure of the forgiveness of his sins and his salvation that one is prepared every moment to die in it.

Now, is it possible that such a living persuasion and knowledge of the inexpressible love of God in Christ Jesus can come into a person's heart without such a heart's being moved and set on fire with flames of love? Is it possible that a person can obtain such a living trust in God's word of grace, such a daring hope in His promise, and such a certainty of his salvation without his heart's becoming happy and having a holy desire to do for others as God has done for him? Oh, certainly not! Consider, if a person, even if he were a miser, once quite unexpectedly received an immeasurable inheritance sent to him; on the day he received it, would he not be happy, friendly, and amenable not only for himself but also toward everyone? But a believer knows that he daily receives the greatest and richest inheritance, namely the forgiveness of all his sins, the grace of God, eternal life and salvation. Therefore the believer can do nothing else; he must daily be happy, friendly, and obliging toward everyone, not begrudging all, even his enemies, their good things, rejoicing over their good fortune, being sad over their adversity, and counseling, comforting, and helping them wherever he can. As God has dealt with him, so he must again do to his neighbor; as God lived, suffered, and shed His blood for him, even though he was an unworthy sinner, yes, His enemy, so the person who in a living way believes this now can no longer live for himself but must live for his neighbor.

That a living, true faith works this in a person we can see in the prophets and apostles and in all true Christians about whom Scripture and church history tell us. As soon as they began to believe from the heart that they found grace with God, so soon they also began to consecrate their whole life to their fellow-redeemed brothers; more and more their whole life became a life of love until death; they were the benefactors of their world, the friends of all men, and they preferred rather to suffer a martyr's death than to silence the Gospel of grace which they preached that also others would get to know Christ and be saved.

Therefore let no one think he has faith if he has not yet come to this love and still lives for himself. Without love, there is no faith. Just as a person is dead when his heart is cold and beats no more, so faith is dead when love is cold and its inner impulses and emotions cease. God's Word says clearly: "For in Christ Jesus neither circumcision nor uncircumcision is of any avail, but faith working through love." Again: "But if anyone has the world's goods and sees his brother in need, yet closes his heart against him, how does God's love abide in him?" And in another place we read: "He who does not love does not know God; for God is Love."

Therefore let no one think: It is surely nice when a Christian is friendly, loving, reconcilable, charitable, and good toward everyone, also toward his enemies and those who offend him; but really, not everyone reaches that point. It is indeed true that not everyone reaches that point, but not because the true faith does not always have this fruit, but because not everyone comes to true faith, because the faith of most is only an empty thought of the heart. The person in whose heart there does not live love to all his fellow redeemed, also to his enemies, may nevertheless boast about faith, but he still does not know the unspeakable grace and love of God in Christ. This sun has not yet arisen on him; the light of faith does not yet burn in him; he is still a child of the night and of death, for Scripture says: "He who does not love remains in death."

Now if we examine ourselves about this, what do we find? O hearer, do you wander through the world as a good Samaritan? Or do you still, like the priest and Levite, pass by your neighbor and live for yourself? Have you already poured your oil and wine in the wounds of your brother, yes, of your enemy? Or have you always thought only of yourself and your desire?—The way you answer will speak the verdict of either life or death.

If you find yourself without true love to your brothers, ah, then it is time that you repent, for then you are still in death; and with your cold, self-seeking heart you will never see life. Yes, if you perhaps have to say to yourself that you not only pass by your brother but are often yourself his tormentor, that you not only pour no oil or wine into his wounds but that you inflict wounds by hurting his feelings, by slander, by fraud and things like that, ah, then be afraid for yourself! For God's Word says: "Anyone who hates his brother is a murderer, and you know that no murderer has eternal life abiding in him." Therefore, although you have not attacked anyone with murderous intent, God nevertheless calls to you in the words of the prophet: "Your hands are full of blood," namely full of the blood of your brother whom you hate in your heart. Ah, repent of your blood-red guilt and, as did the murderer on the cross, turn to the Crucified, that He may still receive also you by grace into His kingdom and still put that love into your heart which flows from His wounds to all sinners.

But you, you dear children of God, who love your brothers, who love them from the heart and gladly want to be an offering for them; you who have a reconcilable heart, a friendly eye, and a charitable hand for everyone; you who consider yourselves only stewards of your goods, which you are to distribute to your own and to the poor; but you who feel how incomplete your love still is; you who have already shed many a bitter tear over your cold heart, over your flesh and blood that does not want to be obedient to the spirit: know that here no person attains to complete love; everything, also love, remains imperfect. Therefore seek comfort not in your poor love but in Christ's rich, complete love; it covers your lack. But the more you will consider this love and sink yourself in it, the more your own love will grow, until it will be complete there when you will see God's everlasting love face to face. Amen.

SERMONS
FOR SPECIAL OCCASIONS

Sermon for the Opening
of a Synodical Convention
Psalm 119:23-25

How Comforted We Can Be in the Face
of All the Reproaches We Experience, as Long
as We Stand on God's Word Without Wavering
(*Lutherische Brosamen*, pp. 452—61)

"Grace to you and peace from Him who is and who was and who is to come, and from the seven spirits who are before His throne, and from Jesus Christ the faithful Witness, the Firstborn of the dead, and the Ruler of kings on earth. To Him who loves us and has freed us from our sins by His blood and made us a kingdom, priests to His God and Father, to Him be glory and dominion for ever and ever. Amen."

Honorable and beloved fathers and brothers in the Lord!

We live in a fearful time of a double apostasy. On the one side a horrible, complete unbelief rules; on the other, a falsified and only apparent faith.

The manifest unbelief of our day is a frightening thing; it keeps uncounted multitudes from the church and swallows up their children like a voracious monster. But more fearful still in many ways is the false faith and apparent faith. For this is within the church itself like a devouring cancer; within the church it fills thousands upon thousands with false hope and, *under the guise of Christianity,* deceives concerning the soul and salvation.

It is true: After the time of the reign of rationalism there has followed within the church a period of more general belief to a certain extent, notably on the part of the servants of the church. In the lecture halls of the universities, in the pulpits of the churches, as well as in books and religious journals, the Christian religion is now again for the most part praised as a religion of supernatural, divine revelation and truth. And, on the other hand, fresh unbelief which rejects all the mysteries and wonders of Christianity is fought against.

But far be it that the representatives of the present so-called believing movement have penitently returned to the doctrine of the first church and the church of the Renewal; rather, with rare exceptions, they expound that the old system, as they call the old, unchangeable Christian faith, no longer can be held in the clear light of newer, deeper investigation, or as they like to say, scholarship. While some frankly say that this or that of the old articles of faith must be given up, others say (although they mean the same thing) that one can indeed let the old foundation stand but that one must build further on it, namely that also in respect to doctrine one must advance and in that way lead the church to necessary perfection. They say that the time when chief importance was placed on a simple, fearful guarding of what had been entrusted—that time of fighting and wrangling about pure doctrine—is fortunately past. And it would only be a hindrance to the revival of the kingdom of God if a person undertook again to conjure up that sad time. They no longer want to hear anything about a church which is the faithful guardian of an inerrant faith; rather, each party finds its glory in *not* maintaining that they have the clear truth but in declaring that they represent only an important particular direction, while they recognize all others with their different doctrines as representatives of equally valid directions.

Therefore today under the name of Christianity and the Christian, yes, the Lutheran Church, an entirely new religion is making its appearance. They have still retained the titles of the old articles of faith and by that means deceive innumerable inexperienced Christians; but they have given them an altogether different meaning. As once in paganism, they change the truth itself into a lie. By the divinity of Christ they understand a certain godliness of His; by the church of the Third Article, in which we believe, they understand a visible institution, namely by the communion of saints and believers they understand a kingdom of those who rule and those who obey; by the office of the ministry they understand a particular privileged position; by the kingly priesthood of all believers they understand the freedom of Christians to engage in pious practices; by the church's hope they mean its future visible glory on earth lasting a thousand years; by the free gracious gift of faith they mean a person's free decision; by death they understand a going to an intermediate state. They no longer regard the doctrine of justification alone by grace through faith as the Alpha and Omega, the heart and soul of all doctrines; rather they regard the perpetual urging and pressing for sanctification and good works now dominant in sermons as a sign that today more living Christianity is being planted and fostered than in the so-called good old days. While under the cloak of a zeal for sanctification the Gospel is emptied of its full comfort, so under the cloak of freedom from the yoke of Old Testament law they rob the eternal law of love of its deep and rich spiritual meaning.

But the most fearful thing about it and the real root of this complete deformity of the whole Christian faith in our time on the part of the pretended believing teachers is their complete defection from the ruling principle of all of Christendom, namely from the principle that the entire Scripture is the Word of the great God. Almost without exception those theologians of our time who want to be considered believers explain that the belief that every word of Holy Scripture is inspired by the Holy Spirit is no longer worthy to be held, an altogether obsolete stance. They say that God's Word is indeed in the Holy Scripture, but God's Word and Holy Scripture are not one and the same thing, but two altogether different things; therefore the correct teaching about Christ must be taken and established not from individual sayings of the Scripture, as one formerly did, but only from the totality of Scripture. To find this right teaching is a matter for the learned or the church. What David in Psalm 11 writes about the manifest enemies applies also to those with pretended faith: "The foundations are destroyed."

Therefore, honored and beloved fathers and brothers, dare we let it concern us that we are overwhelmed with reproaches from all sides because we do not want to know about such apparent belief, do not want to extend its adherents the hand of fellowship, and do not want to pull with them under the same yoke? No, surely not! In this we share the lot of all true children and servants of God in the Old and New Testaments. Let us learn from David how comforted we can be.

Text: Psalm 119:23-25

According to this let us now consider:

How Comforted We Can Be in the Face of All the Reproaches We Experience, as Long as We Stand on God's Word Without Wavering

We can do this

1. *because in it we have the inerrant truth in spite of all our capacity to err;*

142

2. because in it we also have the righteousness which avails before God in spite of all our unworthiness.

I

My brothers, since we not only call ourselves Lutherans but also profess that the teaching and the faith of our Evangelical Lutheran Church is the one, pure, divine truth in all points, we find the reproach coming from many sides, first of all, that in our blindness we manifestly consider ourselves to be infallible.

How? people call to us, are you not also men who can err? Is it not intolerable arrogance that you declare your teaching to be the only true one, and that you reject and condemn every other teaching as false doctrine? Is it not laughable pride that you want to be smarter than all the believing scholars of our time, who together testify that on the basis of the most scrupulous testing they must give up the old teaching in many points? When you compare yourselves with the great chorus of believing learned people of our day, should not Christian modesty demand of you that you assume that you could sooner err than they? Should you not blush when you want to set yourselves up as judges of such men and as censors of their learned writings? And if you want to yield in no point, what do you make of yourselves? What else do you do except to declare yourselves infallible, as does the pope in Rome?

My brothers, there is no doubt: If we were here dealing with matters which could be decided by human learning or astuteness or the power of high offices and positions, we surely would have to lower our eyes in shame as often as we experienced such reproaches; for we must freely confess that we are not only men who, like all, can easily err, but also that as far as learning, astuteness, and high office and position go, we have reason only to humble ourselves before God and man. But here we are dealing with something altogether different. That reproach is therefore not at all pertinent to us.

According to our text, also David had to complain: *"Princes sit plotting against me";* for also he had to hear the reproach, not only from the less important, but also from the *"princes,"* that is, from the highest and wisest of his time, that he was so blind because he considered himself alone to be wise. But what comforted David in the face of this reproach? He himself tells us as he adds: *"Thy servant will meditate on Thy statutes. Thy testimonies are my delight, they are my counselors."* David wants to say: It is not because I consider myself more learned, more astute, and higher in office or position than they, or consider myself infallible, that I adopt no teaching of even the wisest and most respected people of this world,

143

but because the statutes and testimonies of the Lord, because the Word of God, the Highest and Only Wise One, are my infallible and never-failing *"counselors."*

My brothers, that is the reason why we can be comforted in the face of all reproaches which we experience, as long as we stand unwaveringly on God's Word: because, first of all, we have therein the infallible truth, in spite of all our capacity to err.

When people continue to call to us: Do you want to be infallible? we reply: Far be it! But the Word of God on which we stand is infallible. Christ prays in His high-priestly prayer: "Sanctify them in the truth; Thy Word is truth."

Yes, someone says, God's Word is indeed the truth, but is God's Word not in many places dark and therefore very easily misunderstood? Therefore can you not, just as others, err in your *interpretation* of God's Word? Do not all heretics appeal to Scripture, and in the past have not thousands upon thousands who believed in God's Word erred under them?—But, my brothers, indeed one can err although he believes in God's Word, but not in those things in which a person stands firmly on God's Word. God's Word is not dark and capable of being misunderstood, but light, clear, and certain in all articles of faith. Peter writes: "And we have the prophetic Word made more sure. You will do well to pay attention to this as to a lamp shining in a dark place." That also those who believe in God's Word err in articles of faith does not arise because God's Word is unclear and capable of being misunderstood, but because also believers in God's Word only too often, instead of following the clear Word of God, follow their reason, their conceit, their heart, their prejudices, or their human point of view. Therefore our church sings: [Here Walther inserts a hymn verse about the firmness of God's Word].

I ask you: How is it that the whole Reformed Church does not believe in the real presence of the body and blood of Christ in the Lord's Supper? Are Christ's words not plain and clear: "This is My body; this is My blood"? How is it that they do not believe in the regenerative and saving power of Baptism? Are Christ's words not plain and clear: "Unless one is born of water and the Spirit, he cannot enter the kingdom of God," "He who believes and is baptized will be saved"? How is it that they do not believe in the universal grace of God and in the universal redemption of Christ? Are not the words of God plain and clear: "God . . . desires all men to be saved," and "Christ . . . gave Himself for us to redeem us"? How is it that they do not believe in Christ's omnipresence according to His human nature? Are not Christ's words, which He spoke in His state of humiliation, plain and clear: "No man hath ascended up to heaven but he that came down from heaven, even the Son of man which is in heaven" [KJV]? How is it that many who confess to believe in God's Word do not believe in the freedom of Christians from the law about a specific sabbath day? Are the words of God not plain and clear: "Therefore let no one pass judgment on you in questions of food and drink or with regard to a festival or a new moon or a sabbath. These are only a shadow of what is to come; but the substance belongs to Christ"? How is it that today many deny that all believing Christians of the New Testament are priests who originally possess all priestly rights, offices, and powers? Is God's Word not plain and clear: "But you are a chosen race, a royal priesthood, a holy nation, God's own people, that you may declare the wonderful deeds of Him who called you out of darkness into His marvelous light," and "All are yours"? How is it that today many do not want to believe that the congregation is the final tribunal in the church? Are the words of Christ not plain and clear: "If he refuses to listen to them," namely several, "tell it to the church; and if he refuses to listen even to the church, let him be to you as a Gentile and a tax collector"? Why is it that today many reject the teaching that the church of Christ, which is His kingdom and has the promise, is in a true sense no visible institution but an invisible kingdom? Is Christ's word not plain and clear: "The kingdom of God is not coming with signs to be observed; nor will they say, 'Lo, here it is!' or 'There!' for behold, the kingdom of God is in the midst of you"? Why is it that today some dream of a special thousand-year glory of the church at the end of days? Is Christ's word not plain and clear: "When the Son of man comes, will He find faith on earth"? Finally, how is it that today so many make clear teachings of God's Word into open questions whose falsification one must therefore bear in the church? Is God's Word not plain and clear: "A little leaven leavens the whole lump," and "Let him who has My Word speak My Word faithfully, What has straw in common with wheat"?

My brothers, what is the situation when anyone raises the reproach against us that with our insistent holding fast to our doctrine we make ourselves guilty of arrogance by claiming to be infallible?—As long as without wavering we stand on God's Word, we can be comforted in the face of this reproach, for in the clear Word of God we really have the infallible truth in spite of all our capacity to err. God did not give His Word to Christians in order that it should still be submitted to the learned as though only they could open up its meaning. No, the divine Scripture is not a collection of ambiguous oracular sayings and riddles which only man's sagacity can solve for us; rather, God's Word is plain and clear in all articles of faith, brighter than the light of the sun, for it makes the blind see and the fools wise. God's Word is the true, infallible, ecumenical council, for it is the great assembly of prophets and apostles, in which the judging voice of Christ Himself always gives us an unambiguous answer as often as we ask for guidance.

Therefore our opponents may assert that they are fighting only against the infallibility of our human interpretation of the Word of God, which can have more than one meaning; but the doctrine we confess is not our interpretation but nothing else except the clear and infallible Word of the Lord itself, which interprets itself. What God once said to Samuel applies also to us: "They have not rejected you, but they have rejected Me." Oh, how comforted we can therefore be in the face of all the reproaches we experience!

II

Yet, my brothers, we can do this as long as without wavering we stand on God's Word also, in the second place, because in God's Word we have the righteousness which avails before God in spite of all our unworthiness.

Since we not only declare that our doctrine is the one pure divine truth in all points, but also want to enter fellowship in faith and into sacramental and church fellowship only with those who stand with us in the unity of doctrine and faith, some raise the reproach against us that we manifestly by our arrogant self-exaltation consider ourselves better and more worthy than others.

How? some call to us, do you not also belong to those about whom it is written: "All have sinned and fall short of the glory of God"? Is it not a manifest pharisaism that you separate yourselves in this manner? Is it not a sign of rude self-righteousness that you refuse the hand of fellowship offered you? Are there not in your churches black sheep and angry quarrels? Are there not sometimes also among your pastors such as become guilty of serious blunders and mistakes, yes, manifest hirelings on account of whose awful fall into sin the name of the Lord is blasphemed among the heathen? Therefore should you not rather be happy when others are not ashamed to have fellowship with you, instead of refusing those who ask you? Should you not first take out the beam from your eye before you withdraw from others because of the splinter in their eye?

Without doubt also David once experienced similar reproaches in connection with his faithful confession of the truth. Some reminded him of his deep fall and explained his inflexibility in matters of faith as a sign of his impenitence. What did David do then? Among other things, he says further in our text: *"My soul cleaves to the dust; revive me according to Thy Word!"* Far be it that David became unmindful of his deep fall and again ever exalted himself above any sinner; rather the memory of his fall always pressed him into the dust. While his enemies amused themselves over his so-called self-exaltation and impenitence, he was often tired from sighing and watered his bed the whole night and wetted it with tears. But in no way did he doubt, even though such bitter judgments were made about him, but cried out as his soul lay in the dust: *"Revive me according to Thy Word!"* The Word, to which he held without wavering, was his comfort; above all, the word spoken over him by the prophet: "The Lord also has put away your sin; you shall not die." For in that he found the righteousness which avails before God in spite of all his unworthiness.

My brothers, it is the Word which comforts us also in the face of the second reproach, namely that we in intolerable self-exaltation regard ourselves as more worthy than others.

Ah, we ourselves realize it only too well, yes, we know it better than can the sharp eyes of our enemies spying on us, that our Synod has no reason self-righteously to elevate itself above any other fellowship; rather, we know and confess openly before all the world that if God wanted to enter into judgment with us, He would have to reject us. It is not any kind of pretended greater worthiness, holiness, and perfection which we ascribe to ourselves and about which we boast and which comforts us over against the reproaches of our enemies, but nothing except the Word in which God the Holy Spirit announces, offers, gives, and bestows to all who repentantly acknowledge their sins the satisfaction of the Son of God accomplished for the sins of all sinners. As the princes speak against us, we say with David: *"My soul cleaves to the dust; revive me according to Thy Word!"* And we believe firmly that the answer which God gives to this our prayer is the same assurance which Christ once gave His disciples: *"You are already made clean by the Word which I have spoken to you."* [Here Walther has a short hymn stanza about the merit of Christ's suffering, and then quotes *The Lutheran Hymnal,* 528:3:]

> I build on this foundation
> That Jesus and His blood
> Alone are my salvation,
> The true, eternal good.
> Without Him all that pleases
> Is valueless on earth;
> the gifts I owe to Jesus
> Alone my love are worth.

Indeed, our opponents contend that to our necessary humility and repentance belongs above everything else the modesty and peaceable disposition according to which one extends the hand of brotherhood to such as, according to our view, depart from and falsify God's Word. But far be it! Precisely because in the Word alone all worthiness of human beings before God, all safety, and all salvation lie enclosed, therefore this

147

rather belongs to true humility that a person, even though deeply fallen, says with David: "Can wicked rulers be allied with Thee, who frame mischief by statute?" and "Do not I hate them that hate Thee, O Lord? . . . I hate them with perfect hatred." Just because in the Word alone we have found the mercy which has befallen us and daily befalls us, so love to God and our brothers compels us to place the least tittle of that Word, this treasure above all treasures, over all human holiness, wisdom, favor, peace, friendship, and fellowship.

O my brothers, let us also in the future stand without wavering on God's clear and gracious Word! If we do that, we can be comforted in all the reproaches we experience; for in it, I repeat, we have the infallible truth in spite of our capacity to err, and the righteousness which avails before God in spite of all our unworthiness. To the Lord our God be praise and honor eternally. Amen.

Address at the Dedication of Concordia Publishing House

Monday afternoon, Feb. 28, 1870, Holy Cross Church, St. Louis
(*Der Lutheraner*, XXVI, 14 [March 15, 1870], 107—09;
Lutherische Brosamen, pp. 576—82)

Let the beauty of the Lord our God be upon us; and establish Thou the work of our hands upon us; yea, the work of our hands, establish Thou it. Amen.

When 430 years ago, in the year 1440, John Gutenberg, a native of Mainz then living in Strasbourg, by chance pressed the insignia of his heraldic ring in a small tablet of wax and the row of raised letters thus instantly formed met his eye, suddenly like lightening there flashed through Gutenberg's mind the thought that by means of carved or cast letters a whole page of print could be reproduced with a push of the hand; in that instant the art of printing was born, like a newborn child.

This was, my friends, an achievement which not only the children of the world have again and again praised and glorified as highly significant, but one which has always been recognized also by the church as one of the most important achievements in world and church history.

Significant, among others, is Luther's statement about it. "Printing," he once said, "is the highest and last gift through which God advances the cause of the Gospel; it is the last flame before the extinction of the world." The great Strasbourg theologian Conrad Dannhauer writes: "God has sent the art of printing as a midwife, with whose help thousands of letters are born in an instant like Cadmus' armed soldiers." Another orthodox theologian of Strasbourg, John Schmidt, has no scruples about saying in a sermon that the art of printing "was invented by divine inspiration." A third Lutheran man of letters, named Cellarius, even ventures the opinion that through the invention of the art of printing John Gutenberg benefited the world more than did Christopher Columbus 52 years later through the discovery of America. This high regard for the noble art of printing also on the part of the church therefore was the reason that in 1640, the bicentennial of the art of printing, and in 1740, the tricentennial, many churches in Germany publicly and festively conducted services with sermons of praise and thanksgiving and hymns of joy.

149

And indeed properly so, my friends.—How would I find the time if I wanted to mention merely all the most important blessings the world has received through the discovery of the art of printing? Although the invention of gun powder and in our time the application of steam power and electricity have had no less *influence* in changing the world, nevertheless all these and similar inventions have not brought the *blessings* that the art of printing has. Without the art of printing, how many thousand outstanding books of lasting worth either would not have been written or not so widely disseminated or soon lost again! Rightly does the old Dannhauer remind us that in the 60 years following the invention of the art of printing, 1440 to 1500, more books appeared than in all the preceding centuries of the Christian era put together. By 1500 there were no less than 200 printing shops in Germany alone.

But of all books, it is well known that this was especially advantageous for the dissemination of the written Word of God. The first major book published was a Latin *Bible;* the first major book published in German was a German *Bible.* Whereas formerly a person had to pay 400 to 500 Kronenthaler for a parchment copy of the Bible, now the printing press immediately delivered a copy for 60. As easy as it was for the Synod of Toulouse in 1227 to pass its decree that a layman could not even own the books of the Old and New Testament, yes, that in church a layman could read the Psalter and Breviary only in Latin—after the invention of the art of printing and the resultant great multiplication of copies of the Bible, it was impossible to enforce the ban on the Bible as had been done formerly. True, we read that Carlstadt was made a doctor of theology before he had even seen a Bible; true, we read further that Luther was already 18 years old when for the first time in his life he came upon an entire Bible, in the library of the University of Erfurt, and there with joyful amazement saw that it contained more than what he had hitherto found of it in the devotional books used in the churches; true, we read finally that the second Bible Luther found, in the library of his cloister in 1505, was chained down with an iron chain. But soon a change was to come with the help of the constantly improving printing press, and those chains would forever be burst asunder.

Indeed, Gutenberg himself did not realize what a significant instrument he was in the hand of God and why this invention, obvious and close at hand, was delayed until his time; he thought only that he found a rich source of money for himself, which he therefore wanted to keep hidden as much as possible. But soon it would be revealed to the whole world that the art of printing was destined by God to be first a forerunner and then a true servant of the Reformation determined by God. In the year 1415 the

150

Council of Constance had stifled the voice of the faithful witness to the truth, John Hus, in the fire and smoke of the burning stake, and no one imagined that only 25 years later, in 1440, another John would invent an inanimate instrument which would mightily avenge the death and silencing of the holy martyr and would proclaim the suppressed truth in all the world, not with one but with millions of metal tongues.

At the time of the beginning of the art of printing, Christendom looked lamentable. It was then that the Turks finally occupied Constantinople, at that time the chief city of the Christian empire, and so established themselves in Europe to this day. Then also the papacy had won the battle against all the councils which gave themselves the assignment of reforming the church in head and members. Hence the popes now, as demonstrably invincible, thought they could look forward to a further unhindered course of conquest—and no one, not they themselves, imagined that with the letters of the printing press the gun barrels were already cast which soon would bombard the castle of the Roman antichrist and would break through the walls of their doctrines and commandments of men, substituted for the Word of God, and their arrogated stolen rights, and would shake at its deepest foundations the whole antichristian thousand-year-old structure.

For what happened? The man of God, Martin Luther, arose and not only again preached the old Gospel of free grace and the only salvation of all sinners in Christ, but also took up his pen and *wrote* what his tongue proclaimed; but the printing press quickly carried his herald's word, as on wings of the wind, in countless pages into all regions of the earth. Rightly, therefore, old and new theologians call the art of printing "wings of the angel" who, according to the prophecy of the Revelation of St. John, from the year 1517 onward flew through the sky of the Church with the everlasting Gospel. Those 95 theses, the first stones the new shepherd boy gathered from the clear brook of Holy Scripture to throw against the Roman Goliath, were with the help of the printing press spread and read in all of Germany within 14 days, throughout all of Europe within four weeks. It was really, as the childlike Myconius writes, as if the angels themselves were here the messengers. Hereafter Luther wrote one piece after the other, which fell like manna from heaven upon the famished Christians in the wilderness, but on the enemies of Christ like fiery cannonballs bringing death and destruction into their terrified camp. There is no doubt that the invention of the art of printing, only a short time before, was the God-ordained, chosen instrument which 350 years ago should and really did serve the wonderful, speedy progress of the pure Gospel that was again resounding. Already in the year 1519 the renowned

151

and learned book publisher of Basel, Frobenius, reported to Luther personally that he was sending his reformation writings in countless copies to France, Spain, Italy, Brabant, and England, where they would everywhere be voraciously devoured. So, in many respects it is unquestionably to be attributed to the art of printing that the Jesuit Cardinal Bellarmine had to write and publish the following wrathful complaint: "The pestilence of the Lutheran doctrine, which arose in Saxony, has forthwith taken over practically all of Germany. Then it moved north and east, to Denmark, Norway, Sweden, Hungary, etc., and has with equal speed been brought west and south, to France, England, Scotland; it has finally even crossed the Alps and gained a foothold in Italy. The new sect, not satisfied with the western and northern kingdoms, makes bold to sail also to the Orient and the South, to the Greeks, the Indians, even to the new world."

With horror the Roman antichrist and his servants noted what a fearful weapon had been brought into action against them in the form of the printing press. Therefore not only the monks in particular hated the honorable art of printing as something highly dangerous and destructive, but also Pope Alexander VI in 1501 issued a bull in which all were threatened with the ban and other so-called ecclesiastical punishments who sent any sort of book to press without having it examined and approved in advance by censors he appointed. Yes, as late as 1536 papal theologians in Paris ventured to advise King Francis I to abolish and forbid by law all printing establishments in all of France.

But a useless, impotent battle! After God had given the world the splendid gift of the art of printing, He also took care that it would be preserved to the world; and so even today libraries are full of treasuries of books, which are of incalculably more worth than all the gold and silver of the earth; and still the presses work day and night to enrich the world with ever new treasures of books. For that praise be to God in time and eternity!

Yet, my friends, it is true, also Satan and all powers of darkness have seized upon the printing press as a powerful instrument to share with the world also their thoughts and principles. And just now, as never before, Satan's press is incomparably more active than the press of God. Not only does one book after another now leave countless presses, in practically all languages of the world, in which God's Word, yes, the existence of God and His rule itself, and everything holy, everything that is merely moral, is assailed and ridiculed; daily in millions of copies the press now delivers into the hands of millions of readers newspapers in which religion and morals, all divine as well as human ordinances, are mocked and ridiculed and sin, as if it were a joke, is made the object of pleasurable entertainment.

But alas! even those products of the press that do not have the purpose of fighting against religion and morals nevertheless almost without exception now contain much of the soul-destroying poison of unbelief, or false belief, or unchristian or antichristian principles for living. In a word, the press in our day delivers either pure poison for the soul, or else food for the soul which is largely poisoned, on which millions now daily eat eternal death.

But, my friends, shall I on that account perhaps take back what I said at the beginning about the boundless blessing which God with the invention of the art of printing intended for and actually presented to the world and the church? Far be it from me! Why, that is the history and fate of all God's good gifts in the world. God gives them to people for life, and most people use them for their death; God gives them to people for a blessing, and most people change them into a curse; God gives them to people for their salvation, and most people use them for their greater damnation. We see this, above all, in the case of the precious Gospel, of which the holy apostle Paul says that in the case of those who are being saved it is a fragrance from life to life, but for those who are perishing it is a fragrance from death to death. Now just as the Gospel is to be recognized and in all eternity cannot be sufficiently praised as "the power of God for salvation to everyone who has faith," so also the noble art of printing, in spite of all misuse of it to eternal death and destruction, is nonetheless to be recognized and praised as a dear and precious gift of God.

Therefore it is fitting that we have joyfully gathered here for a festive celebration to dedicate a new publishing house with common prayer and praise to God. For this new publishing house of our dear Evangelical Lutheran Synod of Missouri, Ohio, and Other States is to serve not the flesh, not the ungodly thoughts of the world, not error and falsehood, not the teachings of men, in short, not the devil, but also not half God and half the flesh and the world, not half Christ and half the devil, not half the truth and half error and falsehood, not half the Word of God and half the teachings of men, but God alone, Christ alone, the Word and kingdom of God alone, the church of Jesus Christ and the truth alone.

Indeed, this our new synodical publishing house is also to serve for the dissemination of all sorts of good sciences and arts, which contribute something to the furtherance of the temporal welfare of world and country. For the church not only has the duty to be concerned also about this, but the blessing which she thereby institutes for citizens and for government always ultimately flows back upon it, the church. That is why the prophet Jeremiah already called to the church of the Old Testament in the midst of Babylon: "Seek the welfare of the city . . . for in its welfare you will find your welfare." For that reason also Paul commands all Christians to pray "for all men, for kings and all who are in high positions, that they may lead a quiet and peaceable life, godly and respectful in every way." But as to what may be published in our new publishing house, not earthly benefit and advantage, not money, not honor, not popularity, but only God's Word shall decide. With God's Word in hand, faith and love shall stand watch over our publishing house like an angel of God.

Oh, my dear friends, do we not therefore have cause today to arrange for a festival of joy, now that we are at the point of dedicating a press belonging to God? Yes, truly! At a time in which not only the children of unbelief but even some Christians out of selfishness or for the sake of popularity use the noble art of printing to print and sell books which contain the poison of false doctrine—in such a time we must rejoice greatly that the Lord has helped so that today we see before us, built and gloriously completed, a publishing house which shall serve only God. It is a wonder before our eyes.

So then, in conclusion say now with me in your hearts: Our Concordia Publishing House shall be dedicated to God as long as it stands; dedicated to Him, the all-holy triune God, God the Father, God the Son, and God the Holy Ghost. From this institution may nothing go forth except that which serves the glory of this great God and the temporal welfare and eternal salvation of men. Cursed be the hands which write something contrary to God's Word so that it may be multiplied through this press of God! Cursed be those hands which in this institution with knowledge and willingness set type for or print anything contrary to God's Word! Cursed be the hands that offer for sale any literature from this publishing house that has the poison of hell mingled with it! Cursed be this entire house with all its equipment if the devil once succeeds to draw it into his service; God's wrath must then destroy it with fire and wipe it off the earth. On the other hand, blessed be the hands which write for this institution to God's honor and man's salvation! Blessed be the hands that set type and print it! Blessed be the hands that circulate it! But finally may all be highly blessed in time and eternity who in faith have offered and will still offer their trouble and concern, or earthly means, or at least their wishes and prayers for this press of God!

Yes, may the Lord always permit all who go in and out of our Concordia Publishing House to walk under His blessing and protection— and may He guard it according to His almighty power and goodness from all misfortune and make it a place of temporal and eternal blessing until the end of days, through Jesus Christ, the Son of the living God and Savior of the world of sinners. Amen.

Day of Repentance, 1870
Galatians 5:7

We Are No Longer What We Were
(Casual-Predigten und -Reden, pp. 172—82)

God, holy and just God! You are not a God who is pleased with an ungodly life; whoever is evil cannot stand before You. You are a strong, jealous God, visiting the iniquity of the fathers upon the children to the third and the fourth generation of those that hate You. You are a just Judge and a God who daily threatens. If people will not repent, You have sharpened Your sword and stretched Your bow and taken aim and have placed upon it a deadly arrow; You have appointed Your arrows to destruction. Ah! You great and fearful God, with deep shame in our souls we lie today before Your face, for we must lament and confess to You: We are no longer what we were! We have fallen! We have sinned against heaven and before You and are no longer worthy to be called Your children, Your congregation.

Ah! where shall we turn in this distress on account of our sins? Where? No creature in heaven and earth can protect us against Your just wrath. Lord, You holy God, whom we have offended and angered, You Yourself are our City of Refuge to which alone we can flee. Even though we are no longer worthy to be called Your *children,* nevertheless You are and remain our *Father,* and today, on this day dedicated to our general repentance, You Yourself call to us: "Return, faithless Israel . . . I will not look on you in anger, for I am merciful . . . I will not be angry forever."

O You God of grace, who do not desire the death of the wicked, but that he turn from his way and live, today bless the preaching of Your Word about repentance through the powerful working of Your Holy Spirit upon the hearts of us all and make this day a day of our united return and reconciliation with You. Help that there may be no one among us who hardens his heart against the rebuke of Your Word, but that we all give honor to You; that we acknowledge that we have fallen and confess this to You with penitent hearts; that we seek Your grace and hold fast to it in faith. Hear us, Lord, hear us, for the sake of Jesus Christ, Your only begotten Son, our Savior, Mediator, and eternal Advocate. Amen.

Text: Galatians 5:7

My beloved brothers and sisters in the Lord, the Galatian congregations, to whom the words just read are directed, are one of the most fearful
warning examples of the apostolic period. Not only were they established
by the great apostle to the Gentiles, Paul himself, but in the beginning they
also flourished gloriously as did few others of the apostolic congregations.
When Paul came to the Galatians the first time and described Christ to
them, their hearts welled up with indescribable joy at the sound of this
heavenly message. Paul gives them this testimony: "You... received me as
an angel of God, as Christ Jesus .... For I bear you witness that, if
possible, you would have plucked out your eyes and given them to me." At
that time no insult or persecution could disturb their consummate joy in
the Gospel. To remind them of the time of their first love, Paul calls to
them: "What has become of the satisfaction you felt?" And that this their
blessed joy was not simply an excitement of their feeling but the fruit of a
genuine faith in the heart we see from our text as the apostle gives them also
the testimony: *"You were running well."* They therefore showed their faith
also in their life. They had become a model apostolic church. In the midst
of the godless heathen surrounding them they shone, unspotted from the
world, as lights in this world.

But what happened?—False teachers, with a great display of holiness,
sneaked in among them and threw suspicion on the doctrine that faith
alone makes one righteous and saved before God and described how they
could lift them to a higher plane of Christianity as they led them from faith
back to works, from the Gospel back to the Law. And ah! the unfortunate
Galatians did not watch, let themselves be deceived, and fell away. With
indescribable pain the holy apostle heard about this. Therefore he calls to
them in his epistle: "O foolish Galatians! Who has bewitched you, before
whose eyes Jesus Christ was publicly portrayed as crucified?... I am afraid
I have labored over you in vain. .... You are severed from Christ, you who
would be justified by the Law; you have fallen away from grace."

See here the fall of an entire once-flourishing congregation!—But
perhaps you will say: Of what purpose is this example today? Have we also
fallen away from the Gospel? This is my answer: It is true that in doctrine
we have not yet fallen away as did the Galatians; it is true that among us the
Lord has not cast down the lamp of His Word from its place; it is true that
the pure, clear Gospel of righteousness and salvation through faith in Jesus
Christ alone still sounds forth from all the pulpits of our churches. But in
spite of that—how could I remain silent about it today?—in spite of that a
fall has happened also among us. *We are no longer what we were!* What the

holy apostle in our text calls to the fallen Galatians applies also to us: "You were running well; who hindered you from obeying the truth?"

Therefore today, on our annual congregational day of penitence, I call to you in the name of the Lord:

We Are No Longer What We Were!

In connection with this theme, let me set forth three points:
1. *what change has taken place among us;*
2. *what the cause of it is;* and finally
3. *what our present situation today demands of us.*

I

"We are no longer what we were!" That, my beloved brothers and sisters, is what I want to shout deep into your hearts today on our day of repentance and through which I want to wake you up to turn again through God's grace to earnest love and to serious, fervent zeal.

When I call to you today: We are no longer what we were! I do not want to remind you that we have grown from a few to many, that from a poor congregation we have become a wealthy one, that from a despised little group we have become an organization recognized in part even by the world, that we now have more and larger and more beautiful churches, more schools achieving greater things, that we have grown in clarity of Christian knowledge on many points, and have made progress in all kinds of good churchly programs. No, circumstances like this are not for our day of repentance but for our celebration of thanksgiving, for all of these are evidences that also today we must cry out: "The steadfast love of the Lord never ceases, His mercies never come to an end; they are new every morning."

But my call: We are no longer what we were! today should be a call to repentance, for ah! our congregation has experienced not only happy change for which we have the Lord to thank, but also a most sad change on account of which we have reason to weep and lament in earnest repentance.

Or is it perhaps not so?—Surely you will all agree with me: On the question of whether a congregation has gone forward or backward, everything hinges on how things stand, first, in respect to faith in God and, second, in respect to love to the neighbor; for just as only faith and love make a Christian into a genuine Christian, so these two parts alone make a congregation into a genuine congregation.

Therefore I ask you beloved brothers and sisters who nearly 32 years

157

ago helped establish this congregation: How did things stand then and in the immediately following years in respect to our *faith in God?* It is true, as far as proper understanding is concerned, we were in a bad way; many and dangerous errors still darkened our souls. But must we not acknowledge to the glory of God that nevertheless our faith in God was then living and powerful and our highest good and treasure? Had we not emigrated only for the sake of our faith? Had we not, only for the sake of our faith, joyfully left house, home, fatherland, and in the case of many, the best-loved things they had in this world? And what did we seek here? Did we seek, like most immigrants, mountains of gold, a good, comfortable life, honor, and prestige? No, our one real goal was to save our souls, here to live our faith, here to have pure, proper worship services and a genuine Christian school for our children.

We were bloody poor, but that did not deter us on all Sundays and festival days, and at an inconvenient time, from streaming into the haven provided for us by heterodox Christians and from gladly offering our last pennies for the establishment, maintenance, and furtherance of church and school. Although forsaken and covered with disgrace, we did not therefore woo the friendship of the world but were fearfully concerned not to be stained by it and allow it to cheat us out of our heavenly riches. With what zeal at that time we read our little, pure Lutheran paper, while we loathed even to have in our homes papers which ridiculed religion, let alone to kill our precious time with their indecent reading matter for entertainment! Our tireless zeal was to be grounded in the correct doctrine; matters dealing with godly doctrine and the kingdom of God were our best-loved entertainment, and an explanation from God's Word about matters of faith or life seemed to us then as a precious discovery; in our meetings godliness ruled.

But how do we stand now in comparison with that time, first, in regard to our faith in God? Does our congregation still have the form of a congregation in which care for the soul is the highest concern and God's pure Word is regarded as the highest jewel of this life, as the greatest treasure on earth? Ah, we would be liars before God and men if we wanted to assert this. For in the last years have we not been of a mind to cancel one festival day after another, and when a festival day was resolved upon for a weekday, on which money could be earned in business, haven't our churches usually been practically empty? Instead of an eager digging for the gold of the truth in Holy Scripture and in other good books, isn't there now among most of our members a running and rushing after earthly riches, after big business deals, after friendship, honor, and recognition by the world, or after a good, comfortable, carefree, delightful life? It is true,

158

our religious papers are still taken and paid for by our members, for the opinion still prevails that thereby one is supporting a good thing. But who reads them? Who studies them? Who delights in their contents? With only too many the opposite is the case. One finds religious papers dry and has no time for them, but godless newspapers must conscientiously be read; they are the daily nourishment of our immortal spirit. Indeed, the fortunes of the kingdoms of the world interest most people, but, in the case of too many, interest in the kingdom of God is about to die. Indeed, people do things for the improvement of our Christian schools, but for many the important thing about such improvements is greater worldly knowledge; the thorough instruction in God's Word has become an adjunct and an incidental matter. And, finally, what unchristian judgments are now sometimes expressed in our meetings!

Still I ask you further, you old, first members of this congregation: How was it nearly 32 years ago and in the following years, second, with respect to the *love of the brethren?* How we then were inwardly united like a single family! Of how much worth to us was even the least member of the congregation over against an unbeliever, even though a respectable man of the world! How eagerly one helped another in his temporal need and difficulty! What zeal there was to bring also others to God's Word, and what joy if only one soul was won, even though it were a poor wood cutter! How mightily brotherly admonition was practiced, so that as often as a brother wanted to go on wrong ways, immediately many set out to warn and rescue him! How long it was, therefore, before we for the first time had to exercise the necessary ban in our congregation!

But how do we stand today in comparison with that time in respect to this brotherly love? It is true that because of the growing crowd of our members the old familiarity can no longer be present among all members, but do not many all too often manifest indifference, yes, coldness also over against those about whom they know that they are brothers and belong to the congregation? Is it not only too evident that, on the part of many, a respectable child of the world is regarded more worthily and highly than a brother or a sister? How hard it is in our congregation which has become wealthy to make a small loan to a poor man in need! And has not the zeal to win souls practically died out among us? Has not brotherly admonition almost entirely vanished? Does not "backbiting and evil speaking" against brothers and sisters rule in almost all of our meetings?

I intend that these few references persuade also those who until now did not realize it: *We are no longer what we were.* It is true, in the early years of our congregation's existence many injurious things occurred which we had to confess with tears to God on our days of repentance; but ah! the evil which previously, one could almost say, was only an exception has now almost become the rule, and the good which was once about the rule has now practically become the exception; what once only spotted our congregation has now practically become its dress, its character. What the holy apostle tells the Galatian congregations in respect to doctrine: *"You were running well; who hindered you from obeying the truth?"* therefore applies to our congregation in respect to faith and love.

II

Yet, my brothers, after we have now reminded ourselves of some features of the sad change which has occurred in our congregation, let us now, in the second place, seek to explore what *the cause of it is.*

My beloved, as it appeared almost inexplicable that the once so gloriously blooming Galatian congregations, which an apostle had founded, could so quickly be led to apostasy through false teachers, so that the apostle himself calls to them in amazement: "Who has *bewitched* you," it seems almost more inexplicable that our congregation, instead of going forward, has obviously gone backward, although it not only retained the pure, clear teaching but with every year grew richer in doctrine, knowledge, and many glorious gifts. Our congregation, as a memorial to God's mercy, was once wonderfully rescued by God from great spiritual dangers and now for almost 32 years has been blessed richly with spiritual blessings and gifts beyond countless congregations in all of Christendom. Should one not, therefore, think that our congregation necessarily *must* have become the model congregation for all of Christendom? Should one not think that all our members *must* be so strong in faith, so fervent in love, so courageous in witnessing, so free of the love of the world with its goods, joys, and honors, so zealous to live only for God, in short, so genuinely godly as no other Christians in the world? Tell me, what is the reason that, on the contrary, our congregation not only has not grown in all the qualities of a genuine congregation of God but rather from year to year has more and more lost them?

Ah! my brothers, the reason is no mystery; it is only too clear and evident. Shall I tell you what it is? In a few words, it is manifestly this and nothing else: As the Galatian congregations fell because they permitted the Gospel to be falsified and taken from them, so our congregation has fallen because, although we hold to the Gospel, we have changed it through misunderstanding and misuse; for the situation in every congregation depends upon nothing else than its relationship to the Gospel, whether it has it, and if it does, how it understands and uses it.

For more than 30 years on every Sunday and festival day the sweet

160

Gospel of the free grace of God in Christ Jesus and of righteousness and salvation without the merit of works, alone through faith, has been preached. All sources of comfort in the Word and the holy sacraments have been opened up, and all the heavenly blessings of the complete redemption and reconciliation of Christ in their whole, rich fullness have, as it were, been poured into our laps.

But what happened? We have manifestly gotten accustomed to the comfort and have become secure. More and more the thought has crept in: All right, if it is all a matter of grace, why should one trouble himself with repentance? If everything depends on faith, why should a person still work out his salvation with fear and trembling? If Christ has already made satisfaction for all our sins and has earned their forgiveness, why does a person have to be so concerned about every sin? If Christ has already fought for us, conquering the world and the devil, why should a person have to be on guard so earnestly against the flesh, the world, and the devil and fight against them? The thought has crept in: I indeed believe; therefore I am righteous and will be saved even if I have never been converted to God and I can remain a saved Christian even if I do not live in daily contrition and repentance. With this false comfort, as though wearing an iron breastplate, we come to church. Now even if the sharp arrows of earnest sermons of punishment and the Law ring from the pulpit, they no longer penetrate the breastplate of our false comfort. We think this way: We know the secret for becoming saved without having to first seek the kingdom of God and His righteousness; and so those among us who once were zealous Christians become lukewarm, lazy, and entangled with the world, its concerns, goods, and joys. They finally fall into spiritual sleep, impotence, and death; and the others, who were not yet converted Christians, remain without repentance.

This misunderstanding and misuse of the Gospel, and nothing else, is the reason we no longer are what we were, even though the Gospel which makes us righteous, holy, and saved is continually preached and heard. Among us this heavenly seed falls either on the trodden path, and Satan takes it from us; or as on stony ground, and for that reason it does not take root in us; or as among thorns and thistles, and it must therefore be choked in us. For if we received this heavenly seed in a repentant heart, as on good ground, we would bring forth the fruit of a new life with patience some thirtyfold, some sixtyfold, some a hundredfold. Already in the early church and in the church at the time of the Reformation, countless blooming congregations withered again and finally became a desert because of a misunderstanding and misuse of the Gospel; and that's the way also our congregation will go to ruin, if it does not turn around.

161

III

Now the question arises: *What does this our present circumstance therefore demand of us today?* Let me, thirdly, with at least a few words answer this most important, decisive question.

The first thing our situation demands of us is that we do not deny it, but that in deepest humility we admit it before God and men. The most awful thing in God's kingdom of grace on earth is not the sin, the sickness, the fall, but the denial of sin, the excusing and palliation of it, self-justification, hard-heartedness and obduracy in sin. The most awful thing also in our situation would therefore be if we compared ourselves with other congregations and comforted ourselves that it is a lot worse in many other congregations than in ours. Such thoughts would make our evils unhealable. We must rather consider that of us, to whom much is given, much is also required.

Oh, let us therefore today above all appear before the holy God as a fallen congregation in genuine contrition and repentance. Let no one shove the blame on another, let no one exempt himself from the culprits; let everyone come before God today as the guilty member of a congregation burdened with guilt; yes, let all of us as one man say to God: "Lord, we have sinned and done evil before You; we have wantonly despised Your grace; we have fallen." Ah, my brothers, consider this: Today our congregation is like a besieged city, around which because of our unfaithfulness God's threatened displeasure has already gathered like an army demanding our surrender. Oh, let us not defy God in insane blindness, but let God be our Conqueror, and let us give ourselves over to Him as His captive.

Yet, my brothers, we need to think of God not as a king who is provoked to wrath and thirsty for revenge, so that our fate is uncertain, depending on favor or disfavor; no! with the Lord there is forgiveness, that he may be feared. Therefore we must surrender ourselves to Him in a firm faith in His grace alone. Throughout more than 30 years God has demonstrated that He has thoughts of peace toward our congregation and that it is His desire to do good to her, yes, to adorn and crown her here and yonder. Although we have been unfaithful to Him, He has remained faithful to us; He does not want the good work which He has begun among us to lie there, but wants to move it forward and bring it to completion until the day of Jesus Christ. Therefore let us today also confidently say to Him: Lord, tear up our book of debts and from this day forth begin again Your old rule of grace among us.

Oh, if today as one man we return to God repentant and believing, this day will be the day of the rebirth of our congregation and a time of a new visitation of God's grace, and new, great blessings will dawn upon her.

162

It is true that the history of the church shows, as Luther so often mentions, that the flourishing of blessed congregations almost always lasted no longer than a generation. But history shows us also that there have been congregations which for a time repeatedly went backward but which also repeatedly returned to the first love. They always bloomed anew and for many generations, yes, for hundreds of years were God's reservoirs and remained to water the great garden of God upon earth near and far. This hope we should and will firmly grasp before the face of God regarding our dear church in St. Louis, and let nothing take this hope from us.

Arise then, arise, all you brothers and sisters, husband and wife, young and old, parents and children, men and women, young men and maidens, teachers and pupils, preacher and listeners! Arise, let us now as one man draw near to the Lord, and not only with the knees of our body but also with the knees of our heart bow before Him with a broken spirit and believing soul; and as a congregation returning to Him today in the name of Jesus, let us cry to Him for grace and help from the depth of our need because of our sins. Then the Lord will hear us and again raise us up. We will do that in the appointed, old prayers of the church heard a thousandfold in all her troubles and those of the whole world: Lord, have mercy!—Our Father, etc. Amen.

Sermon at the Installation
of Pastor C. G. Stoeckhardt[1]
in Holy Cross Church, St. Louis, Mo.

Third Sunday of Advent, 1878; 1 Corinthians 4:1-5

When Is the Day of the Installation of a Pastor
a Day of Festive Joy for a Congregation?

(*Amerikanisch-Lutherische Epistel Postille*, pp. 19—24)

Lord Jesus, with joy we have gathered in Your holy sanctuary today, because today You are again giving us, Your orphaned congregation, a shepherd. But—how can we hide it from You?—we are rejoicing together with *trembling*. For of what use is all the care and labor of Your children if You do not make them sufficient for it? And what is all our hearing and learning worth if You do not open our hearts? Oh, therefore we pray You, Lord, have mercy, have mercy upon us! Do not look upon our great guilt and the fact that we have deserved that You should take Your Word and its blessing from us; but look upon Your own reconciling blood, shed also for us, which speaks better than the blood of Abel, which also for us cries aloft to You: Mercy! Mercy! Oh, therefore, pour out Your Holy Spirit richly upon Your servant sent to us; fit him out with Your gifts; give him the wisdom which comes down from above; give him power from on high; give him the comfort and peace which the world cannot give; and finally, give him faithfulness and perseverance in doctrine and life, in word and conduct, until his death. But give us, whom You have commanded him to pasture, grace so that we, as often as we hear Your Word from his mouth may receive it as Your Word in honest and good hearts and bring forth fruit with patience, so that he may carry out his office among us with joy and not with grief, and that someday we all may appear with him before the throne of Your glory to praise Your mercy with *one* voice to all eternity. Amen.

Text: 1 Corinthians 4:1-5

In the Lord Jesus, beloved, precious [Holy] Cross congregation! After our previous beloved shepherd, who grew gray and tired in the service of his Lord and Master, laid down his shepherd's staff, a man hurried over land and sea to come to us in response to our call in the name of the Lord. Today he is in our midst, to take up the office of shepherd among us. Although previously he lived in a different part of the world, he has for a long time been inwardly united with us in faith and confession; yes, he has borne with joy the shame of our name and narrowly escaped bonds for the sake of the name of Christ. For that reason a day of festive joy has today dawned upon our congregation. Indeed the day of a pastor's installation is not always a day of festive joy for the congregation.

If the new pastor is a false teacher, the day of his installation is much more a gloomy, dark day for the congregation, a day of misfortune, a day when God visits the children of God with wrath and deep sorrow. For the Lord says: "Beware of false prophets, who come to you in sheep's clothing but inwardly are ravenous wolves." Oh fearful day, therefore, for a congregation when, as now so often happens in our old fatherland, such a false prophet is forced upon a congregation! But it is a still more fearful day for a congregation when the congregation itself according to its own lusts takes to itself such a false prophet. Unfortunately, this happens only too often here in our new fatherland, blessed with complete religious freedom.

Yet, my beloved, one entering the office of the ministry may not be a heretic, but rather one who correctly teaches all articles of the Christian faith, denying none, nor intentionally changing any; but if he is a hireling, who covets the honor but not the burden of the ministry, not the precious *work* of a bishop; if in his office he seeks only himself rather than souls, ease and good days, favor and honor among men, then the day he enters upon his office is anything but a day of festive joy for the congregation, but rather a day of the visitation of divine wrath and bitter sorrow for all the children of God. Oh, deplorable congregation which instead of a pious shepherd receives a hireling! For the Lord Himself says: "A hireling . . . sees the wolf coming and leaves the sheep and flees; and the wolf snatches them and scatters them. He flees because he is a hireling and cares nothing for the sheep."

Permit me therefore in this holy hour on the basis of our text to answer the question:

When Is the Day of the Installation of a Pastor a Day of Festive Joy for a Congregation?

On the basis of our text I answer:

1. *when a pastor comes as a servant of Christ and steward of the mysteries of God; and when*

2. his congregation seeks nothing else of him except that he be found faithful.

I

My beloved, when the holy apostle writes at the beginning of our text: *"This is how one should regard us, as servants of Christ and stewards of the mysteries of God,"* the apostle in the first instance says only how a congregation is to *regard* their upright pastor. At the same time he indicates clearly the qualities which all upright pastors must have; for the way in which a congregation according to God's Word is to *regard* pastors, that they must without doubt *be,* in deed and truth.

But now, according to our text, what must an upright pastor above all be? The first thing the apostle mentions is that he must be a "servant of Christ." A true pastor, over whose arrival his congregation has reason to rejoice, is therefore above all, only that person who has not with power forced his way into the office or has sneaked into the office with cunning and devious ways, but whom Christ Himself has placed into his office. The same apostle testifies to this in clear words also in other places. For example, he writes to the Ephesians: "And His gifts were that some should be apostles, some prophets, some evangelists, some pastors and teachers." But about the false prophets God the Lord Himself complains in the book of Jeremiah the prophet: "I did not send the prophets, yet they ran."

Two thoughts attach to the idea that the pastor is sent by Christ Himself. The first is this, that the pastor is *inwardly* called by Christ to the holy office; namely, that he himself is a sheep of Christ's flock, that he is himself a converted believing Christian, that he himself is going the way to heaven which he should show others, that in his heart the desire burns to bring also to others the costly pearls which he himself has found with such blessed joy; in short, that with David and Paul he can say: "I believed and so I spoke." Or does Christ Himself appoint a blind man as a guide for the blind or the seeing? Never! Rather, Christ says to an unconverted pastor, in the words of Psalm 50: "What right have you to recite My statutes, or to take My covenant on your lips? For you hate discipline, and you cast My words behind you."

The true faith in which the pastor himself stands and the urge which fills his heart to carry out the holy office is, however, as previously stated, only the *inner* call which he himself has received from Christ. To this inner call must therefore come also the *external* call through men. For Christ has given His believing congregation the keys of the kingdom of heaven and therewith also the power, in His name and in His stead, to choose, to call, to ordain and install His servants. *"A servant of Christ,"* or one who has been sent and called by Christ Himself, is not one who like the enthusiasts brags only about the "Spirit" who leads him, but one who can produce the call of the congregation whose shepherd he claims to be.

But, my beloved, the apostle in our text does not call true pastors lords, nor rulers, nor masters, nor authority figures of Christ, but *"Servants* of Christ." Here the apostle uses a word which in the original means "Christ's galley slaves." Christ Himself wants to be and remain the *Captain* of the ship of the church; He Himself wants to be at the helm; pastors should be only the rowers. A true pastor, over whose coming a congregation may rejoice, is therefore only that person who comes not to rule over her but to serve her, not as her master but as her brother. That we have not erred in this interpretation of the words of our text "Christ's *servants,"* we see from many clear statements of Christ Himself as well as of His holy apostles. For example, Christ calls to His disciples: "You have one teacher, and you are all brethren. . . . You know that the rulers of the Gentiles lord it over them, and their great men exercise authority over them. *It shall not be so among you;* but whoever will be great among you must be your *servant,* and whoever will be first among you must be your *slave."* Therefore not only does the apostle Peter as with upraised finger warn the preachers of his day: "Not as domineering over those in your charge, but being examples to the flock," the dear humble apostles say also of themselves: "What then is Apollos? What is Paul? *Servants* through whom you believed, as the Lord assigned to each. . . . Not that we lord it over your faith; we work with you for your joy." Yes, the holy Paul testifies to his Corinthians: "What we preach is not ourselves, but Jesus Christ as Lord, with ourselves as your *servants* for Jesus' sake." Oh, with what joy can and should a congregation therefore welcome such a humble servant of Christ!

Still, my beloved, the apostle says in our text not only: *"This is how one should regard us, as servants of Christ,"* but he also adds, *"and stewards of the mysteries of God."* According to our text, therefore, that is the second thing a true pastor must be: *"a steward of the mysteries of God."*

My beloved, also in these words lie two ideas. First this: A true pastor does not come with his own mysteries, not with the mysteries of his reason and wisdom, not with the mysteries of his heart and his imagination, but only with the mysteries of the great God Himself, revealed in the Scriptures; in short, not with the word of man but only with the Word of God. The writings of the apostles and prophets must be the source from which all that he teaches flows clean and pure. He must not be a proud master but a humble "minister of the Word," as Luke writes (Luke 1:2). He must be able to say with Paul: "I say nothing but what the prophets and

Moses said would come to pass." What God says through Moses must be before his soul night and day: "You shall not add to the Word which I command you, nor take from it." Therefore he must be prepared to suffer hunger, thirst, and nakedness, as well as shame, disgrace, and persecution, yes, even a martyr's death rather than to depart from even a letter of the written Word of God. In this last period of the world's history, through His chosen servant Luther alone, God again kindled, gave, and placed on a candlestick the light of His pure Word for Christendom, and sealed him before the whole world as His prophet. Therefore the watchword of a true preacher of our time must be: *"God's Word and Luther's doctrine pure shall now and evermore endure."* And the glorious, golden confessions of the church named after Luther must also be the confession of his faith and the banner under which he teaches and guards, fights and suffers, conquers and dies.

But, my beloved, in our text the apostle calls faithful preachers not simply proclaimers of the mysteries of God but *"stewards"* of them. This is a matter of great importance. A steward is neither an absolute lord nor a mere dispenser of goods; rather he manages the goods of another and has specific instructions in which he is told to give to each member of the household what he needs. A true preacher over whose coming a congregation can and must rejoice is therefore only that one who not only proclaims God's Word, namely Law and Gospel, to his congregation, purely, clearly, and unabridged, but who also shows himself to be a good *"steward"* over his congregation; namely, one who as the apostle writes in another place "rightly *handles* the Word of truth," or, as Christ says, one who *"gives . . . their portion of food at the proper time"* to the members of the house of God.

Therefore, as soon as a true preacher in the name of Jesus has entered upon his holy office, he takes to his heart each soul entrusted to him, seeks to know each one, and then gives to each just what he needs. If he encounters a person still spiritually dead, who securely goes on living in sin, he tries to awaken and terrify him and therefore proclaims to him the Law. If he encounters a spiritually blind person, who is without true faith and yet thinks he stands in faith, he tries to open his eyes and to bring him to a wholesome knowledge of himself. If he encounters one ignorant of God's Word, he patiently instructs him and teaches him the first letters of the wholesome Word. If he encounters a person weak in faith, he tries to strengthen him in faith, and therefore holds up to him the sweet promises of the Gospel. If he encounters a person troubled by his sin, he seeks to comfort him and paints Christ in all His grace and immense love for sinners before his eyes. If he encounters one who is in danger, he tries to persuade him of the danger in which he stands and warns him of it. If he encounters one living in mortal sin and therefore fallen from grace, he tries to raise that person from his fall and works on him tirelessly with rebuke and comfort. If he encounters a person troubled with doubts about the truth, he tries to make him certain and shows him the firm foundation of the Christian faith. If he meets a person who has gone astray in any way, he goes after him, looks for him, entices him, and with tears pleads with him to turn around; he does not rest until he has brought back the straying sheep to his good Shepherd. To the beginners, or the children in Christ, he gives milk; to the mature, or the fathers and mothers in Christ, he gives strong meat.

All this he does in good and evil days, toward the parents as well as the children, the young men and the young women, the poor as well as the rich, the healthy as well as the sick, the living as well as the dying. He does this not as a stern lawgiver and judge, but as a loving brother, as a true friend, yes, as a compassionate, humble fellow sinner and fellow redeemed. He does all this not only publicly but also privately, not only in the pulpit and at the altar, but wherever God brings him together with those entrusted to him, whether in his house or in theirs, whether at the sickbed or deathbed or finally at God's acre; everywhere he seeks to share some spiritual gift.

A true preacher, then, shows himself as a concerned physician of the soul, sometimes with bitter medicine, sometimes with sweet, sometimes with sharp wine, sometimes with soothing oil, and as a true shepherd of souls sometimes with the staff Beauty, sometimes with the staff Bands [Zechariah 11:7 KJV], as is necessary.

Truly, the day of the entry into office of such a pastor is therefore a day of festive joy for a congregation.

II

Beloved, the apostle continues in our text: *"Moreover, no more[2] is required of stewards than that they be found faithful."*[3] From this we see that something is demanded also of the *congregation* if the day of the pastor's beginning of his work is to be for it a day of festive joy. For the congregation dare look for *"no more"* of their pastor *"than that he be found faithful."* Let me now speak to you about this as my second point.

The first thing a congregation has to pay attention to when a new pastor begins his work in its midst is that small phrase in our text *"no more."* Also among ministers God has distributed His gifts differently. Says Paul: "To one is given through the Spirit the utterance of wisdom; and to another the utterance of knowledge according to the same Spirit; to another faith," namely a heroic faith; "to another prophecy"; namely a special skill in the interpretation of Scripture; "to another the ability to distinguish between spirits; to another various kinds of tongues; to another the interpretation of tongues." Therefore no single preacher has all gifts, but each one has only his particular portion. Even the holy apostles and their helpers did not have the same measure of gifts. For example, to Paul was given especially the gift of deep and rich knowledge; to John, especially the gift to look into the future; to Apollos, especially the gift of ready speech. So also today, one preacher is given especially this gift, another that. Now, just as in the case of a *steward* one does not look for his own property but only for the goods of his lord, so a congregation should not seek in its *pastor* this or that gift, but only the gifts given him by God. If it looks for more, that is not only an injustice, yes, cruelty, but the congregation will be at fault if its pastor does not carry out his office in its midst with joy, but with grief; and that is not good for the members, for then they do not receive the full measure of blessing which God intended.

Yet, my beloved, when our text says by way of warning that one should seek *"no more"* in a pastor *"than that he be found faithful,"* the apostle desires at the same time that a congregation should seek *no less* than this in its pastor. As important as it is that a pastor remain faithful in doctrine and life, so important it is that the *congregation* demand this of him. Woe to the congregation when its pastor wants to remain faithful to the doctrine of God's Word but it, the congregation, demands that publicly and privately he teach something else than God's pure Word! Woe to a congregation when its pastor wants to remain faithful in refuting all errors hurtful to the soul but it, the congregation, demands of him that he remain silent for the sake of temporal peace! Woe to a congregation when its pastor wants to be faithful in rebuking all ungodly living but it, the congregation, demands of him as the Jews of Isaiah's time demanded of their prophets: "speak to us smooth things, prophesy illusions"! Woe to a congregation when its pastor wants to be faithful in the handling of the church discipline prescribed by Christ but it, the congregation, wants to use only the loosing key and not the binding key! Woe to a congregation when its pastor wants to be faithful in not making an evil distinction among his hearers but it, the congregation, demands of him that he be a respecter of persons! Finally, woe to the congregation when its pastor wants to be faithful also in a Christian, godly life, and it, the congregation, either demands of him angelic holiness that will endure no weakness on his part or, at the opposite extreme, demands that he be only a good fellow and with it serve the world and the flesh!

Now then, you dear members of this Cross congregation, today a servant of Christ and a steward of God's mysteries begins his work among you; now look for nothing more or nothing less than that he be found faithful!

Consider this: In a certain sense God's grace has placed it into our hands whether the office which our new pastor wants to exercise among us will be blessed or not. Consider this: As God's steward our pastor must take a fearful oath that he will be faithful; he must pledge nothing less than his soul's salvation to us, the whole church, and his God. Oh, therefore, let us—I adjure you by your salvation—let us not demand of him what God forbids, or forbid him what God demands of him! Consider this: God says to him: Preach My Word without taking away from it or adding to it, or I will one day say to you, "I never knew you; depart from Me you evildoer!" Oh, therefore, let us demand of him only God's Word, the whole Word, the whole counsel of God for our salvation! Consider this: God says to him: "Cry aloud, spare not, lift up your voice like a trumpet; declare to My people their transgressions, to the house of Jacob their sins." "If I say to the wicked, 'You shall surely die,' and you give him no warning, nor speak to warn the wicked from his wicked way in order to save his life, that wicked man shall die in his iniquity; but his blood I will require at your hand"— oh, let us therefore receive our pastor's word with meekness, also when he scolds us. Consider finally: God says to him: "Do not be ashamed of the Gospel; it is the power of God for salvation to everyone that has faith." Oh, let us as poor sinners always open our hearts and ears to this message of joy and accept it in faith!

The flesh, the world, and the devil will trouble our pastor daily. Oh, therefore, let us all, as many of us as can pray, daily remember him in heartfelt prayer! If his courage fails, let us speak to him so that he will take heart! If he becomes weak in faith or in any necessary work, let us encourage him! If sorrow overtakes him, let us comfort him! If he stumbles, let us with a gentle spirit help him up! If we see him faithful in the work in God's house, let us hold him all the more dear for his work's sake and consider him worthy of double honor! If at last he goes joyfully ahead of us on the narrow, rough, and steep way to the heavenly Zion, let us joyfully follow him!

Ah, let us—and this I ask of you in conclusion—let us all under the care and shepherding of our new shepherd return to the first love and cast aside all satiety, lukewarmness, indolence, and all earthly and worldly ideas! As he today swears eternal faithfulness to his Lord, let us also swear with him to remain faithful until death.

Thus, thus, my beloved, this day will be not only a day of festive joy but also will become for him and us all the beginning of a time of renewed visitation of grace and abounding blessing; and the garden of our congregation will green and bloom more lovely all the time and become ever richer in the golden fruits of faith and love, of hope and patience. Then when the Chief Shepherd appears, not only our faithful undershepherd but also we who are entrusted to him will receive the crown of glory that does not fade away.

To that end may Jesus Christ, true God and true man in one undivided person and eternal High Priest of the whole lost world, praised in all eternity, help him and us all. Amen.

Sermon on Predestination
Christmas 1881, Macoupin County, Ill.; Ephesians 1:3-6

Concerning Predestination
(Amerikanisch-Lutherische Epistel Postille, pp. 271—78)

Lord Jesus, You Son of the living God, You have come into this world to save sinners. Thanks, praise, glory, and honor be to You today, on the day of Your gracious and saving birth, that You not only came into the world to save us poor sinners, but also that You as the Good Shepherd followed us, who all like sheep have gone astray, called us to Yourself through the shepherd's voice of Your sweet Gospel, brought us to faith in You, and also preserved us in the same until today. Oh, how in time and eternity can we sufficiently thank You for this? *We* did not seek *You,* but *You* sought *us; we* did not come to *You,* but *You* came to *us.* How have we deserved it that You had mercy upon us rather than millions of others? Ah, it is Your undeserved grace alone that we have to thank for this. You saw us lying in the blood of our sins, and behold, Your heart broke, and You said to us: "You shall live!" Oh, Lord Jesus, *You* today once gave *Yourself* for *us;* today we give *ourselves* to *You.* Here is our heart! Take it, cleanse and adorn it for Yourself as Your dwelling and rule in it until our death. For this, with all angels and archangels, cherubim and seraphim, thrones and dominions, with all blessed and chosen ones, we will in heaven give You thanks, glory, praise, and honor through all eternity. Amen.

Text: Ephesians 1:3-6

In the newborn Savior, heartily beloved brothers and sisters!

On this double festival of Christmas and your church anniversary, you have kindly invited me to come and preach a sermon about predestination. With joy I have accepted your invitation to fulfill your desire, as God gives me grace.

Indeed, some have felt that one should not preach about so mysterious a doctrine as predestination to ordinary Christians, that this is a doctrine only for the educated. But that is a great error. St. Paul writes to

173

Timothy: "*All* Scripture is inspired by God and profitable for teaching, for reproof, for correction, and for training in righteousness"; and to the Romans he writes: "For whatever was written in former days was written for our instruction, that by steadfastness and by the encouragement of the Scriptures we might have hope." If "all Scripture," that is, everything contained in the Old and New Testaments, is never harmful, but "profitable" in many ways, so also the doctrine of predestination, when it is properly treated, can never be harmful but must be highly profitable. For Holy Scripture does not touch upon this doctrine only seldom, here and there, and with difficult words, but it treats it in many places, clearly and fully.

Let me briefly remind you of only a few of the passages in the New Testament which deal with predestination.

First of all, as far as *Christ* Himself is concerned, He refers to the doctrine of predestination on the most varied occasions. First, in order to give a summary of their content, Jesus closed two different parables, that of the laborers in the vineyard and the marriage of the king's son, with the words of *warning:* "For many are called, but few are *chosen.*" Again, when Christ wanted to comfort His disciples over against the hatred of the world, He called to them: "If you were of the world, the world would love its own; but because you are not of the world, but *I chose you out of the world,* therefore the world hates you." Furthermore, when Christ for their own benefit wanted to *humble* His disciples whom He had so highly exalted and to cast down all pride and boasting in their hearts and mouths, He said to them: *"You* did not choose Me, but I chose *you."* Again, when Christ wanted to *strengthen the hearts* of His disciples against the great danger of apostasy in the last time, He said to them: "For false Christs and false prophets will arise and show great signs and wonders, so as to lead astray, *if possible,* even *the elect,"* and thus assures them that this is impossible. Again, when Christ wanted to fill His disciples with *courage* after He told them about the tribulation of the last days, He said: "And if those days had not been shortened, no human being would be saved; *but for the sake of the elect* those days will be shortened." Again, when Christ wanted to sharpen *the certainty that their prayers were heard,* He said to His believing followers: "And will not God vindicate His elect, who cry to Him day and night?" Further, when Christ wanted to prepare the apostles for the defection of their fellow apostle Judas Iscariot, the betrayer, so that they would *not take offense* at the deep, fearful fall of even an apostle, He said to them: "I am not speaking of you all; I know whom I have *chosen."* Finally, when Christ wanted to *strengthen* the believers *in the hope* that on the last day they all would certainly enter eternal life, He said to them:

"And then He will send out the angels, and gather *His elect* from the four winds, from the ends of the earth to the ends of heaven."

As far as the *apostles* are concerned, they followed Christ's footsteps in the teaching about predestination through the enlightenment and guidance of the Holy Spirit. For example, Paul *warns* the Corinthians, so rich in knowledge and other gifts, against presumption, by calling to them: "But God *chose* what is foolish in the world to shame the wise, God *chose* what is weak in the world to shame the strong, God *chose* what is low and despised in the world, even things that are not, to bring to nothing things that are, so that no human being might boast in the presence of God." The same apostle writes the Thessalonians in the first of his letters to them in order to *comfort* them in their tribulations: "For we know, brethren beloved by God, *that He has chosen you.*" In the second letter, while *admonishing,* he adds: "But we are bound to give thanks to God always for you, brethren beloved by the Lord, *because God chose you* from the beginning to be saved." In the same way he *encourages* the Colossians: "Put on then, *as God's chosen ones,* holy and beloved, compassion, etc." The apostle Peter, in order to *strengthen* them *in faith,* calls all Christians together *"a chosen race"* and greets the scattered Christians to whom he writes as *"chosen . . . exiles."* Finally James, in order to *preserve* the rich *from pride,* calls out: "Has not God *chosen* those who are poor in the world to be rich in faith?" These few examples may suffice.

So you see, the doctrine of predestination runs through the whole of Scripture like a golden thread. Christ as well as the holy apostles use this doctrine sometimes to strengthen faith, sometimes to quicken hope, sometimes to comfort, sometimes to encourage, sometimes to humble, sometimes to move to prayer in firm faith, sometimes to warn and to preserve from unbelief, sin, and apostasy. How beneficial and salutary this doctrine must be!

In many passages predestination is talked about although the word is not used, as for example when Scripture speaks of those called according to His purpose, those ordained to eternal life, those given to Christ by the Father, those whom He has redeemed from among men that they should be a kind of first fruits, those whose names are written in heaven, etc. But, I say, apart from these passages, the teaching about predestination is treated in the fullest detail in two chief passages of Holy Scripture, namely in the second half of the eighth chapter of Romans and in the entire ninth, tenth, and eleventh chapters, and secondly, in the first chapter of the Letter to the Ephesians.

I have chosen the last passage as my text for today. Under the guidance of the text let me now speak to you

Concerning Predestination

as on the basis of this our text and with the assistance of the Holy Spirit I answer the following five questions:

1. *Who are those whom God has chosen?*
2. *When did this election take place?*
3. *To what did God choose the elect?*
4. *What are the reasons that moved God to choose them?*
5. *How shall a Christian properly use the correct doctrine of predestination for his salvation?*

I

The first question I have to answer today is this: *Who are those whom God has chosen?*

The holy apostle gives us the answer to this question right at the beginning of our text. The words read as follows: "Blessed be the God and Father of our Lord Jesus Christ, who has blessed us in Christ with every spiritual blessing in the heavenly places, even as He chose *us.*" Now who are those whom God has chosen? The apostle says: "Even as He chose us." But who are the "us" about whom Paul speaks? Obviously in part Paul himself, who wrote these words, in part those *to* whom he wrote this letter, namely the Ephesians who had come to faith.

But now how did Paul conclude that not only he but also the Ephesians belong to those whom God has chosen? The apostle shows this by first writing: *"Blessed be the God and Father of our Lord Jesus Christ, who has blessed us in Christ with every spiritual blessing"* and then immediately adding: *"Even as He chose us."* Obviously the apostle wants to say this: You beloved Ephesians, how could and would I dare to doubt that you, as I, have been chosen by God, when I see that God has already *"blessed us in Christ with every spiritual blessing"?* You have not only been redeemed, as have all people in the world, but through the Word of the Gospel you have also been called and enlightened with the gifts of the Holy Spirit, that is, you have come to true faith in Christ and through this faith have been justified and sanctified! Therefore it is absolutely certain that you also belong to those whom God has chosen.

Just as Paul deals with the Ephesians in our text, he deals in another place also with the Christians in Rome, who on account of their faith had to endure much tribulation. For their comfort Paul calls to them in his letter to the Romans: "We know that in *everything* God works for good with those who love Him, *who are called according to His purpose.* For those whom He foreknew," that is, the elect, "He also predestined to be conformed to the image of His Son, in order that He might be the first-born among many brethren. And those whom He predestined He also called; and those whom He called He also justified; and those whom He justified He also glorified." The apostle wants to say: You beloved Christians in Rome have no reason to doubt that God has chosen also you, for, I ask you, have you not been called through the Word of the Gospel? Have you not through it also come to faith and through faith become righteous before God? And are you not also suffering· persecution on account of your faith? You see, these and no others are the very people whom God has elected.

From these facts, know this, beloved: For believing Christians the doctrine of predestination is not a terrible and frightening doctrine that must raise doubts about whether they will be saved because perhaps they have not been chosen. No, on the contrary, it is the most comforting doctrine there can be, which should make Christians entirely certain of their salvation. Predestination does not hang over believing Christians as a dark, black, threatening storm cloud, so that they must always anxiously ask: "Ah, am I also a chosen one?" No, far from being a dark cloud, the doctrine of predestination is much more a brightly shining sun of grace, comfort, and joy that rises over every person as soon as he has been called by the Gospel and thereby has become a believer.

My answer to our first question: Who are those whom God has chosen? is briefly this: The genuine believers. Therefore we read in the confession of our church, the Formula of Concord: "The eternal election of God or God's predestination to salvation does not extend over both the godly and the ungodly, but *only* over *the children of God,* who have been elected and predestined to eternal life" [Tappert, p. 617].

II

We proceed to our second question: *When did this election take place?*

Also for this question the holy apostle gives a clear answer in our text, when he says: "Even as He chose us in Him *before the foundation of the world.*" Therefore election does not first take place in time. According to God's Word, God did not wait until people were born and living on earth and did not elect them only after He saw that they would be converted and would persevere unto the end. No, before people were born and did any good, yes, before God laid the foundation of the world, before heaven and earth, sun, moon, and stars were created, before anything existed except only God's love, in short, election took place already in *eternity.*

People indeed do many things about which they previously had not thought, let alone resolved to do. But God, who knows and rules all things, already in eternity not only *knew* in advance *everything* He would do in

177

time but also in eternity *resolved* in advance to do it. Therefore in his Second Letter to Timothy Paul says of the grace of the elect, that it was given them "ages ago." Therefore Christ on the last day will say to the elect: "Come, O blessed of My Father, inherit the kingdom prepared for you from the foundation of the world." Therefore our church publicly confesses before all Christendom in the Formula of Concord: "Not only before we had done any good, but even before we were born (in fact, 'before the foundation of the world was laid') God elected us in Christ" [Tappert, p. 631].

O beloved, what a hot and inexpressibly great fire must burn in the heart of God toward us Christians, that He thought about us, took counsel concerning us, and resolved to elect us before we were born, yes, before He created the world, from all eternity! That is a love which is higher than heaven, wider than the earth, deeper than the sea, and as long as eternity. Therefore we must exult with the poet [*The Lutheran Hymnal*, 385:2]:

> It is that mercy never ending,
> Which human reason far transcends,
> Of Him who, loving arms extending,
> To wretched sinners condescends;
> Whose heart with pity still doth break
> Whether we leave Him or forsake.

III

Now let us look for the answer to our third question: *To what did God chose the elect?*

Also for this question we find the answer of the Holy Spirit in our text. For it says: "Even as He chose us in Him before the foundation of the world, *that we should be holy and blameless before Him.* He destined us in love *to be His sons. . . .*"

So there are *two things*, especially, to which God has chosen the elect, namely first, that they from the heart *turn* to Him and, second, that they be His dear *children*. For when our text says that God has chosen us that we should be *"holy and blameless before Him,"* that means nothing else than that God has chosen us so that from the heart we turn to Him; for only through a genuine conversion of the heart can a person be *"holy and blameless before Him."* And now when our text further states: "He destined us in love *to be His sons,"* that means nothing else than that God has chosen us that through faith in Christ we might become His dear children; for only through faith does a person become a dear child of God. Paul writes to the Galatians: "In Christ Jesus you are all sons of God, *through faith,"* and John in the first chapter of his gospel says: "But to all who received Him, who *believed* in His name, He gave power to become children of God."

Now, is it not something glorious to be chosen by God already in eternity to *repentance, conversion,* and *sanctification,* as well as to be predestined to the *adoption of sons* and also to *faith?* For if we are chosen and predestined *to these,* we are also chosen and predestined for *salvation.* Christ says: "He who *believes* and is baptized shall be *saved."* That we are chosen for *salvation* St. Paul says expressly in his Second Letter to the Thessalonians, when he writes: "But we are bound to give thanks to God always for you, brethren beloved by the Lord, because God chose you from the beginning *to be saved,* through sanctification by the Spirit and belief in the truth." Therefore the last confession of our church, namely the Formula of Concord, says:

> God's eternal election, however, *not only forsees and foreknows the salvation of the elect, but by God's gracious will and pleasure in Christ Jesus it is also a cause* which creates, effects, helps, and furthers our *salvation and whatever pertains to it.* Our salvation is *based* on it in such a way that "the gates of Hades" are not able to do anything against it (Matt. 16:18), it is written: "No one shall snatch my sheep out of my hand"(John 10:28), and again: "As many as were *ordained* to eternal life *believed"*(Acts 13:48) [Tappert, p. 617].

Oh, how secure is your salvation, you beloved, chosen, believing children of God! You can exult with Paul Gerhardt [*The Lutheran Hymnal,* 520:5]:

> Though all the powers of evil
> The will of God oppose,
> His purpose will not falter,
> His pleasure onward goes.
> Whate'er God's will resolveth,
> Whatever He intends,
> Will always be accomplished
> True to His aims and ends.

IV

We come now to our fourth question, which is: *What are the reasons that moved God to choose the elect?*

Our text answers also this question clearly in the following words: "He destined us in love to be His sons *through Jesus Christ, according to the purpose of His will, to the praise of His glorious grace* which He freely bestowed on us in the Beloved." From this we see that God had *only two causes* for choosing the elect for the adoption of sons and eternal salvation. According to our text the *first* cause was "the purpose of His will," or *His glorious grace which He freely bestowed on"* them. But the *second* cause was *"Jesus Christ";* that means His most holy merit, won by His life, suffering, and death for all humanity.

179

You see, my beloved, God did not foresee something good in His chosen ones which He regarded and which moved Him to choose them; but rather He saw them in the blood of their sins and yet said: "You shall live!" Also God did not consider that they were already acceptable to Him and for that reason chose them; but, as our text says, "He hath *made* us accepted in the beloved" [KJV]. God also did not regard the fact that they forsook the world through repentance and conversion and for that reason chose them; but, as Christ said to His disciples, He "chose" them "out of the world," that is, out of the *unbelievers* among whom He saw them. God did not even consider their *faith* and choose them because of their faith; but, because no one can give faith to himself, He rather resolved from eternity to work faith in them through the Gospel and to preserve them in the same unto the end.

Therefore our church confesses in its last confessional symbol, namely in our precious Formula of Concord:

> . . . it is written, "He destined us in love to be his sons through Jesus Christ, according to the purpose of his will, and to the praise of his glorious grace which he freely bestowed on us in the Beloved" (Eph. 1:5, 6). It is therefore false and wrong when men teach that the cause of our election is not only the mercy of God and the most holy merit of Christ, but that there is also within us a cause of God's election on account of which God has elected us unto eternal life. For not only before we had done any good, but even before we were born (in fact, "before the foundation of the world was laid") God elected us in Christ . . . [Tappert, p. 631].

Thus far our dear Formula of Concord.

And now I ask you, believing Christians: Is not this doctrine substantiated by your experience?—Who gave you your faith? Perhaps you yourselves? Or was it not rather God the Holy Ghost who worked faith in you through His power and grace? What good have you done to come to faith? It is true, you went to church. But did you not first hurry to church with a *desire* for faith after God had already ignited a spark of faith in your hearts?—It is furthermore true: You did not stubbornly resist. But do you have your heart, which by nature is good or better than that of others, to thank for that? Or do you not rather have God's grace alone to thank, which overcame your resistance and opened your heart, as once it did Lydia's, so that you paid attention to God's Word?—And you who first came to a living, heartfelt faith here in America, did you *therefore* come to America, to come to the true faith? Or did not rather God, the Ruler of your life, lead you to America so that here you might find the heavenly treasure of faith without your seeking it, yes, while you here sought only earthly bread for you and yours? Did you seek God at all? Or did *God* not rather seek *you?* Did *you* come *to God?* Or did not *God* rather come *to you?* What was it—I want to ask each one of you believing Christians again—what was the *cause* that moved God to choose you?—Nothing, nothing good in you but only God's unspeakable grace and Christ's most holy merit. Woe to him who ascribes the cause of his election to himself! He takes from God the honor which is due Him alone.

V

It is time that I hurry to the end now and answer our fifth and last question: *How shall a Christian properly use this doctrine of predestination for his salvation?*

Our text, my beloved, does not give a particularly specific answer to this question, but from the way the holy apostle uses and applies the doctrine of predestination in our text, we can see clearly enough how it is to be used by every believing Christian.

But how does the apostle apply it in our text? First, he uses it to *comfort* the believing Ephesians; second, to *admonish* and to *warn* them. The proper use of this doctrine is concerned with these two ideas alone.

When, first of all, the apostle writes to the Ephesians: *"Even as He chose us,"* he obviously shows that the believers among them should find *comfort* in predestination, namely that they should consider it certain that they belong to the elect. But far be it that he would have them reach this goal by their reason, or by the Law, or to judge by any outward appearance, or to seek to investigate the secret, hidden abyss of divine foreknowledge; he refers them rather to the *"spiritual blessings in . . . heavenly places"* with which God had already blessed them and through which He had revealed His will concerning them. You see, in this way all true Christians should use the doctrine of predestination. Namely, they should think: God has already "called me by the Gospel, enlightened me with His gifts, and sanctified me in the true faith," and until now "kept me" in it. From this I conclude that I am one of the elect. For the way of the general order of grace is the only way on which God leads His elect to salvation; there is no other way. They are chosen in Christ, the Book of Life; in Him alone, therefore, they can and should seek also the Father's eternal election. From the way God *reveals* Himself to them in the Gospel, therefore, they are to know His *hidden* decision which He made concerning them in eternity. Therefore they should confidently say to Christ with the poet: "Let me through Your nail-prints see my predestination," and with Paul joyfully exult: "Who shall bring any charge against God's elect? It is God who justifies; who is to condemn? Is it Christ Jesus, who died, yes, who was raised from the dead, who is at the right hand of God, who indeed intercedes for us? . . . For I am sure that neither death, nor life, nor angels, nor principalities, nor things present, nor things to come, nor powers, nor height, nor depth, nor anything else in all creation, will be able to separate us from the love of God in Christ Jesus our Lord."—Oh, blessed, blessed are Christians who in this way use the doctrine of election and apply it to themselves! There they will find comfort in all temptations of the flesh, the world, and the devil.

In our text the apostle also reminds the Ephesians that they have been elected by God in order that they *"should be holy and blameless before Him."* To a proper use of the doctrine of predestination, therefore, also this belongs that, in the second place, Christians let themselves be *admonished* by it seriously to pursue sanctification and so through good works to "make their calling and election sure," as Peter writes; they should also let themselves be *warned* against misusing this comforting doctrine by becoming secure. If you consider yourself elected, oh, do not forget that you have been chosen not only to the adoption of children and salvation but also to *sanctification.* Consider this: You could do nothing to effect your predestination, but you can do much to move God *not* to elect you from eternity but to reject you. God indeed wants all people to be saved; He has destined no one to damnation; the Calvinists deny God's sun-clear Word when they teach this. No, all human beings have been redeemed by Christ; all should therefore have the Gospel preached to them; to all God also wants to give faith through the Gospel; and all who by His grace have come to faith He wants to keep it and to give them the gift of perseverance. Therefore whoever is lost is lost by his own fault; he is lost not because God did not want to elect him, but only because of his stiff-necked unbelief and his obstinate resistance. Therefore God through the prophet Hosea says clearly and plainly: "O Israel, *thou* hast *destroyed* thyself, but in *Me* is thine *help"* [Hosea 13:9 KJV].

Up then, beloved brothers and sisters in the Lord. You have already patiently borne the theft of your property; and you have rather turned your backs on your old, large, beautiful church and school then to deny the pure teaching of predestination. *Oh, remain steadfast!* What does it matter if you are called fools now if your names are written in heaven?!

Therefore, in conclusion, I call to you in the words of the pious poet: Come then, O Christian, battle until death. Reject everything that will hinder you and dampen your courage. If you want to wear the crown of glory, you must *venture* for Jesus. The beautiful crown will rest only upon the head of the victors! Amen.

Wedding Address for Magdalene, Walther's Daughter,[1] 1862

Numbers 6:24-26

My Threefold Fatherly Blessing upon You

(Casual-Predigten und -Reden, pp. 463—68)

In the name of the holy, highly praised Trinity, God the Father, God the Son, and God the Holy Spirit. Amen.

In Christ, the bridegroom of our souls, heartily beloved *(herzinnig-geliebte)* betrothed!

Oh, the infinite love of God the Father, my heavenly Ruler! Oh, the great kindness of God the Son, my eternal Savior! Oh, the unwavering faithfulness of the Holy Spirit, my divine Comforter! For, you see, it is through the leading and heart-guidance of this thrice holy God that you, my dearest children, stand here at the altar of the Lord. Here you now also stand publicly before many witnesses, sealing the bond of your hearts for the most intimate fellowship until death. My humble and earnest prayer, which in fatherly concern I often sent to God from my quiet room for you, my dear daughter—that, if it be His will, God would one day grant you a pious spouse—that prayer I see answered beyond all that I could ask or think.

Ah, already in my short life I have seen so many marriages which began with the sound of joy and jubilation, whose joy only too soon was changed into weeping and tears of bitter deception. I have also seen marriages which were the beginning of a common service to the world and its vanity. Oh, how fearful I was for you because of these experiences, my dear Magdalene, whom I so inexpressibly love!

But see! God has now taken from my heart all my anxieties about your future earthly lot. He, as your real father, as your Father in Christ, cared for you better than I knew how to do and could have done. Contrary to all my thoughts and presentiments, He brought you a spouse who not only fears the Lord and with joy serves Him in His church, but who is also the legacy of my dearly loved sister. He grew up under my eyes and for a long time has had the right of a child in my heart. He was the playmate of your childhood and the companion of your youth. Therefore you know him and he knows you as brother and sister know each other. Therefore your mutual love does not rest on the deception of momentary and passing impressions. God gave you what your hearts desired. To Him be thanks, praise, and honor in time and eternity.

What shall I do now?—What one prophet, forced by God's threats, once said causes my deeply moved heart, so full of joy at God's goodness, to say: "Behold, I have received a command to bless; He has blessed, and I cannot revoke it." Yes, beloved, with the holy Peter I call to you: "I have no silver and gold, but I give you what I have," namely my blessing.

You surely know that God has commanded all Christians called to inherit a blessing to bless also others in His name. But above all it is the parents whose hands God, rich in grace, has filled so that they, in His name and in His stead, can bless their pious children. And their blessing should not be an empty hope, but yea and amen up in heaven; therefore the wise scribe Sirach says: "The father's blessing builds houses for the children."

So, my dear children, open the hands of your faith in this holy hour to receive my fatherly blessing. I know of no richer and more glorious blessing than the one which Moses in the name of the Triune God gave to the children of Israel, which reads: *"The Lord bless you and keep you; the Lord make His face to shine upon you, and be gracious unto you; the Lord lift up His countenance upon you, and give you peace."*

Yes, let that be also my fatherly blessing upon you, namely:
God the Father keep you;
God the Son be gracious unto you; and finally,
God the Holy Spirit give you peace.

I

My dear children, you yourselves will neither wish nor expect that my fatherly blessing will bring you riches in worldly goods. If I wanted to comfort you with that, I would be a false comforter. Yes, if with that I hoped to make you happy, I could not love you; I would have to hate you; I would have to be your enemy; I would not desire your salvation. For earthly riches never give true comfort, and give no comfort at all when we need help and comfort the most. Riches are also, as the Lord says, nothing but a thornbush in which only too easily the heavenly seed of the only saving Word is choked; and as the holy apostle further testifies, the pursuit of riches is nothing else than temptation and a snare that plunge men into ruin and destruction.

No, it is not earthly riches that my fatherly blessing wants to bring you. However, as we in the Lord's Prayer, after we have prayed in the first

184

three petitions for those things that make us Christians, then immediately ask: "Give us this day our daily bread," so my first blessing indeed also contains temporal gifts. For how does it read? Moses begins with the words: *"The Lord bless you and keep you."* So I call to you first of all: God the Father keep you!

Oh, rejoice; for thereby I place a great gift in your lap. With these words, in the name of the Lord, I give you the comforting, sure promise: God will be the Protector of your whole life. "He will not fail you nor forsake you." Daily He will hear your prayer: "Give us this day our daily bread." You will always have food and clothing; you will never be in want. "You will not be put to shame in evil times; in the days of famine you will have abundance." God Himself will be the father in your home who cares for you. God will also protect you from all evil. He will permit "no evil to befall you, no scourge to come near your tent." For He has already given "His angels charge of you to guard you in all your ways. On their hands they will bear you up, lest you dash your foot against a stone." The angel of the Lord shall encamp around you and deliver you. God Himself will be like a wall of fire round about your house. God will be a friend to your friends and an enemy to your enemies. "A thousand may fall at your side, and ten thousand at your right hand; but it will not come near you." "When you pass through the waters, God will be with you; and through the rivers, they shall not overwhelm you; when you walk through the fire you shall not be burned, and the flame shall not consume you." When you sleep, the Keeper of Israel, who neither slumbers nor sleeps, will watch over you. His goodness will be new to you every morning.

See, that is my first fatherly blessing; that's what I'm saying when I call to you: *"The Lord,* God the Father, *bless you and keep you."*

II

Yet, my dearly beloved children, I believe that in this my first blessing I have taken only your least anxiety from your hearts. For I have the good confidence that you are Christians. But the Christian's most serious concern is not the earthly, but his debt of sin, his evil, corrupt heart. That, that it is which above all fills him with unrest and apprehension as he looks into the future. Will I always remain in God's grace? That, that is his most important question.

But rejoice; the second portion of God's blessing reads: *"The Lord make His face to shine upon you and be gracious unto you."* Therefore also my second fatherly blessing is: God the Son, Jesus Christ, be gracious unto you. Beloved, also this blessing is not merely a pious wish. With this my fatherly blessing on earth God the Son says to you in heaven above:

185

"Take heart, My son; take heart, My daughter; your sins are forgiven." Christ has established a universal, complete, and eternal redemption and has now given the command to proclaim this accomplished redemption to all creatures, and therefore also to you, yes, also to you.

Therefore take heart. Let not your unworthiness tempt you and lead you to despair. "God knows your frame; God remembers that you are dust." Through faith you are in Christ Jesus; but "there is no condemnation for those who are in Christ Jesus." In Him you are God's chosen children. "Who shall bring any charge against God's elect? It is God who justifies; who is to condemn? Is it Christ who died, yes, who was raised from the dead, who is at the right hand of God, who indeed intercedes for us?"

Oh, you blessed children! In faith take the blessing of your father: God the Son be gracious to you! Although in us there is much sin, in God there is much more grace; His helping hand knows no limit, however great our hurt. As often as in the future you will fail and stumble, just do not doubt: Everything has long ago been forgiven. Be certain of this: All your sins have long ago been buried in the grace of Christ, long ago been thrown into the depths of the sea—yes, obliterated like a cloud and like fog, even before they were committed.

Be sure of this, God is not niggardly with His grace; day and night He offers it to you and says: There it is. God's grace will go before you, God's grace will follow you; God's grace will move in with you, and then go in and out with you, work and rest with you, eat and drink with you, wake and sleep with you; and it will vault over you like the spreading heavens, from which you cannot slip away, no matter where you go or no matter where you sit or lie.

Therefore never say: Where shall I find grace? for it is already there. Do not say: Ah, if only I had grace! for you have it already. And if your heart says only no, let God's Word be more sure to you.

III

My dear children, my fatherly blessing has now removed the lack of life's necessities and God's disfavor; should it also take away the cross and trouble of life? Ah, far be it! How could I want to do that? For God's Word says: "Through many tribulations we must enter the kingdom of God." If, therefore, I wanted to take life's troubles from you, I would take from you also the kingdom of God. God's Word says: "Indeed all who desire to live a godly life in Christ Jesus will be persecuted." Therefore if I wanted to free you of all persecution, I would have to desire that you not live godly lives. God's Word says: "For the Lord disciplines him whom He loves and chastises him." Therefore, if I wanted to spare you God's fatherly chastenings and scourgings, I would remove from you also God's love. No, no; I tell you in advance: Also your married estate will prove to be a painful estate; also your wedding happiness and joy will soon be followed by life's burden and mourning and tears.

But do not be afraid, for I have one more blessing, which will make this mourning sweet and blessed for you, and that is: *"The Lord lift up His countenance upon you and give you peace."* Yes, God the Holy Spirit give you peace; that is my last blessing. I am not talking to you about the peace which the world can give and take away, but the peace of the Spirit, which the world cannot receive because it does not see Him or know Him; that peace which exists in the midst of lack of peace in the world and is the blessed city of refuge in the war of the peace-hating world; that peace which passes all understanding and keeps the hearts and minds in Christ Jesus unto eternal life; that peace of the heart in which the Savior holds His spiritual supper with the believing soul, of which the bride in the Song of Solomon says: "He brought me to the banqueting house, sustained me with raisins, refreshed me with apples"; in short, that inner peace by which one tastes and sees that the Lord is good, which is a foretaste of salvation, a little drop of the wine which the Savior will drink new with His own in His Father's kingdom, a beginning of eternal life in the valley of death and tears.

Yes, my children, I bespeak you this peace as my last blessing. If this rules in your heart, you, my dear son, will have strength to love your wife as Christ loved the church, to rule over her in love and to bear her weaknesses; and you, my daughter, will have strength not only to love your husband as your lord but also to honor and to fear him and to be obedient to him in all things. And your marriage will be a happy, a blessed marriage, a lovely picture of Christ's marriage to the church, His eternal bride. And when finally your hour comes, you will fall asleep in peace, to awake there in the mansions of eternal peace.

Therefore may this blessing, the blessing of your fathers and mothers, be our legacy, your earthly dowry which you take with you, your spiritual treasure chest from which you take all that your strength needs, your spare money in the days of need and in the hour of death. For it is not our blessing—oh, believe it—not ours, but the blessing of the triune God, the Father, the Son, and the Holy Spirit, to whom be honor and praise throughout eternity. Amen.

Funeral Address
for Mrs. Caroline Barthel[1]

St. Louis, Mo., July 14, 1881

(Reden gehalten am Sarge
der weiland Frau Caroline Juliane Barthel, pp. 1—7)

Since I have been asked by relatives of the deceased, whose weary limbs this coffin encloses, I cannot deny this request of honor.

It is just 50 years ago that I had the good fortune to be introduced to the family of the deceased by a pious friend. A youth without God behind me and having only recently come to the knowledge of Jesus Christ, a new, unexpected world opened up to me here. I saw a truly Christian family; a family in which Jesus was All in all, in which God's Word was the daily food and drink of the soul and ruled in everything, in which the Lord was served ceaselessly, in which therefore also the heavenly peace of Jesus was poured out on all the members of the family. Here I found my spiritual parents, a father in Christ and a mother in Christ, who assumed my spiritual and physical needs as though I were a son.

Just at that time I lay in heavy spiritual trials; in body and soul I was exhausted, uncertain of and doubting my salvation. At that time no praying helped, no sighing, no weeping, no fasting, no wrestling. God's peace had forsaken my soul. Terrified by the Law, this thought rang in my heart day and night: "Only this concerns me, that I cannot know whether I am a true Christian and You are my Jesus."

At that time it was particularly the dear deceased who carried me in her motherly heart. As often as I stepped over her threshold, there flowed from her mouth not only evangelical words of comfort for me, but also day and night she prayed in fervent prayer for me, a young stranger. And behold! God heard her supplication. Finally I found peace in Christ. And now a bond of blessed fellowship with Christ embraced us that nothing was able to break until her death.

Oh, how it gives me joy to testify publicly to that here. But still more I rejoice that one day before the throne of the Lamb and in the presence of all angels and the elect I will be able to thank her with all my heart for what she once did for me, such a poor person. For I have no doubt that her soul now rests in the bosom of Jesus. It is true that she was a poor sinner surrounded with "weakness within and without"; but by her faith and love she showed herself prepared.

In 1838 the circle of believers to which we belonged came to the conclusion that to save our souls, and particularly the souls of our children, we would have to leave our dear fatherland and emigrate to this far distant and foreign land in the West. At that time the dear deceased did not hesitate for a moment joyfully to leave the highly favorable circumstances in which her whole family lived, in order to serve the Lord here, without scruples of conscience, according to the holy, pure, and inerrant Word.

As great as were the troubles we experienced in the first years; as great as were the trials we experienced here as a result of severe deceptions and of confusion of conscience, which overflowed her conscience as waves of the sea; as hard as was the fight with bitter poverty such as she had never experienced, into which God led her; as cloudy and dark, as hopeless as appeared the future which lay before her—not for a moment did she stray from God's Word and God's gracious guidance. As often as her soul became restless, she said to it: "Why are you cast down, O my soul, and why are you disquieted within me? Hope in God; for I shall again praise Him, my help and my God" (Psalm 42:11). When Satan whispered to her, "The Lord is angry with you," she comforted herself by speaking the word of David: "For His anger is but for a moment, and His favor is for a lifetime. Weeping may tarry for the night, but joy comes with the morning" (Psalm 30:5).

Even when her way grew ever darker, steeper, and thornier, she did not on that account cast away her trust; she waited patiently. In that way she also experienced what the Christian church has always experienced, as it says: "Rejoice not over me, O my enemy; when I fall, I shall rise; when I sit in darkness, the Lord will be a light to me" (Micah 7:8). She never abandoned her hope. By God's grace her life became ever more gracious. Twenty-two years ago her pious spouse was taken from her side. He was a hero of the faith, a true son of Abraham, the father of the faithful. Yet even that could not tear her away from the Bridegroom of her soul, to whom alone she was married for all eternity.

Nor did God tempt her above her ability. Comforted and happy (according to the cheerful disposition which God gave her) and without any care about the future, she could live out her years as a widow in the circle of those who loved her unspeakably much, who considered her the greatly beloved, dearest family treasure; attentive, believing children and children-in-law attended to all her needs and least wishes.

189

The last years and days of her life were indeed accompanied by the miseries and infirmities of old age, but they were also the last witnesses to her living faith. With what inner desire and joy she heard the Word of God spoken to her during the last months, weeks, and days when she was confined to her room! That was her sweetest refreshment. She could not hear enough of it. The last time I was with her, the day before her death, practically all her senses had left her; only now and then a clear moment of consciousness shone forth. She was also for a long time dead to all earthly concerns. When I asked her, among other things, whether she did not rejoice that now soon she would come to Jesus and see Him face to face—then her fallen countenance brightened up, the dimmed eyes began to lighten up, as though having been awakened out of sleep, and she called out, radiant with joy: "Yes, truly! yes, truly!"

Good for her! The Lord says: "He who endures to the end shall be saved." She endured to the end; therefore she is also certainly saved. The Lord says: "Be faithful unto death, and I will give you the crown of life." She was faithful unto death; therefore a crown of life has certainly been given to her. She lived in the Lord and died in the Lord. In life she fought the good fight of true Christians in this evil last time, so full of temptations. Therefore in and with her death she has also triumphed. In her case the precious word of the holy Revelation has come to fulfillment: "These are they who have come out of the great tribulation; they have washed their robes and made them white in the blood of the Lamb. . . . Blessed are the dead who die in the Lord henceforth. Blessed indeed, says the Spirit, that they may rest from their labors, for their deeds follow them!" Therefore let us not weep. At her casket and grave let us rather sing a joyous Hallelujah!

But You, Lord Jesus, who alone brought Your chosen disciple to faith, who alone made her faithful and preserved her on the wonderful way of faith until her end, who finally rescued her from all dangers which threatened her, and brought her into the kingdom that was prepared for her from the beginning of the world, have mercy also upon us! Send us the kind of faith which victoriously conquers sin, the world, death, and hell; make also us faithful and keep also us in faith unto the end. Let the blessing of Your pious and faithful handmaiden rest upon all her children and children's children, and grant that all of us with them may follow her to the glory which You have prepared for all who love Your appearing. Amen.

Notes

Palm Sunday Confirmation Address

1. Walther seems to be referring to Emperor Charles V (1500—58), before whom Luther appeared at the Diet of Worms (1521) and the Augsburg Confession was read at the Diet of Augsburg (1530). He retired to a monastery in 1557.

Installation Sermon

1. Carl (or Karl) Georg Stoeckhardt (1842—1913) had recently come from Germany. He later became a well known professor of exegetical theology at Concordia Seminary, St. Louis.
2. The words "no more" are not generally found in English versions, but are in Luther's German Bible.
3. We have used the KJV's "faithful" rather than the RSV's "trustworthy" because it seems more suited to Walther's use of the German Bible's *treu.*

Wedding Address

1. Magdalene, Walther's older daughter, was born on Nov. 22, 1842. She married Stephanus Keyl, the son of Walther's sister, and therefore her first cousin. The marriage took place in the aula of Concordia Seminary, St. Louis. Stephanus Keyl was born on June 27, 1838, and died on Dec. 15, 1905. Magdalene outlived him. He served as pastor in Philadelphia, Pa., and then for many years as immigrant missionary in New York. The couple certainly was not spared the cross of which Walther speaks in the third part of the sermon. Of their 12 children, 5 died at an early age. For more about Magdalene and Stephanus and their children, see the *Selected Letters* volume in this set.

Funeral Address

1. Mrs. Caroline Barthel, her husband Friedrich Wilhelm, their five children, and her husband's mother came to America in the Saxon immigration. She was 34 years old at the time. They crossed the ocean on the *Olbers* and came up the Mississippi on the steamboat *Selma.* Her husband later became the first treasurer of the Missouri Synod. He died on Feb. 12, 1857. Her son Martin, who was an infant at the time of the immigation, became the first manager of Concordia Publishing House, serving in that capacity from 1869 to 1891.

Bibliography

Der Lutheraner, XXVI, 14 (March 15, 1870).

Walther, Carl Ferd. Wilh. *Amerikanisch-Lutherische Epistel Postille.* Zweite Auflage. St. Louis: Lutherischer Concordia Verlag, 1882.

——. *Amerikanisch-Lutherische Evangelien Postille.* Neunte Auflage. St. Louis: Concordia Publishing House, 1870.

——. *Casual-Predigten und -Reden.* Edited by H. Sieck. St. Louis: Concordia Publishing House, 1892.

——. *Festklaenge.* Edited by C. L. Janzow. St. Louis: Concordia Publishing House, 1892.

——. *Gnadenjahr. Predigten Ueber die Evangelien des Kirchenjahrs.* Edited by C. L. Janzow. St. Louis: Lutherischer Concordia-Verlag, 1891.

——. *Licht des Lebens.* Edited by C. J. Otto Hanser. St. Louis: Concordia Publishing House, 1905.

——. *Lutherische Brosamen.* St. Louis: Concordia Publishing House, 1897.

Walther, C. F. W. and P. G. Stoeckhardt. *Reden gehalten am Sarge der weiland Frau Caroline Juliane Barthel.* St. Louis: Druckerei des Lutherischen Concordia-Verlags, 1881.

*9 7 8 0 7 5 8 6 1 8 2 2 1 *